# AI-DRIVEN TIME SERIES FORECASTING

*Complexity-Conscious Prediction
and Decision-Making*

## Raghurami Reddy Etukuru, Ph.D.

*iUniverse books may be ordered through booksellers or by contacting:*

*iUniverse*
*1663 Liberty Drive*
*Bloomington, IN 47403*
*www.iuniverse.com*
*844-349-9409*

*Because of the dynamic nature of the Internet, any web addresses or links contained in this book may have changed since publication and may no longer be valid. The views expressed in this work are solely those of the author and do not necessarily reflect the views of the publisher, and the publisher hereby disclaims any responsibility for them.*

*Any people depicted in stock imagery provided by Getty Images are models, and such images are being used for illustrative purposes only.*
*Certain stock imagery © Getty Images.*

*ISBN: 978-1-6632-5671-3 (sc)*
*ISBN: 978-1-6632-5673-7 (e)*

*Library of Congress Control Number: 2023918574*

*Print information available on the last page.*

*iUniverse rev. date: 01/24/2024*

# Contents

# 1

# Introduction

Imagine stepping into a labyrinth of numerical patterns, where each turn unveils a unique layer of complexity. Welcome to the world of time series analysis, a domain that presents a complex dance of data where simple mathematical or statistical models often struggle to keep pace. The reality is riddled with complex patterns in time series data, which, like cryptic pieces of a jigsaw puzzle, hold the key to unravelling insightful predictions.

What creates these intricate patterns? The factors are numerous and multifaceted, each adding its own measure of challenge. Let us briefly unravel these complexities. Nonlinearity, a relationship between variables that defies linear predictability, gives rise to these intricate patterns, occasionally inducing chaotic behavior. Nonstationarity, another character, continuously alters statistical properties like trends or seasonality. Meanwhile, volatility clustering gives rise to periods of intense highs and lows, contributing to the complex ebb and flow of variability. Adding another layer to the complexity is the concept of long memory or dependence, where past values continue to exert influence on current values, even across significant time gaps. Then there is asymmetry, reflecting an imbalance in the statistical properties of the series over time, creating unique challenges at different levels or phases.

Complexity takes on a new dimension when we encounter stochastic processes, which, despite their random nature, can still weave patterns so intricate they are hard to predict. These threads of stochastic complexity are indeed challenging to untangle. However, we are not without the tools to navigate this labyrinth. Specialized techniques have evolved to specifically handle these layers of complexity. Nonlinear time series analysis and stochastic volatility models for volatility clustering each serve as a compass to help navigate this challenging terrain. Yet, even with these tools, there remains a degree of uncertainty. This partly makes the study of time series forecasting both challenging and exciting.

As we initiate our exploration into artificial intelligence (AI)-powered time series analysis, anticipate a deep immersion into the realm of numerical patterns. This book aims not just to demystify these complexities but also to harness the power of AI to amplify our comprehension and forecasting abilities. Prepare to decode the enigmas of time series data!

While building upon the intricate world of time series analysis, this book offers solutions to grapple with the complexities associated with forecasting from such data. Readers will find themselves immersed in the rich, diverse universe of AI models. Exploration of their theoretical underpinnings is paired with a tangible grasp of practical knowledge, incorporating code implementations, all to aid in forecasting values amidst complex time series patterns.

The journey begins with an exploration of traditional time series models, such as autoregression (AR), autoregressive moving average model (ARMA), autoregressive integrated moving average (ARIMA), and generalized autoregressive conditional heteroskedasticity (GARCH) models. In tandem with their operational mechanisms being understood, the inherent difficulties presented by these models will be encountered, and a deep dive will be made into the quantitative analysis and interpretation of intricate patterns. Additionally, this book also covers the methods for evaluating complexity in time series data.

Before venturing into the realm of AI and its forecasting prowess, the book sets down a strong foundation, covering the bedrock principles of machine learning, deep learning, and reinforcement learning (RL). This includes a comprehensive overview of accuracy metrics used to assess AI models, along with an introduction to the critical process of hyperparameter tuning.

Raghurami Reddy Etukuru, the author, pioneered the concept of 'Complexity-Conscious Prediction and Decision-Making.' The innovative method, known as 'Complexity-Conscious Prediction,' recognizes and incorporates the inherent complexity in data. It involves assessing the complexity of input data and developing models that are specifically designed to manage this complexity. The aim is to significantly enhance the accuracy of predictions, a factor that is particularly vital in situations where data demonstrates complex patterns and behaviors not adequately addressed by simpler predictive models. Furthermore, Raghurami Reddy Etukuru extended this concept to include decision-making processes, moving beyond just forecasting. By harnessing AI, the decision-making processes that depend on these predictions can be substantially improved.

Raghurami Reddy Etukuru, the author, defines 'Complexity-Conscious Prediction and Decision-Making' as a method that integrates the inherent complexity in data and designs models to improve predictions and decision-making. This approach involves assessing complex data patterns and developing specialized models to manage this complexity, thereby enhancing prediction accuracy and aiding AI-driven decision-making processes.

Complexity-conscious prediction and decision-making in the context of time series forecasting represents a sophisticated, nuanced approach to understanding and predicting temporal patterns. This approach acknowledges the inherent complexity within time series data, which includes nonlinearity, nonstationarity, long-term memory, asymmetry, and stochasticity and the influence of these factors. Rather than using simple linear models that assume independence among observations, complexity-conscious methods seek to capture these intricate, often nonlinear, interrelationships. Techniques such as machine learning methods or even complex deep learning architectures like long short-term memory (LSTM), gated recurrent unit (GRU), and generative adversarial network (GAN) are part of such a complexity-conscious toolkit. The goal is to provide more accurate forecasts by fully acknowledging and integrating the underlying complexity of the data into the predictive model. The aforementioned approach to time series forecasting doesn't just stop at making accurate predictions. Informed by these forecasts, decision-making processes can be enhanced using RL.

As such, the stage thus ventures into the actual development and application of machine learning, deep learning, and RL models to predict future values. Specific machine learning models, like random forest and XGBoost, and deep learning models, including LSTM, bidirectional LSTM (BiLSTM), one-dimensional convolutional neural networks (1DCNNs), 1DCNN-LSTM, 1DCNN-BiLSTM, GRUs, and GANs, were applied to forecast the time series data.

Moving beyond these, the book employs the RL model, soft actor-critic (SAC) model, applied to strategize based on the events evolving within the time series data. As the culminating strand in this intricate landscape, the book delves into the computational dynamics of AI models, adding depth and sophistication to the overall discourse.

Although time series analysis can be applied to various fields, stock forecasting was chosen as a demonstration field due to the easy availability of data. For this purpose, the necessary data was collected from Yahoo Finance, a platform that offers financial information, including stock quotes, commentary, press releases, and financial reports. The stock data obtained from Yahoo Finance consists of a historical record of observations spanning a specific period.

This book aims to be more than a theoretical guide; it is a hands-on toolbox, a practical companion in the often-turbulent journey of understanding and predicting complex time series data. Let us embark on this exciting expedition together!

# 2

# Starting the Clock: An Introduction to Time Series Analysis

A time series is an ordered observation sequence corresponding to specific time points or intervals. Time series data refers explicitly to information tied to time or time intervals and captures the changes or fluctuations that occur over time. It is a type of temporal data expressed in various formats, including dates, timestamps, durations, or as time series. Illustrative examples of time series data encompass historical stock prices, peak temperatures recorded throughout a year, the count of vehicles passing through an intersection over a day, sea levels, sales figures, and profits.

Time series analysis identifies trends, patterns, and cycles within data while also enabling the forecasting of future values. Various statistical and AI techniques examine temporal patterns, identify trends, address seasonality, handle outliers, and generate precise forecasts using time series data. Time series data possesses distinctive characteristics, making it suitable for such analysis.

## 2.1 Characteristics of Time Series Data

For suitable analysis, modeling, and understanding, grasping the key features of time series data is essential. The basic characteristics of time series data are delineated here, while a later section engages in a discussion on the complex patterns inherent to such data.

**Time-dependent**

Time series data is inherently dependent on the order and timing of observations. The values in a time series are recorded chronologically, with each observation associated with a specific time point or interval. The time dimension plays a crucial role in analyzing and understanding the data. The figure below visualizes the time series data for the MERC stock from January 2, 2008, to February 10, 2023.

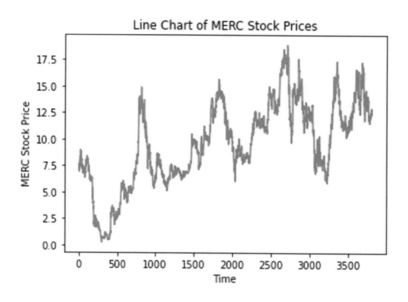

Figure 1: Time Series Data for the MERC Stock.

**Trend**

Time series data commonly showcases a discernible trend, which reflects the long-term direction or tendency of the data over time. Trends can take three primary forms: ascending, descending, or stationary. An ascending trend indicates a consistent increase in values over time, such as when the price of a stock steadily rises. Conversely, a descending trend signifies a gradual decrease in values, like the declining number of people smoking cigarettes yearly. On the other hand, a stationary trend denotes a negligible change in values over time, as seen in a city's population remaining relatively stable without significant growth or decline.

Analyzing trends in time series data helps identify patterns or changes in the data. For instance, an ascending trend in a stock price suggests investors are optimistic, expecting its value to keep rising. Conversely, a descending trend indicates a bearish sentiment, with investors anticipating a decline in value. Trend analysis also aids in forecasting future values. For example, if a stock price has shown a consistent ascending trend over recent years, it suggests the trend may continue. However, it is crucial to note that trends can shift over time, requiring careful monitoring and adjustments to forecasts when necessary.

## Seasonality

Seasonality is crucial in time series data, characterized by recurring and predictable changes that follow a yearly pattern. These patterns can manifest daily, weekly, monthly, or annually, reflecting various factors such as weather conditions, holidays, or human behavior. For instance, the sales of snowblowers tend to rise during winter, while ice cream sales surge in the summer. Similarly, the demand for school supplies typically peaks in the weeks preceding the start of the academic year. Moreover, people are more inclined to dine out on weekends than on weekdays. By recognizing and understanding seasonality, we can effectively analyze and forecast future trends in time series data, enabling businesses to make informed decisions and optimize their strategies accordingly.

Seasonality presents a challenge in time series analysis, as it can obscure the underlying trends in the data. Therefore, detecting and accounting for seasonality is essential to ensure accurate forecasts. Various techniques can be employed for this purpose. One approach involves visually inspecting the data to identify recurring patterns regularly. By examining the data graphically, the seasonal patterns can be spotted. Statistical tests are another tool to detect seasonality, as they analyze the data for significant periodic variations. These tests provide quantitative evidence of seasonality in the data.

Additionally, seasonal decomposition is a technique that breaks down the data into three components: trend, seasonality, and noise. This breakdown helps data scientists understand and model the underlying patterns in the data. By leveraging these techniques, data scientists can detect seasonality, unravel the trends in time series data, and make accurate forecasts and informed decisions.

Once seasonality has been detected in time series data, there are several methods to account for it. One approach is de-trending, which involves removing the trend from the data to isolate the seasonal component. Another method is a seasonal adjustment, where the data is adjusted to eliminate the seasonal component, leaving behind only the trend and noise components. Additionally, modeling can be used to create a model that incorporates the seasonal component, allowing for accurate predictions and analysis. These techniques provide ways to effectively handle seasonality in time series data and ensure the true underlying patterns are captured and utilized in further research.

## Cyclical Patterns

Cyclical patterns are extended fluctuations that lack fixed time frames, unlike seasonality. They can be influenced by economic, social, or environmental factors and may vary in length across cycles. Examples of cyclical patterns include business cycles, which involve alternating periods of economic expansion and contraction over several years; inflation cycles, characterized by rising and falling prices influenced by factors like economic growth; and commodity cycles, reflecting fluctuations in commodity prices driven by changes in supply and demand. Understanding these cyclical patterns provides insights into the dynamics of different systems and helps anticipate changes in economic, pricing, and commodity trends.

## Irregular Fluctuations

Time series data may exhibit irregular fluctuations or random variations that cannot be ascribed to trends, seasonality, or cycles. These fluctuations can arise from unpredictable events, noise, or measurement errors. Analyzing the nature of these fluctuations helps distinguish them from significant patterns within the data. Examples of random changes include unpredictable events such as natural disasters, political events, or economic shocks, as well as noise, a random variation unrelated to any specific factor but stems from the inherent variability of the data. Measurement errors can also contribute to random fluctuations when data is collected or recorded inaccurately. Random changes can pose challenges in identifying meaningful patterns in time series data. However, by carefully examining the characteristics of these fluctuations, it becomes possible to differentiate them in meaningful ways and make informed decisions regarding the utilization of the data.

## Autocorrelation

Autocorrelation in time series analysis refers to the correlation between observation and previous observations at different time intervals. It helps identify dependencies, memory, and persistence within the data, shedding light on its temporal structure. For example, stock prices often exhibit autocorrelation, as today's price is likely to correlate with yesterday's price due to factors like economic news, company earnings, and investor sentiment. By analyzing the autocorrelation of stock prices, investors can gain insights into future market behavior. Similarly, sales data demonstrates autocorrelation, as today's sales are likely to be correlated with yesterday's sales due to customer behavior, promotions, and competition. Analyzing the autocorrelation of sales data helps businesses anticipate customer behavior.

Additionally, weather data exhibits autocorrelation, as today's weather is likely to correlate with yesterday's weather due to atmospheric pressure, temperature, and humidity. Meteorologists leverage autocorrelation analysis to predict future weather patterns. Autocorrelation provides valuable information for understanding and forecasting various phenomena across different domains.

Autocorrelation analysis is valuable for gaining insights into past, present, and future time series data, enabling better decision-making to achieve desired goals. The correlation coefficient, ranging from -1 to 1, measures autocorrelation. A coefficient of -1 signifies a perfect negative correlation, while a coefficient of 1 represents a perfect positive correlation and 0 indicates no correlation between variables. The lag denotes the period difference between correlated variables. Autocorrelation helps identify trends, seasonality, and cycles in data. Positive autocorrelation indicates a trend; negative autocorrelation suggests seasonality, and cyclical autocorrelation signifies a cycle.

Additionally, autocorrelation aids in forecasting future values of a time series. Positive autocorrelation implies future values similar to the current value, while negative autocorrelation suggests anticipated deviations from the current value. Autocorrelation is a versatile tool for understanding, predicting, and leveraging the patterns inherent in time series data.

**Stationarity**

In time series analysis, stationarity is a crucial concept. A time series is considered stationary when its statistical properties, such as mean, variance, and autocorrelation, remain constant over time. Stationarity simplifies modeling and analysis by allowing the use of various statistical techniques. There are three types of stationarity: weak stationarity, where the mean, variance, and autocorrelation of the series are constant over time; strong stationarity, where the mean, variance, autocorrelation, and distribution of the series remain constant over time; and trend stationarity, where the series exhibits a linear increase or decrease in mean over time while maintaining constant variance and autocorrelation.

Not all time series exhibit stationarity. For instance, a time series with a trend is nonstationary because the mean changes over time, while a time series with seasonality is nonstationary because the variance varies over time. To make a time series stationary, various techniques can be applied.

One such technique is differencing, which involves calculating the difference between consecutive values in the series to remove trends and seasonality. Another approach is seasonal adjustment, which entails modifying the series to eliminate the seasonal component. This can be accomplished by using methods like moving averages and regression. Additionally, transformation can be employed by converting the series into a different form, such as taking the logarithm or exponential, to stabilize the variance and autocorrelation of the data. These techniques help transform nonstationary time series into stationary ones, facilitating more reliable analysis and modeling.

**Outliers**

Time series data can contain outliers, data points that deviate significantly from the expected pattern or trend. These outliers can arise from measurement errors, anomalies, or exceptional events. Detecting and handling outliers is essential for accurate analysis and forecasting. Measurement errors, such as typos or sensor malfunctions, can contribute to outliers. Anomalies, unexpected or unusual events like natural disasters or significant economic circumstances, can also result in outliers. Additionally, exceptional events like product recalls or important product launches can cause notable deviations in a time series. Managing outliers improves the integrity of time series analysis, ensuring more reliable insights and predictions.

Detecting and appropriately handling outliers is crucial for accurate time series analysis and forecasting. Failure to address outliers can result in misleading conclusions and inaccurate forecasts. Various techniques exist for outlier detection in time series data. Visual inspection involves identifying data points that significantly deviate from the rest of the data. Statistical tests can be employed to identify data points that exhibit significant differences.

Additionally, specific algorithms and techniques are designed for outlier detection. Examples include Tukey's fences, which identify data points outside the interquartile range; box plots that provide a graphical representation of outliers; and z-scores that identify data points with extreme distances from the mean. These techniques collectively enable effective outlier detection, ensuring the reliability and validity of time series analysis and forecasts.

After detecting outliers in time series data, various methods exist to handle them appropriately. Imputing is a technique where outliers are replaced with estimated values that are considered more probable. Exclusion is another approach where outliers are removed from the analysis entirely. Winsorizing is a method that returns outliers with values closer to the mean, reducing their impact on the overall data. These approaches offer ways to effectively manage outliers and mitigate their influence on time series analysis and subsequent forecasting.

**Multiple Characteristics**

Time series data is complex and encompasses multiple characteristics, including trends, seasonal patterns, cyclical behavior, and irregular fluctuations. By decomposing the time series into its components, we can better comprehend the distinct contributions of each component. This decomposition aids in modeling the data accurately and making reliable forecasts.

## 2.2   Forecasting

Time series forecasting is a crucial technique used in various fields, such as economics, finance, and climate studies, which allows us to predict future data points based on past observations. This field comprises multiple methods, each with unique application domains and complexities. These include univariate time series forecasting, which deals with a single series of data; multivariate time series forecasting, where predictions are based on multiple, interrelated data series; and panel time series forecasting, which uses data collected from multiple entities over the same period. Finally, spatial time series forecasting is a more complex approach that considers spatial correlations between different locations. Understanding these methodologies is pivotal for selecting the most suitable method for any forecasting task.

**Univariate Time Series Forecasting**

Univariate time series analysis is a fundamental method in forecasting that focuses on observing and predicting a single variable over time, like a stock's closing price. Its goal is to identify underlying patterns and trends in the data, which can be systematic fluctuations or general upward or downward trends. Various models capture these aspects and identify unexplained components in the data, known as residuals. While this approach is preferred for its simplicity and minimal computational demand, it has limitations, notably its inability to account for the interrelationships between multiple variables over time.

**Multivariate Time Series Forecasting**

Multivariate time series is the simultaneous observation of multiple variables over identical periods. These variables can pertain to a single entity or multiple interconnected phenomena. For example, in a financial context, one might monitor stock prices, trading volumes, and interest rates concurrently. This monitoring process isn't limited to isolated observation. The variables are tracked synchronously, with data points potentially recorded at intervals ranging from seconds to months, depending on the specific context.

Multivariate time series analysis aims to comprehend the intricate relationships and dependencies among these variables. For instance, one might explore questions like, "Does the stock price increase when trading volumes are high?" or "Does the interest rate impact the volume of shares traded?" The complexity of such analysis escalates quickly due to the possibility of bidirectional, conditional, or temporal relationships among variables.

Taking the above example, recording the daily closing price of a stock, trading volume, and interest rate allows an analyst to decode the interactions between these variables. Suppose interest rates rise; it could trigger a decline in trading volume as borrowing to buy shares becomes costlier. This change, in turn, may impact the stock's closing price. Thus, multivariate time series analysis offers invaluable insights into understanding and predicting complex systems' behavior.

**Panel Time Series Forecasting**

Panel time series, longitudinal time series, or cross-sectional time series is a powerful analytical tool for investigating multiple individuals, entities, or regions over time. This approach involves concurrently studying several units, each recording its time series data over the same time intervals. The structure of panel time series data is rather unique as the data is organized into a panel or grid structure. This gridlike arrangement affords two dimensions of data. The first is the cross-sectional dimension, which refers to the different individuals, entities, or regions; the second is the time dimension, signifying the different time points. For example, a data scientist could observe various countries' GDP growth, inflation, and unemployment rates over several years. Each country would constitute one cross-sectional unit, and each country's time series would represent the GDP, inflation, and unemployment rates recorded annually.

Panel time series data is particularly effective when one is interested in understanding individual or regional differences and how they evolve. This might involve studying the impact of a specific policy on different regions, understanding the growth pattern of various companies in an industry, or analyzing individual behaviors in a population over a certain period. Analyzing panel time series data can provide insights that would not be evident in a simple cross-sectional or time series study. By looking at multiple units over time, one can control for variables that change over time but not between units (time-fixed effects) and variables that vary between units but not over time (unit-fixed effects). This ability to control for fixed effects can provide more robust, reliable findings and allow for a better understanding of cause-and-effect relationships. Moreover, panel data can improve the efficiency of econometric estimates, deal with selectivity bias, and enable dynamic modeling. Hence, the increased richness, complexity, and multidimensionality of panel time series data provide researchers and analysts with a more nuanced and comprehensive understanding of the phenomena under study.

## Spatial Time Series Forecasting

Spatial time series combines both spatial and temporal dimensions. It involves observing and analyzing variables that vary over space and time. Spatial time series data captures how the values of a variable change at different locations over a sequence of periods. An illustrative example of a spatiotemporal time series is remote sensing and satellite imagery. Integrating data from these sources, or other geospatial data, can significantly enrich the analysis and interpretation of spatiotemporal patterns and trends.

Spatial time series analysis considers four fundamental elements: the spatial dimension, temporal dimension, spatial patterns and relationships, and spatiotemporal interactions. The spatial dimension of this analysis points to the specific spatial locations or coordinates where the observations are collected. This information could represent precise points, broader areas, or even continuous surfaces, often visualized through grids or rasters. Meanwhile, the temporal dimension, akin to conventional time series data, monitors the progression and fluctuations of a variable across a set time. This sequence of observations or measurements is recorded at regular or irregular intervals. Spatial time series analysis aims to delve into the spatial patterns and relationships within the data, investigating the variable's distribution across distinct locations and how these distributions morph over time. Through this examination, one can identify spatial trends, spatial autocorrelation where values at neighboring locations are similar, and spatial dependencies.

## 2.3   Applications of Time Series

Time series analysis has a wide range of applications across various fields. Time series techniques are employed in many domains, including financial markets, air pollution control, engineering, transportation, telecommunications, marketing, and more, where analyzing temporal data is crucial for decision-making, forecasting, and understanding dynamic systems.

**Finance and Economics**

Time series analysis is extensively used in finance and economics to analyze stock prices, exchange rates, interest rates, economic indicators, and other financial variables. It helps identify trends, forecast future values, and make informed investment decisions.

For example, analysts look at how the price of a stock has changed every day, month, or year. Analysts try to see if the price goes up or down in response to specific events or follows a pattern, like consistently going up or down over time. They also check if the price changes at particular times, like the end of each month. Suppose they notice the price usually drops at the end of every three months. They can use this pattern to guess the price might drop again at the end of the next three months. To prevent the losses or mitigate the risk, they could sell their stock just before they think the price will drop and repurchase it after it falls, or they might want to hedge.

As such, time series analysis plays a crucial role in quantitative research. Quantitative analysis is a process of evaluating securities using statistical and mathematical models. The statistical and mathematical models use historical returns, stock prices, and trade volume to chart securities movement patterns. While fundamental analysis attempts to show a security's intrinsic value, quantitative analysis aims to gain insight into the future direction of securities. A quantitative approach relies on the concept that the future performance of a security can be determined by reviewing patterns based on past performance data.

The quantitative method is particularly useful when the input data has a faster update frequency and larger data volume. For this reason, quantitative methods offer an effective way of building quantitative trading strategies. Mathematical models and computations help analyze the data on investment prospects at a high throughput rate. Even though larger financial firms such as investment banks and hedge funds use quantitative trading strategies to cope with the large volume of their transactions, individual investors have increasingly turned to quantitative trading in recent years. Quantitative trading strategies employ computer languages to gather historical stock market data from short to long periods. Unlike fundamental analysis, which is suitable for long-term investment, quantitative analysis helps both short-term trading and long-term investment decision-making.

One advantage of quantitative analysis is its unbiasedness, as the mathematical models take human emotion out of the equation. The second advantage of using quantitative analysis is its efficiency, which comes from advancements in computational power to process large data. Since data drives quantitative analysis, it can be used to create models and projections, which can help investors make informed decisions about which stocks to buy, sell, or hold. By using data-driven approaches, investors can potentially identify mispricing in the market and make more informed decisions about their investments. In time series data, time is a significant variable. The variables specific to the transaction are associated with each time point. In the historical data set of stock prices, the open price, closing price, high price, low price, and volume are associated with each trading day.

A multivariate time series has more than one time-dependent variable. Each variable not only depends on its past values but also has some dependency on other variables. This dependency is used for forecasting future values. When applied to stock price prediction, multivariate time series analysis considers the historical prices of multiple stocks simultaneously rather than examining each stock in isolation. This approach can capture the interrelationships and correlations between stocks and sectors, providing more accurate predictions. Alternatively, multiple attributes of the same stock, such as close price, open price, high price, low price, and volume, can be used to forecast a single attribute.

## Environmental Monitoring

The time series analysis helps examine environmental data, including air and water quality information or pollution levels. This method allows for spotting long-term changes, identifying patterns related to different seasons, and understanding how environmental conditions affect ecosystems. For example, outdoor air pollution, which keeps increasing, poses a severe health threat. Pollution levels often cross the limits set by regulatory bodies, raising the risk of health issues like lung cancer, asthma, breathing difficulties, and heart disease.

In the study of air pollution, the pollution levels are collected at different times: every hour, day, month, or year. By looking at this data, data scientists can see how pollution changes over time. They can spot patterns, like if pollution is higher or lower at certain times of day or year. For instance, they might find that pollution is at its worst during busy traffic hours or in winter when people burn more fuel to keep warm. These patterns can help local governments make decisions. If pollution is high during rush hour, they might limit how many cars can be on the road. If it is high in winter, they could encourage people to use greener heating options. Moreover, looking at how pollution levels changed in the past can help predict how they might change. This can help warn people about lousy air days or plan ways to reduce pollution.

We typically gauge air quality by measuring particulate matter. Two common standards are PM2.5 and PM10, which refer to the size of pollution particles. PM10 measures particles less than ten microns in diameter, while PM2.5 measures those less than 2.5 microns. These ultrafine PM2.5 particles can quickly enter the respiratory tract and affect the lungs, causing symptoms like a runny nose, lung irritation, and shortness of breath. Over time, they can impair lung function and lead to asthma. Chronic exposure to PM2.5 can cause long-term health problems, including chronic bronchitis, lung cancer, and heart disease. PM2.5 particles typically originate from car and factory emissions, burning wood, and fossil fuels like oil and coal. They can travel several miles and are also produced by indoor activities, such as smoking tobacco, cooking, burning oil lamps, using fireplaces, and operating kerosene heaters. Other sources include dust from roads, mining operations, and construction sites. Regulatory agencies worldwide set air quality standards. For instance, the U.S. Environmental Protection Agency (EPA) has established the National Ambient Air Quality Standards for PM2.5. Monitoring systems for PM2.5 can help people take the necessary precautions to protect themselves from pollution.

## Other Applications

Time series analysis is a valuable tool used across various fields. In sales and demand forecasting, companies use it to predict future sales, helping them plan better and manage their resources. Weather and climate scientists use this analysis to understand weather patterns and make predictions about things like temperature and rainfall. Energy companies use it to estimate future energy use, leading to more efficient power generation. In health care, it monitors health signals like heart rates and blood sugar levels, which can help diagnose diseases and monitor patients. With the growth of the Internet of things, time series analysis is also used to monitor data from connected devices, helping predict maintenance needs and detect unusual activity. Lastly, it is used in computer network management to help identify congestion, predict future traffic, and improve network performance and security. This shows how versatile time series analysis is, used in many fields to understand trends and make predictions.

# 3
# Exploring Traditional Time Series Models

---

Traditional time series models serve as statistical frameworks aimed at predicting future values of time series, operating under the presumption that past trends can provide insights into future behavior. These models encompass the simplistic moving averages, which calculate the average of time series values over a defined span, and the more complex exponential smoothing that emphasizes more recent data points. The gamut of traditional time series models includes autoregression (AR), moving average (MA), autoregressive moving average (ARMA), autoregressive integrated moving average (ARIMA), and generalized autoregressive conditional heteroskedasticity (GARCH) models.

Traditional time series models offer numerous advantages, notably their simplicity and comprehensibility, facilitating their straightforward implementation. They are efficient tools that enable rapid and cost-effective prediction of future time series values. Furthermore, these models offer versatility, forecasting a diverse array of time series, including those exhibiting trends, seasonality, and cyclical patterns.

While traditional time series models offer distinct advantages, they also possess certain shortcomings. These include a possible deficiency in accuracy when tasked with predicting complex time series patterns. The accuracy of these models can be highly contingent upon the selection of initial parameters, adding a layer of sensitivity. Moreover, these models may not always be the right choice for all forecasting scenarios, especially when the time series manifests complex patterns, possibly driven by external factors like economic shifts or catastrophic events.

## 3.1 Autoregression (AR) Model

The foundational autoregression (AR) time series model operates as a linear equation that uses past observations as inputs to predict subsequent values. It is called autoregressive because it incorporates a regression of the variable on its own lagged or past values to inform future predictions.

Mathematically, an AR model of order p, denoted AR(p), is defined as follows: $X_t = c + \varphi_1 X_{t-1} + \varphi_2 X_{t-2} + ... + \varphi_p X_{t-p} + \varepsilon_t$.

Where:

- $X_t$ is the time series value at time t,
- c is a constant,
- $\varphi_1, ..., \varphi_p$ are the parameters of the model,
- $X_{t-1}, ..., X_{t-p}$ are the values of the time series at times t-1, ..., t-p (the p-lagged values of the time series),
- $\varepsilon_t$ is the error term at time t, and
- p is the order of the AR model (the number of lagged values in the model).

In a simple case of an AR(1) model, the equation reduces to $X_t = c + \varphi_1 X_{t-1} + \varepsilon_t$.

In this model, $X_t$ (the value at time t) is a function of the constant term, the value at the previous time step ($X_{t-1}$), and the error term at time t.

The $\varphi$ coefficients are estimated using the Yule-Walker equations or maximum likelihood estimation. These are typically used to minimize the sum of the squared differences between the left-hand side and right-hand side of the model equation, which is equivalent to the error term, $\varepsilon_t$.

The AR model is grounded in the presumption that future data will resemble past instances, indicating that future events can be inferred from historical ones. Furthermore, the AR model is significantly influenced by temporary fluctuations within time series data, which typically include trends, seasonal, cyclical, and irregular variances, as seen in stock prices. Consequently, an unexpected one-time spike, commonly known as an outlier, can considerably impact all forthcoming value predictions. The AR model postulates the time series data to be stationary, meaning that mean and variance remain consistent over time. If a time series is nonstationary, it can be transformed into a stationary one by differencing the series one or more times. This concept forms the foundation for the autoregressive integrated moving average (ARIMA) model, which blends the AR model with a moving average (MA) model and implements differencing.

## 3.2   Moving Average (MA) Model

The moving average (MA)-based time series models use MAs, calculated as a series of averages of full data subsets. And unlike AR models, MA models utilize past error terms to forecast future terms.

Mathematically, an MA model of order q, denoted MA(q), is defined as follows: $X_t = \mu + \varepsilon_t + \theta_1\varepsilon_{t-1} + \theta_2\varepsilon_{t-2} + \ldots + \theta_q\varepsilon_{t-q}$.

Where:
- $X_t$ is the time series value at time t,
- $\mu$ is the mean of the time series,
- $\varepsilon_t$ is the error term at time t, which are generally assumed to be independent, identically distributed variables drawn from a normal distribution with zero mean,
- $\theta_1, \ldots, \theta_q$ are the parameters of the model, and
- q is the order of the MA model (the number of lagged error terms in the model).

In a simple case of an MA(1) model, the equation reduces to $X_t = \mu + \varepsilon_t + \theta_1\varepsilon_{t-1}$.

In this model, $X_t$ is a linear function of the current error, $\varepsilon_t$, and the previous error, $\varepsilon_{t-1}$.

The parameters of an MA model (the $\theta$s and $\mu$) are typically estimated through methods such as maximum likelihood estimation or similar optimization techniques. The objective is to find the parameter values that maximize the likelihood of observing the data specified in the model. Maximum likelihood estimation (MLE) is a method employed in statistical modeling for parameter estimation. The MLE method operates by identifying the parameters that maximize the likelihood function. The likelihood function assesses the goodness of fit of a statistical model to the data, computing the probability of observing the given data for various sets of parameter values and identifying the parameters that make the observed data most probable.

Consider a straightforward example: a coin is assumed to be tossed to estimate the probability of yielding a head. The coin is then tossed, and the outcomes are recorded. After 100 tosses, the results include 60 heads and 40 tails. Utilizing the MLE method, the probability of achieving a head is estimated to be 60/100, or 0.6. This is due to the maximization of the probability of the observed data (60 heads in 100 tosses) under this parameter value (0.6).

However, the MLE method assumes the data is independently and identically distributed, which means each data point is generated independently from the same distribution. Finding the maximum likelihood function in more complex scenarios may involve solving complicated mathematical equations, often requiring numerical methods or optimization techniques.

The MA model boasts several advantages, such as its simplicity facilitates quick understanding and implementation. It proves effective for short-term forecasting when the data demonstrates a consistent mean or lacks a trend. Unlike other models, the MA model offers robustness against outliers as it averages these unexpected spikes or drops over a given period. Furthermore, the MA model aids in noise reduction and smooths out data fluctuations, thereby easing the identification of underlying trends.

While the MA model offers several advantages, it also has notable drawbacks. Its effectiveness diminishes for long-term forecasting, particularly for data exhibiting trends or seasonality, as it assumes future values hinge solely on present and past errors. The model's accuracy can be sensitive to the window size selection, which denotes the number of periods used for averaging, making its appropriate choice crucial yet potentially challenging. Furthermore, MA models are not designed to account for trend and seasonality in the data and perform best with stationary data, where statistical properties such as mean and variance remain constant over time.

## 3.3 Autoregressive Moving Average Model (ARMA) Model

As the name suggests, ARMA combines two components: AR and MA. The AR part involves regressing the variable on its own lagged values; that is, previous data points in the series are used to predict the next one. The MA part models the error term as a linear combination of error terms occurring contemporaneously and at various times in the past.

An ARMA(p, q) model is represented as $X_t = c + \varphi_1 X_{(t-1)} + \varphi_2 X_{(t-2)} + ... + \varphi_p X_{(t-p)} + \varepsilon_t + \theta_1 \varepsilon_{(t-1)} + \theta_2 \varepsilon_{(t-2)} + ... + \theta_q \varepsilon_{(t-q)}$.

Where:
- $X_t$ is the current observation,
- $c$ is a constant term,
- $\varphi_1, \varphi_2, ..., \varphi_p$ are the coefficients for the lagged observations,
- $\varepsilon_t$ is the error term at time t, and
- $\theta_1, \theta_2, ..., \theta_q$ are the coefficients for the lagged error terms.

The ARMA model is often used to analyze and forecast time series data by estimating the parameters (coefficients) of the model. The appropriate values for the orders p and q can be determined using statistical techniques like the Akaike information criterion (AIC) or the Bayesian information criterion (BIC).

The AIC is a statistical measure used for model selection. It estimates the relative quality of different statistical models for a given data set. While comparing two or more models, the one with the lowest AIC value is typically chosen as it is assumed to have the best fit. However, the AIC does not provide a test of a model in the sense of testing a null hypothesis; instead, it provides a means for model selection.

AIC takes into consideration both the goodness of fit of the model and the complexity of the model. The formula for AIC is $AIC = 2K - 2\ln(L)$.

Where:

- K is the number of model parameters (number of variables in the model plus the intercept) and
- L is the likelihood of the model, that is, the probability the given model produced the observed data.

A lower AIC score is better, suggesting a model with a good balance of complexity and fit to the data. It is helpful when we have several different models and must choose the best one. However, one limitation of AIC is that it relies on a particular sample of data and does not account for the uncertainty in the parameter estimates. This means that different samples could lead to other best models. Moreover, it is a relative measure of model fit, not an absolute one, so it does not tell us how well the best model will predict future data. It only tells us that it is the best of the models considered.

The Bayesian information criterion (BIC), also known as the Schwarz information criterion, is used to select a finite set of models. It is based on the principle of parsimony, which encourages choosing the simplest model that adequately explains the data. Similar to the AIC, the BIC estimates the quality of a model by considering both the model's complexity and its fit to the data. However, the BIC penalizes model complexity more heavily than the AIC. This means the BIC may favor simpler models than AIC if both models explain the data equally well.

The formula for BIC is $BIC = \ln(n) * k - 2 * \ln(L)$.

Where:

- n is the number of observations or the sample size,
- k is the number of parameters estimated by the model, and
- L is the likelihood of the data given in the model.

Just like AIC, a lower BIC value indicates a better model. When comparing models, the model with the lowest BIC is preferred.

While both AIC and BIC are used for model selection, their relative importance might vary depending on the situation. For example, if the focus is on predictive accuracy, one might prefer the AIC. However, the BIC might be more appropriate if the goal is to identify the most probable model given the data and set of candidate models. It is worth noting that the BIC assumes the true model is within the set of candidate models, which may not always be true.

The ARMA model possesses several advantages. It showcases flexibility by capturing AR and MA behaviors in a time series, allowing it to model a wide array of patterns and dependencies within the data. Its relative simplicity facilitates easy understanding and implementation; the need to estimate only a few parameters for the AR and MA components makes it more interpretable than complex time series models. ARMA models' forecasting capabilities make them valuable for predicting future time series values, with the model's parameter estimates generating forecasts and confidence intervals that offer essential insights for planning and decision-making. Moreover, ARMA models come equipped with various diagnostic tools like residual analysis to evaluate the model's goodness of fit and help identify any residual patterns or dependencies in the data not captured by the model.

The ARMA model also has certain drawbacks. It necessitates that the time series is stationary, that is, its statistical properties like mean, variance, and covariance remain constant over time. Nonstationary characteristics in the time series, such as trends or seasonality, might need additional preprocessing steps, including differencing or seasonal adjustments, to meet this requirement. Parameter estimation in an ARMA model can prove challenging, especially with larger or more complex datasets. The process often includes computationally intense optimization techniques that can be sensitive to initial parameter values. Choosing the appropriate orders (p and q) for the ARMA model can be intricate, as incorrect selections could lead to poor model fitting and inaccurate forecasting. While statistical criteria such as AIC and BIC can guide this process, it may still require trial and error. In addition, ARMA models can be susceptible to outliers or extreme data values, significantly affecting parameter estimation and potentially leading to less-than-optimal model performance.

## 3.4  Autoregressive Integrated Moving Average (ARIMA) Model

The autoregressive integrated moving average (ARIMA) model is an extension of the ARMA model that incorporates differencing to handle nonstationary time series data. The ARIMA model combines three components: AR, differencing (I), and MA. Since the ARIMA model takes the lagged moving averages, lagged AR parts, which are differenced, smoothen out the effect of outliers of different seasonality.

The AR component models the relationship between an observation and a linear combination of its previous values. It assumes the current value of the series is a weighted sum of the previous p values, where p is the order of the AR component. The differencing component transforms a nonstationary time series into a stationary one. Differencing involves computing the differences between consecutive observations. It removes trends and seasonality, making the series stationary. The differencing operator is denoted by the symbol $\Delta$ (delta). Mathematically, differencing is represented as $\Delta X_t = X_t - X_{(t-1)}$.

Where:
- $\Delta X_t$ is the differenced series at time t,
- $X_t$ is the original series at time t, and
- $X_{(t-1)}$ is the previous observation.

Differencing can be applied multiple times (denoted as d) to achieve the desired level of stationarity. The order of differencing, denoted as d, represents the number of times differencing is performed.

The MA component models the dependency between an observation and a linear combination of its past error terms. It assumes the current value of the series depends on a linear combination of q-lagged error terms, where q is the order of the MA component.

The ARIMA model combines the AR, differencing, and MA components to handle nonstationary time series. An ARIMA(p, d, q) model is represented as $\Delta^d X_t = c + \varphi_1 \Delta^d X_{(t-1)} + \varphi_2 \Delta^d X_{(t-2)} + ... + \varphi_p \Delta^d X_{(t-p)} + \varepsilon_t + \theta_1 \varepsilon_{(t-1)} + \theta_2 \varepsilon_{(t-2)} + ... + \theta_q \varepsilon_{(t-q)}$.

Where:
- $\Delta^d X_t$ is the differenced series of order d,
- c is a constant term,

- $\varphi_1, \varphi_2, ..., \varphi_p$ are the coefficients for the lagged differenced observations,
- $\varepsilon_t$ is the error term at time t, and
- $\theta_1, \theta_2, ..., \theta_q$ are the coefficients for the lagged error terms.

The parameters (coefficients) of the model can be estimated to analyze the patterns and correlations and forecast future values of the time series. The appropriate values for the orders p, d, and q can be ascertained using AIC, BIC, or visual data inspection techniques. In practice, to determine the optimal orders (p, d, q) for an ARIMA model using AIC or BIC, the AIC or BIC values for different combinations of p, d, and q would typically be calculated and the model with the lowest AIC or BIC value chosen. This process aids in identifying the model that provides the optimal trade-off between goodness of fit and complexity for the given data.

ARIMA models offer a range of advantages in time series analysis. They offer great flexibility, capturing a broad spectrum of time series patterns and dependencies, including trend, seasonality, and autocorrelation, incorporating differencing and making them effective with nonstationary time series data. The models' precise mathematical formulation and parameter interpretation aid in understanding the influence of past values (AR component), past error terms (MA component), and handling of nonstationarity (differencing component), making results easier to interpret.

ARIMA models are extensively used for time series forecasting; once fitted to historical data, they can generate future value forecasts, supporting decision-making, planning, and resource allocation. Additionally, these models are equipped with diagnostic tools for assessing model goodness of fit. Residual analysis, a method of examining model residuals' patterns and distribution, can be used to validate assumptions and identify unaddressed patterns or dependencies.

ARIMA models, while advantageous, come with certain drawbacks. These models necessitate a relatively long and clean time series dataset for accurate parameter estimation, and insufficient data points or missing values can result in unreliable estimates and inaccurate forecasts. The selection of appropriate orders (p, d, q) can prove challenging, often involving exploring multiple combinations of orders and comparing goodness-of-fit metrics like AIC or BIC. This process can be time-consuming and necessitates domain expertise. Sensitivity to outliers is another drawback, with extreme data values significantly impacting parameter estimation and potentially leading to suboptimal model performance, necessitating preprocessing and outlier handling techniques. The computational complexity of estimating ARIMA model parameters can also be intensive, particularly for large datasets or higher-order models. Optimization algorithms typically used to maximize the likelihood function can be time-consuming and demand efficient algorithms and computational resources.

Though the ARIMA models are robust and widely used, they assume linearity and may not capture complex nonlinear relationships in some time series data.

## 3.5   Autoregressive Conditional Heteroskedasticity (ARCH) Model

When the assumptions regarding the data, such as stationarity and the independence of errors, are not met, the accuracy of forecasts produced by the ARIMA model may be compromised. However, the autoregressive conditional heteroskedasticity (ARCH) model offers a solution to this problem by incorporating conditional volatility, also known as heteroscedasticity, instead of assuming constant volatility. Combining aspects of the AR and MA models, the ARCH model focuses on the disturbance terms and their relationship to the data. By considering the effects of changes in the data, the ARCH model can effectively capture the dynamics of volatility clustering, wherein periods of high volatility are followed by similar periods and vice versa. An essential characteristic of the ARCH model is its ability to accommodate time-varying volatility, making it particularly well-suited for analyzing financial and economic time series that exhibit such behavior.

The ARCH model is typically represented as ARCH(p), where p represents the order of the model. Let us look at the formulation of a simple ARCH(1) model:

$$\varepsilon\_t = \sigma\_t * Z\_t$$
$$\sigma\_t^2 = \alpha_0 + \alpha_1 * \varepsilon\_(t-1)^2$$

In the above equations:
- $\varepsilon\_t$ represents the error term or the residual at time t,
- $\sigma\_t$ represents the conditional standard deviation or the conditional volatility at time t, and
- $Z\_t$ is a standardized random variable with mean zero and unit variance.

$\alpha_0$ and $\alpha_1$ are parameters that need to be estimated. $\alpha_0$ represents the constant term, and $\alpha_1$ represents the coefficient of the lagged squared residual.

In an ARCH(1) model, the conditional variance at time t ($\sigma_t^2$) is modeled as a linear combination of a constant term ($\alpha_0$) and the squared residual at the previous period ($\alpha_1 * \varepsilon_{(t-1)}^2$). The parameter $\alpha_1$ determines the persistence of the volatility. If $\alpha_1$ is close to zero, the volatility quickly reverts to its long-term average, while larger values of $\alpha_1$ imply more persistent volatility.

Various methods can be used to estimate the parameters of an ARCH model, including MLE or generalized method of moments (GMM). The estimation process involves optimizing the likelihood function or moment conditions to find the values of $\alpha_0$, $\alpha_1$, and potentially other parameters that maximize the model's fit to the data.

ARCH models are widely used in financial time series analysis, such as modeling stock market returns, exchange rate volatility, and asset price volatility. They provide insights into the clustering and persistence of volatility, allowing for better risk management and forecasting in financial markets.

The ARCH model offers several advantages in modeling and analyzing time series data with changing variance. One of its key benefits is its ability to capture volatility clustering, where periods of high volatility tend to be followed by similar periods. This feature allows for a more accurate representation of the time-varying volatility patterns observed in many financial and economic time series. Additionally, ARCH models provide flexibility in modeling by adjusting the model order, allowing for the capture of various degrees of persistence and autocorrelation in the conditional variance. The estimation of ARCH model parameters is efficient, with methods like MLE or GMM providing reliable estimates that capture conditional variance dynamics.

In risk management and portfolio optimization, ARCH models prove helpful as they accurately model volatility patterns, aiding in estimating measures such as value-at-risk (VaR) and expected shortfall (ES) for decision-making and risk assessment. Diagnostic tests associated with ARCH models enable the evaluation of model fit adequacy, helping identify potential misspecifications. Moreover, ARCH models facilitate forecasting future volatility, crucial in applications such as option pricing, risk assessment, and constructing trading strategies. Overall, ARCH models offer a comprehensive framework for modeling and analyzing time series data with changing variance, providing valuable insights into volatility dynamics.

While advantageous, the ARCH model has several limitations and disadvantages. First, it assumes linearity between conditional variance and lagged squared residuals, which may not hold for complex and nonlinear relationships in some time series data. The ARCH model may not accurately capture extreme events or outliers significantly impacting volatility. Model selection challenges arise when determining the appropriate order, and incorrect specification can lead to inadequate fit and inaccurate volatility estimates. The performance of ARCH models can be sensitive to assumptions about the error distribution, often assuming normality.

Additionally, a large number of parameters in higher-order ARCH models require more data and computational resources. Finally, ARCH models are primarily designed for short-term forecasting and may be less accurate for longer-term forecasts or when complex patterns and structural breaks are present. Combining ARCH models with other techniques or employing more sophisticated models may be necessary for improved forecasting.

## 3.6  Generalized Autoregressive Conditional Heteroskedasticity (GARCH) Model

The generalized autoregressive conditional heteroskedasticity (GARCH) model extends the ARCH model, enabling the capture of dynamic changes in volatility over time and providing greater flexibility for modeling heteroskedasticity in time series data. Similar to how ARIMA generalizes ARMA models, GARCH generalizes ARCH models. The GARCH model determines the best predictor of variance in the next period by considering a weighted average of the long-run average variance, the predicted variance, and new information available in the current period. This framework allows for a more comprehensive understanding of volatility patterns in the data.

The GARCH model incorporates two main components: the AR and the MA. Let us discuss the GARCH(1,1) model, one of the most commonly-used versions. The GARCH(1,1) model can be represented as follows:

$$\sigma_t^2 = \omega + \alpha \varepsilon_{(t-1)}^2 + \beta \sigma_{(t-1)}^2$$

$$\varepsilon_t = \sigma_t * Z_t$$

In the above equations:

- $\sigma_t^2$ represents the conditional variance at time t and
- $\omega$ is a constant term representing the long-term average of the conditional variance.

$\alpha$ and $\beta$ are parameters that need to be estimated. $\alpha$ represents the impact of the lagged squared residual on the current conditional variance; $\beta$ represents the impact of the lagged conditional variance on the current conditional variance. $\varepsilon_t$ represents the standardized error term or residual at time t, and $Z_t$ is a standardized random variable with mean zero and unit variance.

In the GARCH(1,1) model, the conditional variance ($\sigma_t^2$) is modeled as a linear combination of three terms: a constant term ($\omega$), the impact of the lagged squared residual ($\alpha \varepsilon_{(t-1)}^2$), and the impact of the lagged conditional variance ($\beta \sigma_{(t-1)}^2$). The parameters $\alpha$ and $\beta$ determine volatility shocks' persistence and decay rate.

The GARCH model captures volatility clustering, persistence, and autocorrelation in the conditional variance. It addresses some limitations of the ARCH model, such as incorporating the impact of lagged conditional variance on the current volatility. By estimating the parameters of the GARCH model, one can gain insights into the time-varying volatility patterns in the data and generate more accurate volatility forecasts. GARCH model parameters can be estimated using MLE or other optimization techniques. The parameters that best fit the model to the data are obtained by maximizing the likelihood function.

The GARCH model has several variations, including extensions like exponential GARCH (EGARCH) that allow for asymmetric effects in volatility and threshold GARCH (TGARCH) that incorporate threshold effects in volatility modeling. These variations offer additional features to capture more complex dynamics in time-varying volatility. The GARCH model and its variations are widely used in finance, economics, and other fields where modeling and forecasting volatility are essential, such as risk management, option pricing, and portfolio optimization.

The GARCH model provides several advantages for modeling and analyzing time series data with changing volatility. First, it explicitly captures volatility clustering, where periods of high volatility are followed by similar periods. This allows for an accurate representation of time-varying volatility patterns. GARCH models offer flexibility by adjusting model orders, accommodating various degrees of persistence, leverage effects, and asymmetry in conditional variance. Efficient estimation methods like MLE provide reliable parameter estimates capturing volatility dynamics. GARCH models can capture asymmetry and leverage effects, essential in financial modeling where positive and negative shocks may impact volatility differently. These models find extensive applications in risk management, enabling VaR and ES estimation. GARCH models excel in volatility forecasting, providing insights for risk assessment, option pricing, portfolio optimization, and trading strategies. Diagnostic tests allow for model validation, detecting autocorrelation and identifying potential misspecifications or outliers.

While the GARCH model offers advantages, it is essential to consider its limitations and disadvantages. Firstly, selecting appropriate orders for a GARCH model can be complex, and incorrect specifications can lead to inadequate fit and inaccurate volatility estimates. Sensitivity to initial values can also impact parameter estimation, requiring careful consideration and experimentation. Computational complexity arises, particularly in larger models or with high-frequency data, demanding efficient algorithms and computational resources. Larger models with more parameters increase the risk of overfitting, necessitating sufficient high-quality data. GARCH models assume linear relationships, limiting their ability to capture complex nonlinear volatility dynamics. Structural breaks in volatility patterns may also be challenging for GARCH models to capture adequately. The assumptions of GARCH models, such as distributional assumptions, need to be evaluated, and alternative specifications can be explored to enhance robustness.

# 4

# Quantifying Complex Patterns of Time Series

Complex patterns in time series data present challenges for prediction using simple mathematical or statistical models. These patterns can arise from various factors, including nonlinearity, nonstationarity, long memory or dependence, asymmetry, and stochasticity complexity. Nonlinear relationships between variables or time points can generate intricate patterns, including chaotic behavior. Nonstationarity refers to changing statistical properties, such as trends or seasonality. Volatility clustering leads to high and low volatility clustering periods, contributing to complex variability. Long memory or dependence means that past values influence current values, even from distant time points. Asymmetry represents a lack of symmetry in the statistical properties of the series over time or between different levels or phases. Finally, the time series can exhibit complex patterns that are difficult to predict, known as stochastic complexity.

Complex patterns can be classified into deterministic, stochastic, and mixed. Deterministic complex patterns arise from nonlinear deterministic systems characterized by complex and chaotic behavior. Despite following specific rules, these systems can appear random due to their sensitivity to initial conditions and nonlinearity. A well-known example is the weather system, which adheres to deterministic physical laws but exhibits complex and seemingly unpredictable patterns due to its chaotic nature. On the other hand, complex stochastic patterns occur when a random process generates data. Even simple stochastic processes can produce intricate patterns. For instance, a random walk, a basic stochastic process, generates a complex, nonrepeating pattern that can be challenging to differentiate from a deterministic chaotic process. Financial market data, including stock prices, is often modeled as stochastic processes and can exhibit complex patterns. Lastly, mixed complex patterns are observed in real-world scenarios where time series data combines deterministic and stochastic elements. An example is the El Niño phenomenon, a climate pattern involving deterministic components governed by physical laws and stochastic factors stemming from random disturbances.

Complex patterns, whether they are deterministic, stochastic, or mixed, manifest in time series data across various scientific fields, where variables exhibit seemingly unpredictable and nonlinear fluctuations. Illustrative examples include financial markets, where stock prices, exchange rates, and commodity prices demonstrate chaotic behavior with irregular and unpredictable movements. These time series display characteristics of chaos, such as sensitive dependence on initial conditions, despite certain regularities like trends and cycles. Meteorological data, known for their chaotic nature, offer another example, exemplified by the famous "Lorenz attractor" derived from differential equations that model weather patterns. This discovery showcased the high sensitivity of weather to initial conditions, now referred to as the "butterfly effect." Ecological systems also exhibit chaotic behavior, as seen in predator-prey models, where population sizes fluctuate in a complex and nonlinear manner. In health sciences, disease patterns such as influenza or COVID-19 outbreaks and the sequence of a patient's heartbeats can display chaotic patterns. Additionally, traffic flow in congested networks frequently demonstrates chaotic behavior.

To quantify the complex patterns observed in data, various methods can be employed to assess their characteristics, such as nonstationarity, nonlinearity, long memory or dependence, asymmetry, and stochasticity. Although time series analysis can be applied to various fields, stock forecasting was chosen as a demonstration field due to the easy availability of data. For this purpose, the necessary data was collected from Yahoo Finance, a platform that offers financial information, including stock quotes, commentary, press releases, and financial reports. The stock data obtained from Yahoo Finance consists of a historical record of observations spanning a specific period.

## 4.1 Nonstationarity

Nonstationarity in time series data implies the statistical properties of a sequence of observations change over time. These statistical properties include measures such as the mean, variance, and autocorrelation. Nonstationary processes contrast with stationary processes, where these properties are constant over time. Nonstationarity can manifest in trend, unit root, or heteroskedasticity.

**Trend Stationarity**

The series exhibits a deterministic trend, while the fluctuations around this trend are stationary. In other words, the series may increase or decrease over time, but how it wiggles around the trend remains constant. If the trend is eliminated, the resulting residual series becomes stationary. A simple mathematical form for a stationary trend series might be $Y\_t = \alpha + \beta t + \varepsilon\_t$.

Where:

- $Y\_t$ is the value of the series at time t,
- $\alpha$ is a constant,
- $\beta$ is the trend, and
- $\varepsilon\_t$ is a stationary error term.

## Difference Stationarity (or Unit Root)

Difference stationarity is a stronger manifestation of nonstationarity, characterized by the series attaining stationarity only through differencing. In other words, the series possesses a unit root, implying it maintains a nonstationary behavior until the appropriate differencing is applied. A unit root is a property of stochastic processes or time series models in which one or more parameters equals 1. It is a critical concept in econometrics and time series analysis because it is often associated with nonstationarity. A time series with a unit root is typically characterized by a pattern of random walk, meaning its future values cannot be predicted accurately from its past or present values. This is because shocks to the system (random perturbations) have permanent effects and will not diminish over time.

The most common example is a random walk, $Y\_t = Y\_(t-1) + \varepsilon\_t$.

Where:

- $Y\_t$ is the value of the series at time t,
- $Y\_(t-1)$ is the value at time (t-1), and
- $\varepsilon\_t$ is a random error term.

The series Y is not stationary, but the difference series, $\Delta Y\_t = Y\_t - Y\_(t-1)$, is stationary.

In mathematical terms, let us consider a simple autoregressive model of order 1 (AR(1)): $Y_t = \alpha + \beta Y_{(t-1)} + \varepsilon_t$.

Where:

- $Y_t$ is the value of the time series at time t,
- $Y_{(t-1)}$ is the value of the time series at time (t-1),
- $\alpha$ is a constant,
- $\beta$ is a coefficient of the lagged variable $Y_{(t-1)}$, and
- $\varepsilon_t$ is the error term at time t.

In this model, if $\beta = 1$, we say the time series $Y_t$ has a unit root.

If a time series has a unit root, it is nonstationary and has an unpredictable pattern with statistical properties that vary over time. This can be problematic for econometric analysis, as many standard statistical techniques require that data be stationary. In such nonstationary cases, it may be necessary to transform the data (e.g., through differencing) to achieve stationarity before applying traditional statistical analysis methods.

## Changing Variance (or Heteroskedasticity)

The series might have a constant mean but changing variance over time. The changing variance or heteroskedasticity refers to situations where the variability or dispersion of the series changes over time. This means that the series' volatility is not constant; there can be periods of high volatility and periods of low volatility. This is common in many financial time series, such as stock prices or exchange rates. For instance, during times of economic crisis, financial markets often become more volatile, leading to larger changes in prices from one day to the next. Conversely, during more stable periods, price changes might be relatively small.

## Measuring Nonstationarity

An Augmented Dickey-Fuller (ADF) test helps assess the historical data's nonstationarity. The ADF test, a variant of the Dickey-Fuller test, is a statistical tool primarily used to ascertain the stationarity of a time series. It checks for the existence of a unit root in a time series and is recognized as one of the most effective techniques to distinguish between stationary and nonstationary time series. The ADF test tests the null hypothesis that a time series has a unit root (i.e., is nonstationary). If the test rejects the null hypothesis, it suggests the time series is stationary. If it fails to reject the null hypothesis, it suggests the time series has a unit root and is nonstationary. The p-value obtained from the test interprets the stationarity, where a value less than 0.05 signifies stationarity, while a value exceeding 0.05 implies nonstationarity of the time series.

The figure below visualizes the time series data for the MLM stock from January 2, 2008, to February 10, 2023. From the figure, it is observed that the series has complex patterns. The ADF test resulted in a p-value of 0.93, indicating significant nonstationarity.

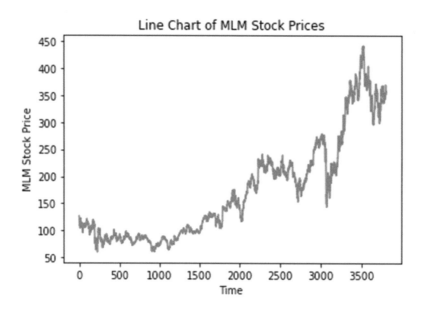

Figure 2: Time Series Data for the MLM Stock.

## 4.2   Nonlinearity

Nonlinearity in time series data refers to situations where changes in the series' output are not directly proportional to input changes. In other words, the relationship between past and future values of the series is not a straight line, and small changes in the input can lead to disproportionally large changes in the output or vice versa. Nonlinear time series display diverse and intricate behaviors, including cycles that vary in length, amplitude changes, and chaotic dynamics. Unlike linear sine or cosine waves with constant cycle lengths, nonlinear time series can exhibit cycles that fluctuate in duration over time. The amplitude, representing the size of these cycles, may also undergo changes, resulting in increased or decreased volatility within the series.

Additionally, certain nonlinear systems can exhibit chaotic behavior, whereby the time series appears random but is governed by deterministic rules. Chaotic systems are susceptible to initial conditions, causing even minor differences in starting values to yield vastly divergent outcomes, rendering long-term prediction nearly impossible. Nonlinear models can be challenging to estimate and interpret, as they often have multiple parameters and may include complex interactions between variables. They can also be more prone to overfitting than linear models.

The Lyapunov test can scrutinize the stability of a dynamical system and the nonlinearity within the time series data. This test utilizes the Lyapunov exponent, a measure that quantifies the divergence rate of trajectories in close proximity within a dynamic system. This indicates the degree of nonlinearity in the time series. If the Lyapunov exponent is positive, it suggests the system is in a state of chaos, implying that trajectories close to each other will exhibit exponential divergence as time progresses. Consequently, even minimal variances in the starting conditions can drastically alter long-term outcomes.

The figure below visualizes the time series data for the SEE stock from January 2, 2008, to February 10, 2023. From the figure, it is observed that the series has complex patterns. The Lyapunov test resulted in a Lyapunov exponent of 0.0027, indicating significant nonlinearity in time series data.

Figure 3: Time Series Data for the SEE Stock.

## 4.3 Long-Term Memory

The concept of long-term memory in time series data refers to the dependence of a current observation on historical observations from a significant distance in the past. This characteristic goes beyond what is typically observed in many common time series models like AR or MA, where the dependencies usually exist over a short or fixed period. In long-memory processes, these dependencies decay more slowly and can extend far into the past.

When a time series displays long-term memory, it retains a certain degree of persistence or memory of its past values. If the series experienced a high value in the past, it is more likely that future values will also be high and, similarly, for low values. This dependency can extend over surprisingly long periods, hence the term "long-term memory." This feature is particularly prevalent in various natural and social phenomena. For example, in finance, the volatility of financial returns can show long memory, meaning that periods of high volatility tend to be followed by similarly volatile periods and the same for low volatility.

The detrended fluctuation analysis (DFA) technique is employed to ascertain the presence of long-term memory within the time series. This method is primarily utilized to determine the long-term correlations or fluctuations within a time series signal. The Hurst exponent, an outcome of the DFA method, helps quantify the correlation traits of a time series. If the Hurst exponent exceeds 0.5, it implies the time series exhibits a positive correlation and displays long-term persistence. Conversely, a Hurst exponent below 0.5 signifies the time series is anti-persistent, indicating smaller ones likely follow larger fluctuations. A Hurst exponent is precisely equal to 0.5, denoting that the time series lacks any correlational properties.

The figure below visualizes the time series data for the JBLU stock from January 2, 2008, to February 10, 2023. From the figure, it is observed that the series has complex patterns. The DFA test resulted in a Hurst exponent of 1.49, indicating significant long-term memory in time series data.

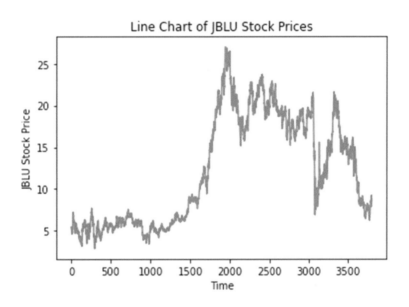

Figure 4: Time Series Data for the JBLU Stock.

## 4.4   Asymmetry

Asymmetry in time series data refers to when the statistical properties of the data are not the same across different levels or periods. This is in contrast to symmetric time series, where the properties of the data remain the same regardless of time shifts. There are several ways in which asymmetry can manifest in time series data. Nonlinear dependencies in a time series can lead to asymmetries. For example, a series might exhibit more substantial dependencies or more extreme values in one direction than another.

In financial time series, it is common to observe that negative shocks, like a decrease in price or return, lead to a greater increase in volatility (risk) than positive shocks of the same magnitude, a phenomenon often referred to as the "leverage effect." In some time series, the seasonal patterns may not be symmetric. For example, in a series of monthly sales data for a retail store, the sales increase leading up to the December holiday season may be more rapid than the decrease afterward. Some time series may exhibit trends that are not symmetric. For example, the series might increase faster than it decreases or vice versa.

Skewness is a statistical measure that can quantify the degree of asymmetry of a probability distribution and, by extension, a time series. In a time series context, skewness can be used to analyze whether the distribution of the data points in the series is symmetric (having a skewness close to 0) or if it leans toward one side, either to the right (positive skewness) or the left (negative skewness). If a time series has a positive skewness, the distribution's right tail is longer or fatter than the left one. Practically, this means that exceptionally large values are more likely than exceptionally small ones. For instance, a positive skew in a daily sales data time series might indicate occasional days with very high sales, but days with very low sales are less frequent or extreme. On the other hand, if a time series has a negative skewness, it means the left tail of the distribution is longer or fatter than the right one. This would mean that the series has occasional exceptionally low values, but the high values are less extreme or less frequent. The formula for skewness is $E[((X - \mu)/\sigma)^3]$.

Where:
- E denotes the expectation operator,
- X represents the values in the time series,
- $\mu$ is the mean (average) of the time series, and
- $\sigma$ is the standard deviation of the time series.

Understanding the skewness of a time series can be very important in forecasting and modeling. Many time series models assume the errors are normally distributed, implying zero skewness. If the skewness is significantly different from 0, these models may not be appropriate, and data transformations or different models may be needed.

The figure below visualizes the time series data for the PENN stock from January 2, 2008, to February 10, 2023. From the figure, it is observed that the series has complex patterns. The calculated skewness is 2.4, indicating significant asymmetry in time series data.

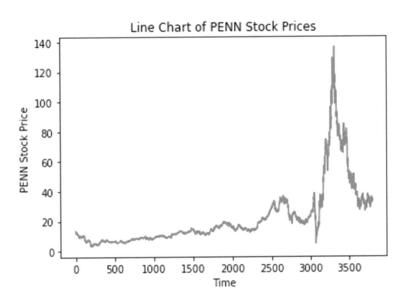

Figure 5: Time Series Data for the PENN Stock.

## 4.5   Stochasticity

Stochasticity refers to the randomness or unpredictability inherent in a process. A stochastic time series is one where the future state is determined not solely by the current state but also incorporates an element of randomness. In other words, the evolution of a stochastic time series is probabilistic. For example, consider the daily closing prices of a stock in the financial markets. Each day's closing price (tomorrow's price) depends on today's price but also on many other factors that introduce randomness, such as news about the company, economic indicators, geopolitical events, and so forth. We can model this using a stochastic process because the future stock price, while related to the current price, also involves a degree of unpredictability.

In the analysis of a stochastic time series, various elements require attention. The trend, for instance, represents the long-term direction the series is moving, demonstrating a gradual increase, decrease, or possibly no change at all. Seasonality, another key feature, denotes regularly repeating patterns in the data occurring at fixed time intervals, such as daily, monthly, or annually. This aspect accounts for time-driven events like seasonal sales spikes in retail. Cycles, in contrast to seasonality,

41

refer to patterns in the data not confined to a fixed length. These can embody fluctuating phenomena like business or economic cycles that lack a defined, regular period. Finally, there are random or irregular movements. These changes in the time series can't be attributed to trend, seasonality, or cycles and are often considered noise, or the random error component of the series. These irregularities contribute to the stochasticity, or unpredictability, inherent in the time series.

Entropy can provide a measure of the predictability of the time series. Entropy is a concept that originated in thermodynamics and information theory, which can be used to quantify the level of uncertainty, disorder, or randomness—in this context, the stochasticity—in a dataset. A lower entropy suggests a more predictable (less stochastic) time series, while higher entropy corresponds to more disorder or randomness (greater stochasticity). In a perfectly deterministic system, entropy would be zero because future states can be predicted with certainty from current states. While there exists variations of entory, Shannon entropy is widely used to measure the uncertainty.

The equation for Shannon entropy is $H(X) = - \Sigma\, p(x) \log_2 p(x)$.

Where $p(x)$ represents the probability of an event $x$. The sum is over all possible events.

The figure below visualizes the time series data for the FIZZ stock from January 2, 2008, to February 10, 2023. From the figure, it is observed that the series has complex patterns. The calculated entropy is 7.75, a figure exceeding 90 percent of the maximum possible entropy. This maximum entropy was determined as the logarithm of the number of unique elements within the time series data, that is, log(len(np.unique(time_series_data))). The high entropy indicates the time series is highly unpredictable, further indicating a high degree of stochasticity.

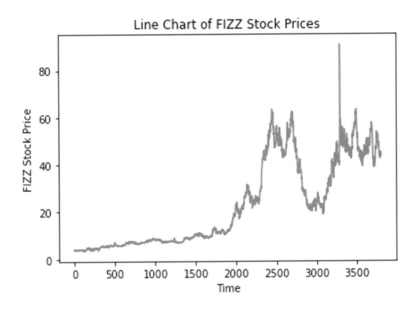

Figure 6: Time Series Data for the FIZZ Stock.

## 4.6   Multiple Characteristics

While the above examples demonstrated a single characteristic for each stock, they often exhibit all complex patterns: nonstationarity, nonlinearity, long memory or dependence, and asymmetry.

The figure below visualizes the time series data for the IESC stock from January 2, 2008, to February 10, 2023. From the figure, it is observed that the series has complex patterns. The measures are as listed.

- ADF p-value: 0.89
- DFA Hurst exponent: 1.47
- Lyapunov exponent: 0.0037
- Skewness: 1.32
- Entropy: 7.25

The measures reveal that the time series exhibits the characteristics of nonstationarity, nonlinearity, long memory or dependence, asymmetry, and stochasticity.

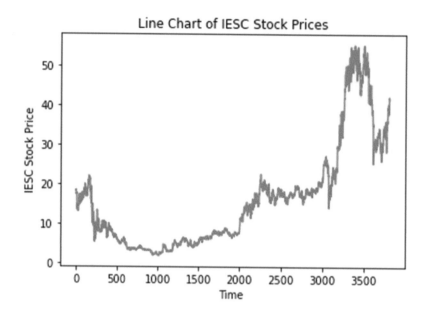

Figure 7: Time Series Data for the IESC Stock.

## 4.7   Code Used to Measure the Complex Patterns

Following is the Python script, used to quantify the complex patterns in time series data. It has utilized essential libraries. The goal of this script is to analyze the predictability and statistical properties of a time series data, more specifically, a dataset of stock prices. It starts by importing the necessary libraries, including NumPy for numerical computation, pandas for data manipulation, statsmodels for statistical modeling, scipy for scientific computation, matplotlib for data visualization, and nolds for nonlinear time series analysis. The dataset used in this script, ticker.csv (where ticker corresponds to a given stock), consists of closing prices of a certain stock over time. It is loaded into a pandas DataFrame, and two distinct series, Date and Close, are separated for further analysis.

The script employs various statistical tests and metrics to analyze this time series data. First, the ADF test is used to check the stationarity of the series. The Hurst exponent and Lyapunov exponent, derived using DFA, are calculated to measure the nonlinearity and long memory in the data, respectively. Skewness is also calculated to measure the asymmetry of the data distribution. Next, the entropy of the time series data is calculated. Entropy is a statistical measure of randomness that can be used to characterize the predictability of a series. Based on the entropy, the time series is categorized into being highly unpredictable, moderately unpredictable, or fairly predictable.

A line chart is plotted to visually represent the changes in stock prices over time. The graph title and axes labels are appropriately set, and the plot is displayed using matplotlib's show function.

```python
import numpy as np
import pandas as pd
import statsmodels.tsa.api as ts
import scipy.stats as ss
import matplotlib.pyplot as plt
import nolds as nl
from scipy.stats import entropy
df = pd.read_csv('ticker.csv')
date_data = df['Date']
time_series_data = df['Close']
adf_p_value = ts.adfuller(time_series_data)[1]
print("ADF P-Value ", adf_p_value)
dfa_hurst = nl.dfa(time_series_data)
print("DFA Hurst Exponent ", dfa_hurst)
lyapunov_exponent = nl.lyap_r(time_series_data)
print("Lyapunov Exponent ", lyapunov_exponent)
skewness = ss.skew(time_series_data)
print("Skewness ", skewness)
value, counts = np.unique(time_series_data, return_counts=True)
ent = entropy(counts)
print(f"Entropy ", ent)
max_entropy = np.log(len(np.unique(time_series_data)))
if ent > 0.9 * max_entropy:
    print("The time series is highly unpredictable, likely indicating a high degree of stochasticity.")
elif ent > 0.5 * max_entropy:
    print("The time series is moderately unpredictable, suggesting a mix of stochastic and deterministic behavior.")
else:
```

```
print("The time series is fairly predictable, likely indicating deterministic behavior with low
stochasticity.")
plt.plot(time_series_data, color='green')
plt.title(f"Line Chart of {ticker} Stock Prices")
plt.xlabel("Time")
plt.ylabel(f"{ticker} Stock Price")
plt.show()
```

# 5

# Demystifying Machine Learning

Machine learning operates distinctly compared to conventional algorithms, leveraging historical data to develop algorithms that optimize the combination of features and weights. This approach deviates from the predefined rules and instructions in traditional algorithms. Predictive analytics is one prominent application of machine learning, empowering intelligent, data-driven decision-making. Machine learning-based predictive analytics is advantageous over traditional predictive analytics by effectively capturing and utilizing the relationships between explanatory and predicted variables from past occurrences to anticipate unknown outcomes. Real-time fraud detection in credit card transactions practically illustrates machine learning's capabilities.

Furthermore, machine learning allows grouping or clustering of items based on shared characteristics. This attribute proves beneficial in comprehending consumer preferences and behavior in the retail industry, aiding in preventing out-of-stock situations. By employing machine learning, consumers can be grouped based on their purchasing patterns, allowing retailers to effectively align their inventory with consumer preferences.

Machine learning empowers machines to identify patterns by utilizing a subset of historical data known as the training dataset. This dataset encompasses both input and corresponding outcomes from past occurrences. By comprehending patterns from the training dataset, the machine constructs an algorithm capable of predicting future outcomes based on incoming data. To achieve this, the machine examines the relationship between input and output within the training dataset, enabling it to generate predictions for the test dataset. The model's generated outcome is then compared against the actual outcome in the test dataset. Through an iterative process, the machine fine-tunes the model parameters, continuously learning until the predicted outcome aligns with the true outcome within the test dataset. This training process ensures the machine gains proficiency in accurately predicting outcomes based on input data.

Machine learning encompasses three main methods: supervised, unsupervised, and semi-supervised. Each technique serves distinct purposes and operates with different data types.

Supervised learning predicts outcomes based on specified features and relies on labeled data. This method is commonly employed for regression and classification tasks. Supervised learning algorithms learn patterns and relationships by leveraging the labeled data to make accurate predictions. In the case of regression, the objective is to predict outcomes based on numeric data. For instance, consider predicting the temperature for the next few days. A regression model can be trained to forecast the temperature values by analyzing historical temperature data. Based on the numeric temperature predictions, this allows us to anticipate whether the upcoming days will be cold, warm, or hot.

On the other hand, classification involves assigning incoming input to specific categories. The algorithm requires the numeric data to be transformed into categorical labels to perform classification. Using the temperature example, we can convert the numeric temperature values into categories such as "cold," "warm," or "hot" based on predefined ranges. This enables the classification algorithm to determine the appropriate category for each input. Classification algorithms include logistic regression, naïve Bayes, support vector machine, k-nearest neighbors, and decision tree. On the other hand, a random forest algorithm comes in both the forms of regression analysis and classification and is considered suitable for nonlinear analysis.

In contrast, unsupervised learning focuses on detecting patterns within a dataset and categorizing the data without using labels. This method utilizes unlabeled data, earning its name "unsupervised" as the algorithms are unaware of the underlying patterns in the data. Typical applications of unsupervised learning include anomaly detection and clustering. Clustering involves grouping data elements into multiple categories based on their similarities, allowing for the identification of cohesive clusters within the dataset. Unsupervised learning encompasses various applications, including clustering, where similar data points are grouped based on intrinsic properties, such as customer segmentation for targeted marketing; anomaly detection, which identifies unusual patterns like cybersecurity breaches; dimensionality reduction for visualizing and understanding high-dimensional data; and association rule mining, uncovering relationships in datasets like market basket analysis for cross-selling and optimizing product placement in retail settings. These unsupervised learning techniques facilitate the exploration of data patterns, anomaly identification, feature reduction, and discovery of meaningful associations without relying on labeled data.

Semi-supervised learning represents a hybrid approach that combines supervised and unsupervised learning elements. It leverages labeled and unlabeled data to make predictions, utilizing the labeled data for guidance while extracting different patterns and insights from the unlabeled data. Semi-supervised learning offers versatile applications across various domains. In text classification tasks, semi-supervised learning can significantly reduce labeling efforts while preserving classification accuracy. This is achieved by labeling a small subset of documents and leveraging the knowledge gained from them to propagate labels to unlabeled data. Similarly, in image recognition, semi-supervised learning enhances performance by initially training the model using a set of labeled images and then applying this knowledge to classify unlabeled images, thereby improving accuracy without requiring an extensive labeling of the entire dataset. For fraud detection, where it is critical to identify fraudulent transactions, semi-supervised learning proves invaluable. Models are trained using labeled fraudulent instances, and the patterns learned from these instances are used to identify potential fraud in unlabeled data, minimizing the need for a large number of labeled instances. Semi-supervised learning also finds its use in recommendation systems, where only a portion of user-item interactions or preferences is labeled. By training the model with this labeled data and utilizing the acquired knowledge, personalized recommendations can be generated for unlabeled interactions, reducing the reliance on fully-labeled data. In this way, semi-supervised learning bridges the gap between labeled and unlabeled data, enabling efficient and accurate learning with reduced labeling efforts. This approach proves particularly advantageous when acquiring large amounts of labeled data is challenging or costly.

## 5.1   Linear Regression

Linear regression predicts a continuous outcome variable, also called the dependent variable, based on one or more predictor variables, also called independent variables. It models the relationship between two variables by fitting a linear equation to the observed data. The steps to performing linear regression are the following:

In simple linear regression, the dependent variable is predicted using a single independent variable. The relationship is given by the equation: $Y = b_0 + b_1{*}X + e$.

Where:

- Y is the dependent variable,
- X is the independent variable,
- $b_0$ is the Y-intercept (value of Y when X = 0),
- $b_1$ is the slope of the line (change in Y for each one-unit change in X), and
- e is the error term (difference between the actual and predicted value).

In multiple linear regression, the dependent variable is predicted using more than one independent variable. The equation becomes $Y = b_0 + b_1 X_1 + b_2 X_2 + \ldots + b_n{*}X_n + e$.

By finding the line of best fit, that is, the line that minimizes the sum of the squared errors, also called residuals, the linear regression optimizes the prediction. This is also known as the method of least squares.

Linear regression operates under several key assumptions that are critical for its implementation. It assumes a linearity in the relationship between independent and dependent variables, meaning that changes in the independent variables correspond to consistent changes in the dependent variables. It also presumes independence among observations, implying that each observation comes from the same distribution and does not depend on the other observations. Another assumption, homoscedasticity, stipulates that the variance or dispersion of errors is the same across all levels of the independent variables. Additionally, it assumes normality in the prediction errors, indicating the distribution of errors follows a normal distribution. These assumptions underpin the efficacy of linear regression in numerous fields include, but are not limited to, finance and economics, where it is applied to model and predict various phenomena.

## 5.2  Logistic Regression

Logistic regression is a popular statistical technique used for binary classification problems, where the goal is to predict the probability of an instance belonging to a specific class. It is widely employed in various fields, including machine learning, epidemiology, finance, and social sciences.

In logistic regression, a binary dependent variable or target variable (commonly denoted as y) that can take two values, 0 and 1, is used. The objective is to predict the probability of y being 1 given a set of input features (commonly denoted as x). The logistic, or sigmoid function, is used in logistic regression to transform the linear combination of input features into a value between 0 and 1.

The sigmoid function is defined as $\sigma(z) = 1 / (1 + e^{\wedge}(-z))$, where z represents the linear combination of input features and model coefficients (known as weights).

**Hypothesis Function**

Predictions in logistic regression are made using a hypothesis function that combines the sigmoid function and the linear equation: $h(x) = \sigma(w_0 + w_1 x_1 + w_2 x_2 + ... + w\_n x\_n)$.

Here, $w_0$, $w_1$, $w_2$, ..., w_n represent the coefficients or weights associated with each input feature, and $x_1$, $x_2$, ..., x_n are the corresponding feature values.

The logistic regression model is trained through a process of optimizing its parameters (weights) with the goal of minimizing the discrepancy between the model's predicted probabilities and actual class labels found in the training data. This is generally accomplished using a method known as MLE or, alternatively, through the minimization of a cost or loss function, like the cross-entropy loss. An algorithm named gradient descent is frequently used for iteratively updating the model weights. This algorithm determines the gradients of the cost function concerning the weights and subsequently adjusts the weights in the direction that reduces the cost. This iterative procedure continues until either convergence is achieved or a predefined stopping criterion is fulfilled. Once the training phase is complete, the model can make predictions on new, unseen data. A decision boundary, which separates the two classes based on predicted probabilities, is established. This decision boundary hinges on a threshold probability, typically set at 0.5.

Instances with probabilities above this threshold are classified as belonging to one class, while those below are classified as belonging to the other class. In some scenarios, regularization techniques such as L1 (lasso) or L2 (ridge) regularization can be employed in logistic regression to curb overfitting and enhance the model's ability to generalize to unseen data. This involves constraining the weights from attaining excessively large values by incorporating a penalty term.

## 5.3    Ridge and Lasso Regression

Ridge and lasso regressions are extensions of linear regression, where a penalty term is added to the cost function to minimize overfitting and improve the model's generalization. This process is known as regularization.

Ridge regression is a type of linear regression that introduces a small amount of bias into the regression estimates to reduce the standard errors. This method, also known as L2 regularization, uses a penalty term to discourage the coefficients of the regression model from reaching large absolute values, a situation that indicates overfitting.

The ridge coefficients minimize a penalized residual sum of squares: Minimize ($\Sigma$ [y(i) − $\Sigma$ $\beta$(j)*x(I,j)]$^2$ + $\lambda\Sigma$ $\beta$(j)$^2$).

Here, $\lambda \geq 0$ is a complexity parameter that controls the amount of shrinkage: the larger the value of $\lambda$, the greater the amount of shrinkage. The coefficients are shrunken toward 0 (and each other). This shrinkage has the effect of reducing variance and can lead to significant improvement in model performance on testing data.

Ridge regression works best in situations where the least square estimates have high variance. So it will shrink the coefficients for least important predictors, very close to 0. But it will never make them exactly 0; hence, the final model will still include all those predictors.

Lasso regression (least absolute shrinkage and selection operator) also uses a penalty term, but with a key difference from ridge regression. Lasso uses an L1 penalty, which can force some coefficients to be exactly equal to zero. This means the lasso can exclude useless or irrelevant variables from a model.

The Lasso coefficients minimize a penalized residual sum of squares: Minimize ($\Sigma$ [y(i) − $\Sigma$ $\beta$(j)*x(I,j)]$^2$ + $\lambda\Sigma$ |$\beta$(j)|).

Here again, $\lambda \geq 0$ is a complexity parameter that controls the amount of shrinkage. When $\lambda$ = 0, no parameters are eliminated. But when $\lambda = \infty$, all coefficients are shrunk toward 0.

In other words, Lasso simultaneously performs variable selection and regularization. Therefore, it can be particularly useful when dealing with high-dimensional datasets with many predictors or when dealing with predictors that exhibit a high degree of multicollinearity.

## 5.4   Naïve Bayes

Naïve Bayes is an algorithm based on the principles of Bayes' theorem. It is commonly used for classification tasks and is known for its simplicity, efficiency, and effectiveness, especially in text categorization and spam filtering. At the core of naïve Bayes is Bayes' theorem, which provides a way to calculate the probability of an event occurring given prior knowledge of related conditions. The theorem incorporates the prior probability of an event and likelihood of observing certain conditions given that event.

The theorem is defined as P(A|B) = (P(B|A) * P(A)) / P(B).

Where:
- P(A|B) is the posterior probability of event A given event B,
- P(B|A) is the likelihood of event B given event A,
- P(A) is the prior probability of event A, and
- P(B) is the prior probability of event B.

Naïve Bayes makes a strong assumption known as the "naïve" or "strong" independence assumption. It assumes the features used for classification are conditionally independent of each other, given the class variable. This simplifying assumption enables efficient calculations and makes the algorithm well-suited for high-dimensional datasets.

During the training phase, naïve Bayes learns the statistical relationships between the features and target classes from a labeled dataset. It estimates the prior probabilities and conditional probabilities based on the observed frequencies or probabilities in the training data. Categorical features are typically represented as counts or frequencies, while numerical features may be discretized into bins or transformed into categorical variables.

In the classification phase, naïve Bayes calculates the probability of each class given the observed features using Bayes' theorem. It evaluates the likelihood of the features given to each class, multiplies them with the corresponding prior probabilities, and normalizes the results to obtain the posterior probabilities for each class. The class with the highest posterior probability is assigned to the instance using a decision rule, often called the maximum a posteriori (MAP) rule. To handle cases where a feature value has not been observed in the training data, naïve Bayes incorporates Laplace smoothing, also known as additive smoothing. This technique adds a small constant value to all observed counts, preventing zero probabilities and accounting for unseen feature values during classification. It performs well when the naïve assumption of feature independence holds reasonably well.

## 5.5   Support Vector Machine (SVM)

Support vector machine (SVM) is a robust supervised machine learning algorithm for classification and regression tasks. It is widely used due to its effectiveness in handling complex datasets. SVM aims to find an optimal hyperplane in a high-dimensional feature space that can best separate the different classes of data points. The hyperplane is selected to maximize the margin, the distance between the hyperplane and closest data points from each class. These closest data points, called support vectors, are crucial in defining the decision boundary.

SVM is particularly effective in scenarios where the data is not linearly separable in the original feature space. To handle such cases, SVM employs the kernel trick. The kernel function allows mapping the data into a higher-dimensional space, where finding a linear hyperplane that separates the classes becomes easier. Standard kernel functions include the linear kernel, polynomial kernel, and radial basis function (RBF) kernel.

In the training phase, SVM learns the optimal hyperplane by solving an optimization problem. The objective is to minimize the classification error and maximize the margin. This is typically achieved by solving a quadratic programming problem with the help of optimization techniques such as sequential minimal optimization (SMO).

Once the SVM model is trained, it can predict the class labels of new, unseen data points. The position and orientation of the hyperplane determine the decision boundary. Data points on one side of the hyperplane are classified into one class, while those on the other side belong to the other class. During prediction, the model evaluates the position of the test data relative to the decision boundary to assign class labels.

SVM offers flexibility and generalization capabilities by using different kernel functions and tuning hyperparameters. It can handle datasets with a high number of features and is less affected by outliers compared to some other algorithms. However, SVM's performance can be sensitive to the choice of the kernel function and hyperparameters, and it may become computationally expensive with large datasets.

## 5.6 K-Nearest Neighbor (KNN)

K-nearest neighbors (KNN) is a supervised machine learning algorithm for classification and regression tasks. KNN stores the labeled training dataset during the training phase without explicit model training or parameter estimation. To make predictions, KNN identifies the K-nearest neighbors in the training dataset based on a chosen distance metric, such as Euclidean or Manhattan distance. The value of K, determined by the user, is the number of neighbors considered. KNN employs majority voting among the K neighbors to assign a class label to the new data point for classification. The class label most frequently among the neighbors is assigned to the point. In regression tasks, KNN predicts the target value for the new data point by averaging the target values of its K-nearest neighbors.

KNN can optionally be modified to assign weights to the neighbors based on their distances. Closer neighbors have higher weights, indicating a stronger influence on the final prediction. This is known as weighted KNN. Selecting the optimal value of K is crucial, affecting the model's bias-variance trade-off. A smaller K can result in a more flexible model that may overfit the training data, while a larger K can lead to a more stable model but potentially increased bias. The optimal K value is typically determined through hyperparameter tuning using cross-validation or other evaluation techniques.

KNN has several strengths, including its simplicity, versatility, and ability to handle multiclass classification problems. It can capture complex relationships in the data and adapt to different decision boundaries. However, KNN can be sensitive to the curse of dimensionality and may suffer from reduced performance as the number of features increases. It can also be computationally expensive for large datasets due to the need for distance calculations.

## 5.7   Decision Tree

A decision tree is a machine-learning algorithm used for classification and regression tasks. The decision tree algorithm constructs a model of decisions based on actual values of attributes in the data. The structure of a decision tree is similar to a flowchart where each internal node represents a test on an attribute, each branch represents the outcome of this test, and each leaf node represents a class label or a decision. The topmost node in the decision tree is called the root node. It learns to partition the data based on the values of the attributes. The partitions form a subset of the data, further divided by subsequent nodes in the tree. The way the tree is split at each node is determined by a function that measures the impurity or uncertainty of the data. The goal is to minimize this impurity in the data. The most common impurity measures are Gini impurity, entropy, classification error for classification trees, and mean squared error, mean absolute error, and so forth for regression trees.

Let us take a simple example of how a decision tree might work for a classification problem. Assume a dataset of various animals is presented, characterized by two features: "Number of legs" and "Can fly." The classification of each animal as a "bird," "mammal," or "insect" is desired. Initially, the data might be split based on the "Can fly" feature by the root node. If an animal possesses flight capability, it might be classified as a bird or an insect. If flight is impossible for the animal, it is likely categorized as a mammal. The next split in the data might be made at the subsequent node, dependent on the "Number of legs" feature. If the animal can fly and is equipped with two legs, it is likely classified as a bird. If flight is possible and more than two legs are present, an insect is a probable classification. Following the tree's branches from the root node to a leaf node, a decision or classification is ultimately reached for each animal.

Decision trees are a versatile machine learning tool applicable to various problems. They are employed in credit scoring models, analyzing multiple factors like income, debt, and credit history to evaluate the risk of lending money to borrowers, with higher credit scores suggesting lower default risks. In fraud detection, decision trees aid in identifying fraudulent transactions by considering transaction amount, fund source, and customer behavior. For medical diagnoses, decision trees assist doctors by considering patient symptoms, medical history, and test results to ascertain the most probable diagnosis. In marketing, they facilitate customer segmentation, dividing customers into groups based on shared characteristics, thus informing targeted campaigns, new product development, and customer service improvements. Moreover, decision trees are used in risk assessment models, determining the likelihood of adverse events and information pivotal for insurance, investments, and other financial decisions.

In the realm of time series data, decision trees prove their multifaceted utility across various tasks. They serve as classifiers, capable of categorizing time series data into distinct groups, like classifying stock prices as "buy," "sell," or "hold." They are invaluable tools for forecasting, predicting future data values, such as projecting the stock price for the next day. Additionally, decision trees excel in outlier detection, identifying data points significantly deviating from the norm due to either data errors or rare events. Furthermore, they facilitate segmentation, grouping similar data points together, a marketing and customer analysis technique often employed.

Although decision trees are powerful and versatile tools for analyzing time series data, they come with limitations. They can overfit a scenario where the model excessively learns the training data, impairing its ability to generalize to new data. Overfitting can be mitigated through pruning or regularization of the decision tree. Moreover, decision trees can be computationally expensive to train, especially with large datasets, as they must evaluate all potential data splits.

These challenges aside, decision trees remain beneficial in time series data analysis due to their interpretability and adaptability to various tasks.

## 5.8  Ensemble Methods

Ensemble machine learning methods combine multiple models' predictions to improve the overall performance. The main principle behind ensemble methods is that a group of weak learners can come together to form a strong learner. They aim to increase the model's accuracy, robustness, and stability. Some common types of ensemble methods include:

- Bagging: Bootstrap aggregating, or simply Bagging, involves creating multiple subsets of the original dataset, training a model on each subset, and combining the predictions. Each subset is created by sampling with replacement so some instances may be repeated in each subset. Bagging reduces variance and helps avoid overfitting. A popular example is the random forest algorithm.

- Boosting: Boosting trains models in sequence, where each new model is trained to correct the errors made by the previous ones. Boosted models convert weak learners into strong learners by emphasizing misclassified instances with higher errors. Examples include AdaBoost, gradient boosting, and XGBoost.

- Stacking: Stacking involves training multiple models and combining their predictions using another machine learning model, the meta-learner or second-level learner. The idea is to leverage the strengths of each model in the ensemble.

- Voting: Voting can be done in two ways, hard and soft. In hard voting, the final prediction is a majority vote among the models. In soft voting, probabilities predicted by each model are averaged to get the final prediction.

Each method has strengths and weaknesses and is suited to different problems and datasets. They can often provide a significant boost in performance compared to single models, especially on complex problems with large amounts of data.

## 5.9  Random Forest

Random forest is an ensemble learning method that constructs a multitude of decision trees at training time and outputs the average of their predictions at test time. It is used for both classification and regression tasks. Random forests are built using bagging, which involves repeatedly sampling the training data with replacements and then building a decision tree on each bootstrap sample. The final model is then created by averaging the predictions of the individual trees. Bagging has two main benefits. First, it helps to reduce the model's variance, making it less likely to overfit the training data. Second, it helps to improve the model's accuracy by averaging the predictions of multiple trees.

Random forest takes a bootstrap sample of the original dataset (i.e., a random sample with replacement). This process is done multiple times, generating multiple sets of data. For each bootstrap sample, a decision tree is built. However, unlike standard decision trees, where every feature is considered at each split, only a random subset of features is considered at each split in the tree. The split in the tree is then made on the best feature in this subset. This randomness in feature selection injects diversity into the ensemble and helps to reduce overfitting. For a classification problem, each tree in the forest gives a vote for the class, and the class with the most votes is chosen as the final prediction. For a regression problem, the average prediction of all trees is taken as the final prediction.

Random forests offer several advantages in machine learning applications, including high accuracy, particularly with high-dimensional data. They exhibit robustness against overfitting, an issue commonly observed in single decision trees, thus ensuring more reliable performance. Unlike more complex algorithms such as neural networks, random forests retain considerable interpretability, making them easier to understand and use. With versatility among their key strengths, they are adept at handling classification and regression tasks.

Despite their benefits, random forests do present some disadvantages. They can be computationally costly, particularly when training on large datasets, making them less optimal for time-sensitive applications or resource-limited environments. Their performance can be sensitive to hyperparameter selections, including the quantity of trees and their respective depths, which might require careful tuning. Furthermore, they may not always be the ideal choice for every machine learning problem, with other algorithms, such as neural networks, potentially offering greater accuracy or efficiency for specific tasks.

## 5.10    Adaptive Boosting (AdaBoost)

This is one of the first and most simple boosting algorithms. It works by assigning weights to instances and updating these weights at each iteration. The goal is to emphasize the misclassified instances in previous iterations. AdaBoost algorithm can be used for both classification and regression problems. It is a meta-algorithm, meaning it is an algorithm that builds other algorithms. In the case of AdaBoost, it builds a robust classifier or learner by combining a number of weak classifiers or learners.

AdaBoost regressor iteratively builds a series of weak learners. AdaBoost assigns weights to the training data points in each iteration based on how well the previous weak learner predicted them. The data points mispredicted are given higher weights, while the data points correctly predicted are given lower weights. This ensures the next weak learner will focus on the data points that were difficult to predict. The weak learners are then combined to form strong learners. The strong learner is a weighted sum of the weak learners, with the weights determined by the AdaBoost algorithm.

AdaBoost regressor offers several advantages over other machine learning algorithms when tackling regression problems. Notably, it can enhance the accuracy of weak learners, turning them into a stronger prediction model. Compared to other algorithms for regression, AdaBoost is less susceptible to overfitting, thereby maintaining a good balance between bias and variance. Additionally, the implementation and tuning of AdaBoost are relatively straightforward, making it a user-friendly tool for machine learning practitioners.

While the AdaBoost regressor offers certain advantages, it also comes with disadvantages. It can be computationally intensive to train, which might make it less feasible for large datasets or in resource-constrained environments. The performance of AdaBoost can be negatively impacted by noisy data, reducing its robustness. Furthermore, optimally tuning the algorithm's hyperparameters can be challenging, potentially affecting the algorithm's overall performance and efficiency.

## 5.11   Gradient Boosting Machine (GBM)

Gradient boosting works by fitting a new model to the residual errors of the previous model and then adding this new model's predictions to the ensemble's output. It can be used with any differentiable loss function, and the "gradient" in the name comes from the fact that the algorithm uses gradient descent to minimize the loss.

Gradient boosting machine (GBM) can be used to solve both classification and regression problems. It is a type of ensemble learning algorithm that builds a model by combining multiple weak learners. GBM works by iteratively building a series of weak learners. In each iteration, GBM fits a decision tree to the residuals of the previous weak learner. The residuals are the errors that the previous weak learner made. The decision tree is fit using a greedy algorithm, which means it tries to find the best split at each node in the tree that minimizes the error. The weak learners are then combined to form strong learners. The strong learner is a weighted sum of the weak learners, with the weights determined by the GBM algorithm.

Both GBM and AdaBoost are boosting algorithms that can be used to improve the accuracy of weak learners. However, there are some key differences between the two algorithms. GBM builds a model by iteratively fitting decision trees to the residuals of the previous weak learner. GBM uses a greedy algorithm to find the best split at each node in the tree. AdaBoost builds a model by iteratively assigning weights to the training data points based on how well the previous weak learners classified them. AdaBoost uses a weighted majority vote to combine weak and strong learners. AdaBoost can be more difficult to implement and tune than GBM.

## 5.12   Extreme Gradient Boosting (XGBoost)

Extreme gradient boosting (XGBoost) is an optimized distributed gradient boosting library designed to be highly efficient, flexible, and portable. It offers several useful features like regularization, tree pruning, handling missing values, and parallelizable learning. XGBoost algorithm can be used for regression and classification problems. It is an implementation of gradient boosting machines created by Tianqi Chen, offering several advanced features designed for efficiency, flexibility, and improved performance.

XGBoost operates on the principle of boosting, combining numerous weak learners, typically decision trees, into a robust learner by sequentially adding new models to rectify the errors made by the existing ensemble. It implements the gradient boosting framework, which utilizes gradient descent to minimize the loss as new models are integrated. Whenever a new tree is added, it identifies the optimal splits in the data to minimize the loss, that is, the difference between the actual and predicted values.

The XGBoost algorithm differentiates itself by incorporating regularization (L1 and L2) and deters overfitting by penalizing complex models, a feature not typically emphasized in other gradient-boosting algorithms. Furthermore, it employs parallel processing, harnessing multiple CPU cores, making it faster than comparable gradient-boosting methods. It handles missing values through an in-built routine that learns the best path for such instances over time. Regarding tree pruning, XGBoost grows the tree to the max_depth and prunes backward until the improvement in the loss function falls below a certain threshold, contrasting the GBM method, where trees are grown to a set depth. Finally, XGBoost includes built-in cross-validation capabilities, enabling the user to perform cross-validation at each iteration of the boosting process and determine the optimal number of boosting iterations in a single run.

XGBoost offers several advantages, including high predictive accuracy and ability to handle diverse data types, missing values, and outliers. It incorporates a regularization term to prevent overfitting, uses parallel processing for faster computation, and includes built-in cross-validation to determine the optimal number of boosting iterations. However, it also has disadvantages: it can be computationally intensive, especially with large datasets, and sensitive to noise and outliers. Moreover, tuning can be difficult due to the number of hyperparameters involved and may require significant computational resources and expertise.

## 5.13   Light Gradient Boosting Machine (LightGBM)

Light gradient boosting machine (LightGBM) is another gradient-boosting framework that uses tree-based learning algorithms. It is designed to be distributed and efficient with a faster training speed and lower memory usage. LightGBM improves on traditional gradient boosting techniques by using a novel technique of gradient-based one-side sampling (GOSS) and exclusive feature bundling (EFB).

LightGBM, similar to XGBoost, operates on a gradient-boosting framework, utilizing a decision tree-based learning algorithm. It sequentially fits new models to the residuals of preceding models, which are then summed together to yield the final prediction.

Distinct from other tree-based algorithms that typically grow trees level-wise (breadth-first), LightGBM adopts a leaf-wise (depth-first) approach. It prioritizes the leaf split that results in the maximum loss reduction or gain. While this may produce a more complex tree, it offers a more significant reduction in loss than level-wise growth. The LightGBM framework also incorporates EFB, an effective technique for handling high-dimensionality categorical features. EFB bundles exclusive features, those not taking non-zero values concurrently, to optimize memory usage and expedite computation.

Furthermore, LightGBM utilizes GOSS to manage large datasets. Instead of using all the data points in each iteration, it employs a smaller subset, enhancing the speed and reducing memory usage of the LightGBM framework. Instances with larger gradients or errors are preferentially selected for training, thereby improving learning on instances that produce large errors. LightGBM also natively handles missing values and supports categorical features, reducing the necessity for extensive data preprocessing. Lastly, it supports GPU learning and parallel learning, and it can split the tree across features and data points to hasten the learning process.

Despite its many advantages, LightGBM does present some limitations. It can be sensitive to overfitting, particularly when dealing with small datasets, potentially leading to suboptimal performance. Moreover, while it is quicker than several other algorithms, it can still demand substantial computational resources when handling large datasets or intricate models. Another notable challenge associated with LightGBM is the complexity and time-consuming nature of tuning its hyperparameters. It requires a solid understanding of the algorithm to effectively optimize these parameters, adding to the intricacy of its deployment.

## 5.14  CatBoost

CatBoost is a boosting algorithm that uses gradient boosting on decision trees with innovative strategies like ordered boosting, categorical features processing, and several speed and scale enhancements. It is primarily known for its ability to handle categorical variables and robust performance across various datasets. CatBoost, akin to XGBoost and LightGBM, is based on a gradient-boosting framework that employs decision tree-based algorithms. It functions by iteratively training numerous weak models, specifically decision trees, each progressively learning from the errors of its predecessors.

A notable aspect of CatBoost is its unique capability to directly handle categorical features, eliminating the need for extensive preprocessing or one-hot encoding. It deploys a proprietary algorithm to convert categorical values into numerical ones while preserving the statistical properties of the category. This efficient transformation results in enhanced performance and less memory usage. In addition, CatBoost employs a technique known as "ordered boosting." Unlike conventional boosting methods that calculate the values for new trees in a random order, ordered boosting computes the values in a distinct order, effectively minimizing overfitting by reducing bias.

CatBoost also stands out for its automatic handling of missing values, which saves the user from the need for explicit preprocessing to address them, simplifying the overall model-building process. Further, it is robust to hyperparameters, not requiring exhaustive hyperparameter tuning, and can provide satisfactory results with default parameter settings. This feature makes CatBoost a user-friendly option for beginners and reduces the time required to develop the model.

While CatBoost comes with several advantages, it does have certain potential drawbacks. Even though CatBoost tends to perform well with default parameters, understanding and tuning more complex parameters can prove challenging, necessitating deep model knowledge. Training CatBoost models can also be computationally intensive and time-consuming, particularly when dealing with large datasets, and this might make it slower compared to other gradient-boosting libraries. Despite its adept handling of categorical variables, ensuring these variables do not exhibit high cardinality (excessive unique values) remains crucial, as this could impact the model's performance.

# 6
# Demystifying Deep Learning

Deep learning harnesses the synergy of artificial neural networks (ANNs) and computational capabilities provided by graphics processing units (GPUs). While the concept of neural networks emerged in the 1960s, the practical application of the theory was limited due to insufficient computational power. However, in 2006, Hinton and his colleagues published a seminal study that unveiled the deep learning (DL) technique. This marked a resurgence in the interest and research in ANNs, which effectively reemerged under deep learning.

ANN algorithms are computationally-intensive models that mimic the brain's neural network structure. They are nonlinear and nonparametric, capable of learning independently, with varying degrees of supervision, to perform tasks such as prediction, classification, and decision-making. One edge that ANNs have over traditional models is their flexibility to model complex nonlinear relationships without making explicit assumptions about the data-generating process. Additionally, ANNs are highly valued as universal function approximators. They can approximate a wide array of functions with high accuracy, leveraging the power of parallel information processing derived from the data.

GPU is a specialized electronic circuit designed to rapidly manipulate and alter memory to accelerate the creation of images in a frame buffer intended for output to a display device. Initially engineered for rendering 2D and 3D computer graphics, GPUs have evolved into powerful processing units capable of executing complex mathematical and geometric calculations at high speeds. They operate using parallel processing, which makes them incredibly efficient for tasks requiring the same computation to be performed on large amounts of data simultaneously, such as AI models, scientific research, and video game graphics. This ability to perform multiple calculations concurrently makes GPUs particularly suited for computational tasks beyond their traditional role in graphics rendering.

ANNs, modeled after the human brain, provide the foundational structure for deep learning algorithms. They consist of layers of interconnected nodes, or neurons, that process information and pass it forward, enabling the network to learn from and predict data. However, training these networks involves heavy computational loads due to the high dimensionality of the datasets and complexity of the models, making it time-consuming and computationally challenging on traditional CPUs. This is where GPUs come into the picture. They are equipped with thousands of cores that can handle thousands of threads simultaneously, facilitating highly parallel computation, which significantly accelerates the training process of deep learning models. The GPUs' ability to perform multiple calculations concurrently makes them ideally suited to handle the massive matrix operations and linear algebra calculations required in deep learning algorithms, thus making the synergy of ANNs and GPUs fundamental to the growth and advancements of deep learning.

ANNs are structured into three main interconnected layers: the input, hidden, and output layers. Each layer consists of units known as nodes, or artificial neurons. The input layer accepts data and transmits it to the subsequent hidden layer. Each hidden layer, in turn, processes the received information and passes it to the next hidden layer, if there is one, or directly to the output layer in the absence of additional hidden layers. The hidden layers imbue the network with the capacity to analyze intricate nonlinear relationships, amplifying the network's flexibility and computational power. Each artificial neuron within the network comprises weighted inputs, known as synapses, and an activation function that calculates the output based on the input received. The ultimate result of these calculations is then transmitted as a singular output from each neuron.

In an ANN, weights are critical parameters that represent the strength or intensity of the connection between two neurons. They are not simply signals or information but govern how data is transformed through the network. The input layer does not perform computations but merely passes the inputs, multiplied by their corresponding weights, to the next layer, usually the first hidden layer. The calculations performed within the hidden layers involve the summation of the product of these inputs and their corresponding weights, to which a bias term is often added. The bias term allows for greater flexibility in the model by enabling it to fit the data better. If additional hidden layers exist, these weighted sums, often called weighted inputs, are passed to the next hidden layer.

The output layer then uses an activation function. This mathematical function transforms the weighted inputs into a desired output format, such as a class in classification problems or a continuous value in regression problems. Depending on the activation function used, it introduces nonlinearity to the model, which is essential for learning from complex data. The output (Y) of a neuron can be represented mathematically as follows: Y = activation_function($\sum$(weight * input) + bias).

The above sum is calculated over all inputs to a neuron. Therefore, the actual computation depends on the number of inputs and specific activation function used. The process of adjusting weights and biases to minimize the error between the network's prediction and the actual value is accomplished through a method called backpropagation, in combination with an optimization algorithm, like stochastic gradient descent.

Based on the calculated output (Y), the activation function is pivotal in an ANN by determining whether and to what degree a neuron gets activated. Each activation function applies a distinct mathematical operation to its input, with nonlinear activation functions serving the critical purpose of introducing nonlinearity into the network. This enables the network to learn and model intricate, nonlinear relationships between the inputs and outputs, thus empowering it to comprehend complex patterns within data.

Among the nonlinear activation functions frequently employed in ANN are tanh, rectified linear unit (ReLU), leaky ReLU, sigmoid, and softmax. Each of these has specific characteristics that make them suitable for various problems. For example, ReLU and its variant, leaky ReLU, are often used in the hidden layers of deep neural networks due to their ability to mitigate the vanishing gradient problem. In contrast, sigmoid and softmax are frequently used in binary and multiclass classification problems.

On the other hand, linear activation functions, such as the identity function, do not introduce nonlinearity and can only model linear relationships between inputs and outputs. This constraint significantly restricts the network's ability to capture more complex patterns and relationships inherent in the data. In contrast, incorporating nonlinear activation functions enhances the neural network's expressive power, enabling it to model and decipher complex correlations and trends in the data.

ANN can vary significantly based on their architecture, the number and arrangement of neurons, the type of connections between neurons, and the learning rules they employ. This diversity allows different types of ANN to be optimized for specific tasks or data types. Some common types of ANN include feedforward neural networks (FNNs), recurrent neural networks (RNNs), convolutional neural networks (CNNs), and autoencoders, each with unique advantages and typical applications. Let us delve into the specifics of each of these types.

## 6.1   Feedforward Neural Networks (FNNs)

Feedforward neural networks (FNNs), also known as multilayer perceptrons (MLPs), are among the simplest types of ANNs. They have a single input layer, one or more hidden layers, and an output layer. The data flows in one direction through the network, from the input layer to the output layer. Despite their simplicity, they can model complex nonlinear relationships and have seen wide usage across numerous applications, from image recognition to natural language processing (NLP).

A FNN is an architecture that comprises an input layer, one or more hidden layers, and an output layer. Each layer consists of multiple neurons or nodes. The layers are interconnected in that each node connects to every node in the next layer with a certain weight. This structure gives the network the ability to learn from input data. The feedforward name comes from how information travels through the network: it moves in one direction—from the input layer, through the hidden layers, and finally to the output layer—with no loops or cycles.

The starting point of a neural network is represented by the input layer. A single feature from the dataset corresponds to each neuron in this layer. For example, in the case of dealing with images, an input neuron could be tied to each pixel. In the case of text data, each word or character might be linked to an input neuron. The network is concluded by the output layer. The number of neurons in this layer is determined by the task. In a binary classification task, such as identifying if an email is spam, typically one output neuron is used. For multiclass classification, like distinguishing whether an image is of a cat, dog, or bird, typically one output neuron per class is utilized. The hidden layers are located between these two layers. In these layers, the input data is learned to be interpreted by the network in a manner that facilitates accomplishing the task. In the case of a hidden layer, each neuron processes the outputs from all neurons in the preceding layer or the input data in the case of the first hidden layer. The outputs are multiplied by a learned weight and added together, and then an activation function is applied. The neuron's output for an input or set of inputs is determined by activation functions.

FNNs learn via backpropagation, combined with an optimization technique like gradient descent. The process begins when the network makes predictions on the training data. To quantify these predictions' accuracy, a loss function is used to compute the discrepancy between the network's predictions and actual values. The output of this loss function represents the error of the network. The essence of backpropagation is to distribute this error back through the network, which is why it is called backpropagation. Starting from the output layer, the error is passed back toward the input layer, layer by layer. During this process, each neuron's contribution to the error is computed based on the weights of its connections to other neurons. This procedure effectively determines how much each neuron is responsible for the error.

Once the network has computed the error contributions for all neurons, it uses an optimization technique, such as gradient descent, to adjust the weights of the connections between neurons. This adjustment minimizes the loss function, improving the network's predictions. Gradient descent iteratively updates each weight in the direction most decreases the loss function. In simple terms, it is like descending a hill in the direction of the steepest slope to reach the bottom, where the bottom represents the minimum of the loss function. This whole procedure—forward propagation of inputs, computation of loss, backpropagation of error, and weight adjustment—is repeated many times throughout the network's training. Each repetition is known as an "epoch." With each epoch, the network becomes better at making accurate predictions, honing its ability to learn from the underlying patterns in the data.

FNNs do come with a set of drawbacks. For instance, their inability to handle temporal or sequential data due to their feedforward structure makes them unsuitable for tasks where the order of inputs is crucial, such as time series prediction, NLP, or speech recognition. More advanced architectures like RNNs and LSTMs were developed to respond to this limitation. Despite their ability to model nonlinear relationships, FNNs often struggle with complex patterns. Achieving success with intricate patterns requires them to be deep or wide, leading to potential overfitting and computational inefficiencies. Overfitting, especially in deep or wide FNNs, is when the network learns the training data too well and performs poorly on unseen data. Techniques like dropout, early stopping, or regularization are frequently employed to counter this.

FNNs are often criticized for lacking interpretability, earning them the black box moniker. Their decision-making process can be opaque, making understanding the reasoning behind specific predictions challenging, an issue in scenarios requiring clear interpretability. Moreover, unlike CNNs with an in-built feature extraction mechanism, FNNs often require manual feature engineering. Training FNN also presents challenges due to issues like vanishing or exploding gradients, particularly in deeper networks. These problems arise during backpropagation, making the network difficult to train.

## 6.2   Activation Functions

An activation function in a neural network is a mathematical function applied to a neuron's output, or activation. This function introduces nonlinearity into the output of a neuron. Without activation functions, even a deep neural network would be equivalent to a single-layer linear model because the composition of linear functions is still linear. The purpose of an activation function is to map the output of a neuron to a form that can be understood and processed effectively by the next layer. This mapping often involves limiting the neuron's output to a specific range of values. Activation functions also play a key role in backpropagation, the method used to train a neural network. During backpropagation, the derivative or gradient of the activation function is required to compute the gradient of the loss function with respect to the parameters of the network. Therefore, activation functions used in neural networks must be differentiable.

### 6.2.1   Properties of Activation Functions

**Nonlinearity**

Activation functions must be nonlinear to ensure the neural network can learn from errors and make adjustments. If the activation function is linear, the derivative would be a constant, and all network layers would look identical, essentially rendering a deep network no more powerful than a single layer.

## Continuously Differentiable

In the training of ANN, parameters or weights of the model are adjusted using optimization methods like gradient descent. This adjustment aims to minimize the difference between actual results and predictions made by the model, as measured by a cost or loss function. Determining the direction and magnitude for parameter adjustment to decrease the loss is done by calculating the derivative, or rate of change, of the loss function with respect to each parameter, often referred to as the gradient. To facilitate this calculation, every component of the loss calculation, including the activation functions in the neural network, needs to be differentiable. This means a derivative must exist at every point, and the derivative function must be continuous. If an activation function isn't continuously differentiable, reliable gradient calculation may not be possible, making gradient-based optimization methods potentially unreliable or unusable.

## Monotonicity

Monotonicity refers to an activation function increasing or decreasing continuously without any fluctuations. If an activation function is monotonic, it ensures the error surface of a single-layer neural model will be convex. In a convex error surface, there is a single minimum value. This characteristic simplifies optimization as it avoids local minima, facilitating the efficient training of the neural network.

## Approximation to the Identity

For tasks involving binary classification, the output is required to correspond to one of two classes, often denoted as 0 or 1. In such scenarios, an activation function approximating the identity function is necessary to ensure the outputs fall within the desired range. This necessity is particularly pronounced for the last layer of a neural network model, where the generation of appropriately ranged predictions is vital.

### 6.2.2 Types of Activation Functions

The types of activation functions include, but are not limited to, sigmoid, hyperbolic tangent (tanh), rectified linear unit (ReLU), leaky ReLU, parametric ReLU (PReLU), exponential linear units (ELUs), softmax, and Swish.

## Sigmoid

The sigmoid activation function, also known as the logistic function, outputs a value between 0 and 1, making it especially useful for models where the output is a probability that an input point belongs to a certain class.

Mathematically, the sigmoid function is expressed as $f(x) = 1 / (1 + \exp(-x))$. The shape of the function is an "S" curve ranging from 0 to 1. At the extremes (negative infinity, positive infinity), the Y values will approach but never reach 0 or 1, respectively. Around $X = 0$, the function is linear.

The sigmoid function has several important properties. Being nonlinear, it permits the network to learn from its errors, a crucial aspect since the primary principle of neural networks revolves around learning from mistakes. It also offers a smooth gradient due to its differentiable nature, facilitating efficient computation of gradients necessary for backpropagation. Furthermore, the sigmoid function allows for clear predictions in binary classification tasks, as an output close to 0 or 1 can be distinctly classified into either of the two categories.

While the sigmoid function is widely used in neural networks, it has certain drawbacks. One major issue is the vanishing gradient problem, which occurs when the function's input values are very high or low, resulting in little to no change in the prediction. This can cause the network's learning process to stall or slow down considerably, hindering accurate forecasts. Additionally, the sigmoid function's outputs are not 0-centered, meaning gradients could be positive or negative. This can lead to undesirable zigzagging dynamics during the gradient updates for the weights, potentially slowing down the convergence of the network during training.

## Hyperbolic Tangent (Tanh)

The hyperbolic tangent, or tanh, activation function is another traditional function used in neural networks. Like the sigmoid function, tanh is an S-shaped curve. However, the output of tanh is 0-centered, meaning it can return values between -1 and 1. This makes it more practical for certain types of data and in certain neural network layers, particularly in hidden layers.

Mathematically, the tanh function is expressed as $f(x) = (2 / (1 + \exp(-2x))) - 1$.

## Rectified Linear Unit (ReLU)

The rectified linear unit (ReLU) is widely used in the hidden layers of neural networks. The popularity of ReLU can be attributed to its simplicity and performance across a wide range of network architectures and datasets.

Mathematically, the ReLU function is defined as $f(x) = \max(0, x)$. This means the function returns x if x is greater than 0 and 0 otherwise.

Despite appearing linear, the ReLU function possesses a bend at the origin (x=0), categorizing it as nonlinear and enabling the network to represent nonlinear transformations. Compared to the sigmoid and tanh functions, ReLU is computationally efficient due to its simplicity and lack of expensive exponential operations. Furthermore, ReLU leads to sparse activation, meaning only a few neurons are activated at any given time. This light activity makes the network more efficient and computationally easier to manage.

## Leaky ReLU

The leaky rectified linear unit (Leaky ReLU) is a variant of the standard ReLU activation function that attempts to fix one of the main problems with ReLU, the dying ReLU problem. In a standard ReLU activation function, the output for inputs less than 0 is 0, which means that once a neuron gets a negative input, it is stuck and unlikely to become active again, effectively "dying" and no longer able to learn. To mitigate this problem, the leaky ReLU function has a small positive slope for negative inputs, meaning that even when the input is less than 0, the output is a small, non-zero value.

Mathematically, the leaky ReLU function can be expressed as $f(x) = \max(0.01x, x)$. This equation means that if x is greater than 0, the function behaves like a standard ReLU function and will output x. However, if x is less than 0, the function will output 0.01x, a small, negative number. The 0.01 is not a fixed value and can be adjusted as a hyperparameter, though a value of 0.01 is used in most contexts.

The leaky ReLU possesses several significant properties. It is a nonlinear function, much like ReLU, allowing the network to learn and comprehend complex data patterns. Unlike ReLU, leaky ReLU helps prevent dying neurons by assigning a small negative value when x < 0, thereby maintaining neuron activity. Additionally, similar to ReLU, leaky ReLU is computationally efficient compared to the sigmoid or tanh activation functions due to the straightforward nature of its operations.

## Parametric ReLU (PReLU)

The parametric rectified linear unit (PReLU) is another type of activation function that is a modified version of the ReLU activation function. PReLU was introduced to solve the dying ReLU problem and is used mainly in CNNS. In ReLU, the output is 0 when the input is negative, while in leaky ReLU, this is replaced with a small negative slope. PReLU improves upon this idea by making the leakage coefficient into a parameter that the network learns. This allows the network to learn the coefficient of leakage that is most beneficial.

Mathematically, the PReLU function is defined as:

$$f(x) = x, \text{ for } x >= 0$$
$$f(x) = ax, \text{ for } x < 0$$

Here, a is the parameter that the network learns. It is not a predetermined constant like in leaky ReLU but is learned during the training process through backpropagation. This means the network can adapt to learn the most helpful leakage coefficient for the given task.

PReLU offers a number of significant properties. PReLU, like ReLU and leaky ReLU, is a nonlinear function that enables the network to learn complex patterns and data. Its distinct feature lies in its adaptability, as it learns the parameter a during training, allowing it to adjust based on the data, which could lead to an optimized model. Furthermore, PReLU prevents dying neurons similarly to leaky ReLU by providing a non-zero output for negative input values, effectively mitigating the dying ReLU problem. One potential risk with PReLU is that adding another learnable parameter increases the risk of overfitting, especially when working with small datasets.

## Exponential Linear Units (ELU)

The exponential linear unit (ELU) is another modified version of the ReLU activation function. It is designed to smooth the approximation toward the function around negative inputs and, as a result, speed up learning and generalization in deep neural networks. In the ReLU, the output is 0 for negative inputs, while in the ELU, this is replaced with a small negative value derived from an exponential function for x < 0.

Mathematically, the ELU function is defined as:

$$f(x) = x, \text{ for } x >= 0$$
$$f(x) = a(\exp(x) - 1), \text{ for } x < 0$$

In this definition, a is a hyperparameter defining the maximum negative saturation amount for the ELU function. A typical value for a is 1.

The ELU function, akin to its peers such as ReLU, leaky ReLU, and PReLU, is nonlinear in nature. This trait endows the network with the capacity to learn and simulate intricate patterns found in data. One of the significant advantages of the ELU function is its capability to avert the issue of dead neurons, a common problem encountered with other counterparts. This is achieved by introducing a non-zero output for instances with negative input values. Furthermore, the ELU activation function is designed with a negative region, effectively pushing the mean outputs closer to 0. As a result, it provides more normalized outputs, thereby expediting the learning process.

**Softmax**

The softmax function operates on each element of the input vector and computes its exponential value. It then normalizes these exponential values by dividing each element by the sum of all exponential values. This normalization ensures the resulting values lie between 0 and 1 and sum up to 1, representing probabilities.

Mathematically, given an input vector $z = [z_1, z_2, ..., z_n]$, the softmax function calculates the output vector $y = [y_1, y_2, ..., y_n]$ as follows: $y_i = \exp(z_i) / (\exp(z_1) + \exp(z_2) + ... + \exp(z_n))$.

The softmax function amplifies the relative differences between the input values. Larger values in the input vector will correspond to larger probabilities in the output vector, while smaller values will have smaller probabilities. This property makes softmax suitable for multiclass classification problems where the goal is to assign an input to one of several mutually-exclusive classes.

The output vector produced by softmax can be interpreted as a probability distribution, allowing us to make predictions by selecting the class with the highest probability. Additionally, the probabilities provide a measure of confidence or certainty for each class prediction.

Softmax is sensitive to the scale of the input values, and large input values can lead to large exponential values and potentially numerical instability. To address this, techniques like numerical stabilization or normalization of the input values are often applied before applying softmax.

**Swish**

The Swish activation function is a self-gated activation function introduced by researchers at Google. The term "self-gated" means the function controls its information flow. Compared to other activation functions like ReLU or tanh, Swish tends to work better in deeper networks.

Mathematically, the Swish function is defined as $f(x) = x * sigmoid(\beta x)$.

In this definition, $x$ is the input to the function, and $\beta$ is a learnable parameter. When $\beta = 1$, the Swish function equals the sigmoid-weighted linear unit (SiL) activation function. If $\beta$ is set to 0, Swish becomes the identity function $f(x) = x$. During training, $\beta$ can be updated via backpropagation. Also, $\beta$ can be set as a constant that is not updated during training, effectively making Swish a scaled version of the logistic sigmoid function.

### 6.2.3 Choice of Activation Function

- The choice of activation function may also depend on factors such as training speed, vanishing or exploding gradients, computational efficiency, nonlinearity, saturation, and dead neurons.
- Training Speed: Some activation functions, like ReLU, allow for faster convergence during training, leading to faster model development times.

- Vanishing/Exploding Gradients: Sigmoid and tanh activation functions can lead to vanishing or exploding gradients, which can severely slow down training or cause it to fail entirely. ReLU and its variants help to mitigate this issue.
- Computational Efficiency: Simpler functions like ReLU are more computationally efficient to calculate, which can be an important consideration when training large models or working with large datasets.
- Nonlinearity: Activation functions introduce nonlinearity into the model, which is critical for learning complex patterns in the data. The degree and type of nonlinearity the activation function introduces can affect the model's learning capability.
- Saturation: Activation functions like sigmoid and tanh can saturate with very large or very small inputs, causing gradients to vanish. This is less of an issue with functions like ReLU.
- Dead Neurons: In ReLU activation, if the input is negative, the output is 0, and during backpropagation, the weights are not updated. This is known as a "dead neuron." Variants of ReLU, like leaky ReLU or PReLU, help to mitigate this issue.

## 6.3   Recurrent Neural Networks (RNNs)

Recurrent neural networks (RNNs) are tailored to identify patterns in data sequences, such as text, genomes, handwriting, or spoken word. Contrary to traditional FNNs that process inputs independently, RNNs leverage their internal state or memory to process sequences of inputs. This ability, facilitated by feedback loops, allows RNNs to remember information from previous inputs, making them adept at tasks where order is crucial and learning long-term dependencies in data. The fundamental feature of RNNs that distinguishes them from feedforward networks is their hidden state, which acts like memory. It allows information to be passed from one step in the sequence to the next. A common metaphor for explaining RNNs is a conveyor belt that runs parallel to the neural network, carrying information along as the network processes the sequence.

RNNs structure commences with an input vector representing the specific data input at a given time step. For instance, in NLP, an input might be a one-hot encoded vector of a word. The computation is carried out in the hidden or recurrent layer, which takes the input data and the prior hidden state to produce the new hidden state. The activation function utilized for this computation. The resulting hidden state, often perceived as the memory of the RNN, captures information from previous time steps.

Within a simple RNN, two sets of weights exist: one for the inputs, frequently denoted as U, and another for the previous hidden state, usually denoted as W. These weights, which are learnable parameters updated during training, are shared across all time steps, a unique feature of RNNs that enables the processing of sequences of variable length. The output at a specific time step, often labeled as V, is typically calculated using the hidden state. Depending on the task, such as multiclass classification, an activation function like softmax might be applied to the output. Some RNNs generate an output at every time step, while others produce an output only at the final time.

After computing the output, the error is determined by comparing the predicted output to the actual one. This error is then backpropagated through the network, updating the weights (U, W, V) using gradient descent or other optimization algorithms. Visualizing RNNs can be facilitated by imagining them as an FNN unrolled over time. This representation treats the input, hidden state, and output at each time step as separate nodes at each unrolled step, clarifying the temporal sequence of computations in the RNN. The output from the hidden layer influences not only the output layer but also the subsequent step in the sequence as it is fed back into the hidden layer.

Much like FNNs, RNNs employ activation functions, with the tanh function being a common choice due to its centeredness around 0, aiding in faster model convergence. The choice of the activation function, however, can vary based on the application and data characteristics. Training RNNs, a more complex task than training traditional feedforward networks, uses backpropagation through time (BPTT), which entails unrolling the entire network over time before applying standard backpropagation. This can lead to two issues: vanishing gradients, where the network forgets the long past due to small, multiplying gradients during training, and exploding gradients, where the gradients become excessively large, leading to a weight explosion in the network. This typically occurs when the activation function cannot contain the output within a specific range.

RNNs are particularly effective for tasks where sequence and context play significant roles, finding widespread application in language modeling (e.g., generating text), machine translation, speech recognition, and time series prediction. RNNs are powerful models capable of handling complex sequential data, which makes them highly versatile across numerous applications. However, these networks come with challenges, including training difficulties due to vanishing and exploding gradients and the heavy computational resources they require, particularly when processing longer sequences.

Despite their capabilities, standard RNNs struggle with processing long sequences, encountering problems like the vanishing gradient and exploding gradient, which can destabilize training and lead to poor models. Additionally, RNNs can be computationally intense and time-consuming to train due to their sequential computation nature that inhibits parallelization. RNNs are also often limited by their one-directional context maintenance, requiring more complex structures like bidirectional RNNs for tasks where future context is essential. Moreover, like many other deep learning models, RNNs lack interpretability, with their decision-making processes often referred to as black box models, which can be problematic in applications where understanding the reasons behind predictions is critical. Large training data is required to prevent overfitting and ensure good performance, along with the inherent difficulties in structuring data, tuning the model, and debugging potential issues during training.

To address the vanishing gradients issue in RNNs, variations such as LSTM and gated recurrent units (GRUs) have been developed. The LSTM functions similarly to a standard RNN but also incorporates a mechanism akin to a conveyor belt, which can carry information across multiple time steps without processing it. This conveyor belt is regulated by gates controlling whether the information is discarded and replaced with the current input or preserved and carried forward to the next step, effectively enabling the LSTM to retain information over extended periods and alleviating the vanishing gradients problem. On the other hand, the GRU, a simplified LSTM variant, integrates the forget and input gates into a singular update gate and merges the cell state and hidden state, offering comparable performance to LSTMs on various tasks but with enhanced computational efficiency and simplicity.

## 6.4 Long Short-Term Memory (LSTM) Networks

Various strategies and alternative architectures have been designed in response to the challenges posed by traditional RNNs. Among these, long short-term memory (LSTM) networks stand out. Constructed as a variant of RNNs, LSTMs are explicitly designed to circumvent problems related to long-term dependencies, also known as the vanishing gradient problem. Their ability to retain information over extended time frames makes them especially efficient for tasks involving long sequences. The effectiveness of LSTMs in retaining information over a long duration is attributed to a mechanism of gates. These gates manage the flow of information, deciding when the data enters, remains, and exits the LSTM cell. By doing so, they ensure the preservation of information over time and alleviate the issues associated with vanishing gradients.

The centerpiece of LSTM networks is the cell state, a structure that resembles a horizontal line running along the top of the LSTM diagram. This cell state functions similarly to a conveyor belt, facilitating the flow of information with minimal disruptions or changes, thanks to the limited linear interactions along its path.

LSTM networks, while maintaining this chainlike architecture, possess a unique repeating module structure. Instead of a single neural network layer, an LSTM module comprises four layers, each interacting distinctively. Within an LSTM cell, three types of gates are present: the input gate, the forget gate, and the output gate. These gates serve as checkpoints for data, determining what information should be allowed to pass through. They operate using sigmoid activation functions, which yield output values ranging from 0, signifying that no data should be allowed through, to 1, implying that all data can pass.

The forget gate plays a pivotal role in managing the cell state. It evaluates the previous hidden state and current input, generating an output between 0 and 1 for each number in the cell state. Here, a 1 signifies complete retention of information, while 0 calls for total discarding of the corresponding data. Subsequently, the input gate updates the cell state with new information. This gate comprises two components. A sigmoid layer, the input gate layer, determines which values should be updated. Concurrently, a tanh layer creates a set of new candidate values, which could be potentially added to the state.

Finally, the output gate is responsible for the final output from the cell. However, this output is a regulated version based on the cell state. Initially, a sigmoid layer decides which parts of the cell state will be outputted. This is followed by processing the cell state through a tanh function to constrain the values between -1 and 1 and multiplying it by the output of the sigmoid gate. This process ensures that only the components determined to be retained are included in the output.

LSTM networks hold several advantages, making them popular in handling complex sequential tasks. Primarily, LSTMs are adept at overcoming the vanishing gradient problem and effectively learning long-term dependencies. This capability allows them to maintain their state over extended sequences, which proves highly beneficial in scenarios such as time series forecasting and NLP. LSTMs also exhibit flexibility as they can efficiently process inputs of varying lengths, adapting seamlessly to changes in sequence lengths across different data batches. This adaptability is particularly useful in tasks like text translation, where the length of the input sequence can significantly vary.

LSTM networks' inherent ability to retain prior information using their cell state makes them an advantageous choice for tasks where temporal dynamics are critical. Furthermore, much like other neural networks, LSTMs can be trained end-to-end using standard backpropagation techniques. Given enough data and computational resources, this enables them to learn complex tasks directly from raw input data. LSTMs also showcase robustness against noise, as their ability to discern between essential and discardable information allows them to cope effectively with irrelevant input data. Finally, the LSTM design's modularity, enabling the stacking of cells into layers in a neural network, allows these models to be adapted to different architectures, facilitating the modification of the model's complexity as per requirements.

## 6.5  Bidirectional Long Short-Term Memory (BiLSTM) Networks

Bidirectional long short-term memory (BiLSTM) networks are an extension of traditional LSTM networks, a special kind of RNN capable of learning long-term dependencies. The distinct advantage of BiLSTMs over standard LSTMs lies in their ability to process data in both directions. This dual processing enables them to understand the context of the data by capturing both past and future information. This feature makes BiLSTMs especially potent for tasks where the entire data sequence is crucial for accurate predictions, such as in NLP tasks like sentiment analysis or named entity recognition.

The first LSTM, the forward LSTM, processes the data chronologically from the first data point to the last. This method allows the model to capture and store past information. In contrast, the second LSTM, termed the backward LSTM, interprets the data in reverse, beginning from the last data point and working back to the first. This approach provides the model with a view of future information relative to any point in the sequence. After processing the data independently, the hidden states of the forward and backward LSTMs are merged, typically through concatenation. This merging step ensures that past and future contexts are considered for each data point in the sequence, effectively creating a comprehensive representation of the sequence. This dual-direction processing offered by BiLSTMs makes them particularly effective in tasks where understanding the context from both ends of the sequence is crucial, such as language translation or sentiment analysis.

BiLSTM networks offer several advantages in sequence prediction tasks. They provide a more comprehensive understanding of a sequence by considering past and future inputs for each time step. This context-rich perspective, in turn, leads to more accurate results, particularly in tasks like named entity recognition or part-of-speech tagging. Moreover, BiLSTMs often surpass unidirectional LSTMs in performance due to their capability to capture overlooked information by a unidirectional LSTM. Additionally, while the theoretical possibility of parallel computations for forward and backward passes within a layer remains unexploited mainly in current deep learning frameworks, this independent processing of forward and backward states offers potential for future efficiency gains. Like their unidirectional counterparts, BiLSTMs effectively handle long sequences and mitigate the vanishing gradient problem. However, it is worth noting that the doubled parameter count in BiLSTMs could lead to greater computational expenses, and their reliance on future data could limit their applicability for real-time predictions.

## 6.6    Gated Recurrent Units (GRUs)

Gated recurrent units (GRUs) form a specific class of RNNs introduced to the world by Cho and others in 2014. The development of GRUs stemmed from the need to address the vanishing gradient problem, a common obstacle hampering standard RNNs from learning long-term dependencies effectively. The vanishing gradient problem presents a considerable challenge in deep learning, causing gradients to become infinitesimally small as they are backpropagated through time. This makes the network forget the distant past and prevents it from learning correlations between temporally distant events. GRUs were designed with specific architectural modifications to surmount this issue, making them more apt for handling tasks involving long sequences.

The core structure of a GRU comprises two types of gates: update gates and reset gates. These gates, essentially vectors containing values between 0 and 1, play a crucial role in governing the flow of information within the GRU. They determine what information should be stored in the memory, what should be discarded, and what should be used for producing the output, all tailored to the specific task.

The update gates, one of the two gate types in a GRU, play a critical role in managing the extent to which past information, from previous time steps, should be carried forward to the future. Their function can be seen as balancing between preserving the current memory and introducing the new input. In essence, the update gate decides the proportion of the previous hidden state that should be retained versus the amount of new information that should be incorporated. On the other hand, reset gates decide the quantum of past information that needs to be forgotten. They regulate how much of the past state should be combined with the current input to suggest a new hidden state. This gate allows the model to drop past non-essential information and keep only what is crucial for predicting future elements.

One significant distinction that sets GRUs apart from their close relatives, the LSTM units, is how they handle their internal states. GRUs simplify the architecture by combining the cell and hidden states into a single entity, making the model less complex and computationally more efficient. In contrast, LSTMs maintain separate cell and hidden states, contributing to a more complex structure. Moreover, while LSTMs use three types of gates input, forget, and output to manage the information flow, GRUs streamline this process by using just two gates, update and reset, contributing to their efficiency.

GRUs offer several advantages, making them popular in sequence learning tasks. Notably, they are more computationally efficient than LSTM units due to having fewer parameters, which can result in faster training times and potentially needing less data to generalize effectively. Their reduced complexity often translates into comparable performance to LSTMs, particularly in tasks not requiring the modeling of excessively long sequences. The streamlined structure of GRUs, with fewer components than LSTMs, can also make them easier to understand and implement. Furthermore, similar to LSTMs, GRUs are designed to counter the vanishing gradient problem, enabling them to capture long-term dependencies effectively. The gating mechanism in GRUs aids in retaining important information while discarding irrelevant details in a sequence. However, it is important to note that the choice between GRUs and LSTMs typically depends on the specific application at hand and the computational resources available. In particular scenarios, the added complexity of LSTMs might be advantageous, whereas, in others, the simplicity and efficiency of GRUs may prove more suitable.

## 6.7  Convolutional Neural Networks (CNNs)

Designed with image processing in mind, convolutional neural networks (CNNs) excel in understanding spatial correlations within images. Their unique architecture makes them highly suitable for tasks like image processing, computer vision, and interpreting visual data. The conventional structure of a CNN includes a sequence of distinct layers that convert the input data into the desired output, emphasizing the importance of spatial relationships in the images.

**Convolutional Layer**

The convolutional layer is a fundamental component of CNNs and is responsible for extracting high-level features from input data, such as images. It achieves this through the process of convolution, a specialized linear operation. At its core, the convolutional layer applies a set of learnable filters to the input. Each filter is small but extends through the full depth of the input volume. During the forward pass, the filters slide across the width and height of the input volume, performing convolution by computing dot products between the filter entries and input. This process generates a two-dimensional activation map. The output volume is formed by stacking these activation maps together.

Filters, also called kernels, are used in convolutional layers. These filters are small weight matrices that slide over the input data, performing convolution at each location. The weights in these filters are adjustable parameters that the network learns during training. The sliding of the filters over the input data is determined by the stride, which defines the amount of movement at each step. A larger stride value means the filter moves in larger increments, affecting the spatial size of the output volume. Additionally, padding can be applied to the input volume by adding zeros around the border. This padding helps control the output volume's spatial size and is often used to maintain consistent dimensionality.

By applying different filters, each producing its feature map, the convolutional layer generates multiple feature maps stacked together to form the output volume. These feature maps capture various high-level features present in the input data. The role of the convolutional layer in a CNN is to extract features from the input image or data. It preserves the spatial relationship between pixels through convolution by learning features using small squares of input data. As the network goes deeper, the filters cover larger portions of the input, enabling the learning of more complex and abstract visual features.

In the initial layers of a CNN, the filters may learn to detect edges or specific colors. However, as the layers become deeper, the filters are activated by more intricate patterns, such as shapes. Furthermore, in even deeper layers, the filters might respond to patterns that may not be visually recognizable to humans but are relevant for the specific task the CNN is being trained for, such as classifying images as cats or dogs.

**Activation Layer**

Like in other ANNs, an activation function is used to introduce nonlinearity into the model. Without an activation function, no matter how many layers the network has, it would behave just like a single-layer network because the composition of linear functions is still linear. The network can learn more complex mappings from inputs to outputs by introducing nonlinearities. After the convolution operation in a CNN, an activation function is applied to the output of each neuron, the dot product of the input and the weight vector. There are several types of activation functions used in CNNs, and the choice of activation function can significantly affect the model's performance.

## Pooling Layer

A pooling layer is commonly added in CNNs after convolutional layers to reduce the spatial dimensions of the input volume while keeping the depth dimension unchanged. This reduction serves several purposes in the network architecture. First, it helps decrease the computational complexity of the network by reducing the number of parameters and memory requirements. Second, pooling layers enable the network to achieve a form of translation invariance, focusing on the presence of features rather than their exact spatial location. Last, pooling layers prevent overfitting by providing an abstracted form of the output, summarizing the features in the input.

Two main types of pooling operations are used in CNNs. The most common one is max pooling, which extracts subregions of the feature map (typically two-by-two pixel tiles) and retains the maximum value within each region while discarding other values. Max pooling provides robust feature representation, invariant to small translations and distortions. On the other hand, average pooling takes the average value within each subregion instead of the maximum, resulting in a smoother and more generalized representation of the input. It can help prevent overfitting by providing a less detailed view of the features. The pooling operation has no trainable parameters, unlike the weights in convolutional or fully connected layers. As a result, the pooling layer is often referred to as a fixed layer, as it does not involve learning.

## Fully Connected Layer

The fully connected layer, also known as the dense layer, is typically positioned at the end of a CNN and is responsible for producing the final classification results. Neurons in this layer have complete connections to all activations in the previous layer, similar to traditional MLPs. Its main function is to translate the high-level filtered images from earlier layers into a format that enables the determination of the image class or precise identification of features.

The fully connected layer's structure involves neurons connected to all outputs of the preceding layer. It takes an input volume, which could be the output of a convolution, ReLU, or pooling layer. It generates an N-dimensional vector, where N represents the number of classes the network needs to classify. For instance, in a binary classification problem, N would be 2, and the neuron with the highest activation output indicates whether the input belongs to class 0 or 1.

The fully connected layer plays a crucial role in performing high-level reasoning by incorporating the features extracted by convolutional and pooling layers. It combines these features across the image to identify broader patterns and make decisions. The layer's output probabilities are commonly used to classify input images.

In a fully connected layer, each neuron has associated weights and biases. The weights determine the influence of a particular feature in the decision-making process, and they are learned during training through backpropagation. The bias term allows for shifting the activation function to the left or right, which can be crucial for effective learning and decision-making. Fully connected layers have the advantage of being able to learn global patterns by connecting to all numbers in the previous volume. However, they also come with some disadvantages. One such disadvantage is their computational expense, particularly when working with large volumes of data, as they involve a large number of parameters. Additionally, fully connected layers have the potential for overfitting, where the model becomes too specialized to the training data and performs poorly on unseen data. To address these issues, mitigating techniques like dropout can be employed, randomly dropping out or deactivating certain neurons during training, reducing the number of parameters, and alleviating the problems of computational expense and overfitting.

CNNs offer several advantages in their design and application:
- Local invariance: CNNs exhibit translation invariance, enabling them to recognize patterns regardless of their positions in the image. Pooling layers contribute to this property by enhancing the network's generalization of patterns across different locations.
- Efficiency of images: CNNs leverage the inherent 2D structure of images, preserving the spatial relationships between pixels. This contrasts fully connected networks that treat images as flat vectors. By considering the spatial arrangement, CNNs can better capture local patterns and relationships within the image.
- Parameter sharing: CNNs employ shared filters across the entire image, significantly reducing the number of parameters that need to be learned. This sharing of parameters enhances the model's ability to generalize and improves computational efficiency, making CNNs more practical for large-scale applications.
- Hierarchical pattern learning: CNNs facilitate hierarchical pattern learning with their multiple layers. The network learns more complex structures and high-level concepts

starting from low-level features like edges. This hierarchical representation allows CNNs to capture and understand intricate patterns within the data.

- Versatility: While CNNs were initially designed for image analysis, they have demonstrated effectiveness in various other data types exhibiting a gridlike topology. This includes time series and text data, where the gridlike structure can be interpreted, allowing CNNs to extract meaningful patterns and make predictions in these domains.

## 6.8   One-Dimensional Convolutional Neural Network (1DCNN)

A one-dimensional convolutional neural network (1DCNN) is a CNN variant that uses a single spatial dimension. While 2DCNNs are commonly used for image processing tasks where spatial dimensions are height and width, 1DCNNs are often used for time series data analysis, NLP, and signal processing. The primary difference in 1DCNNs is that the convolution operation slides across only one dimension.

A 1DCNN structure encompasses several layers. It starts with the input layer, which receives the input sequence as a 2D array with dimensions (sequence_length, num_channels) representing the number of time steps in the sequence and the observational values at each time step, respectively. The convolutional layer(s) utilize filters/kernels that slide across the temporal dimension of the input data, generating feature maps that highlight important features. These feature maps are typically passed through activation layer(s) like ReLU to introduce nonlinearity. The pooling layer(s) follow, downsampling the feature maps to reduce spatial dimensions and computational complexity while retaining crucial information. Finally, fully connected layer(s) interpret the features and produce the final output, often incorporating a softmax activation function for classification tasks to generate class probabilities. Due to their distinctive properties and advantages, 1DCNNs are highly efficient for time series analysis. These include:

- Feature learning: 1DCNNs can automatically learn and extract meaningful features from raw time series data, eliminating the need for labor-intensive manual feature engineering.
- Temporal invariance: 1DCNNs can recognize patterns within time series data, irrespective of their temporal position. This temporal invariance property is particularly beneficial as it enables the detection of patterns occurring at different time points.

- Local focus: The filters employed in 1DCNNs focus on local regions of the input data, enabling the modeling of temporal dependencies. This makes them well-suited for capturing trends, seasonality, and other time-dependent patterns within time series data.

- Efficiency: Compared to other deep learning models, such as RNNs or LSTM networks, 1DCNNs have fewer parameters, resulting in faster training times and improved computational efficiency.

- Downsampling capabilities: 1DCNNs utilize pooling layers to downsample the time series, reducing its length and emphasizing the most relevant features. This simplifies the problem, mitigates computational complexity, and helps prevent overfitting.

- Scalability: 1DCNNs exhibit scalability to process long sequences effectively. Unlike RNNs and LSTMs, which can encounter challenges with vanishing or exploding gradients when handling lengthy sequences, CNNs do not suffer from this issue and can handle long sequences more efficiently.

- Handling multivariate time series: 1DCNNs can handle multivariate time series, where each time step comprises multiple features or measurements. By learning to extract features from each measurement and modeling the relationships between them, CNNs can effectively analyze and understand complex interactions within multivariate time series data.

1DCNNs offer distinct advantages that make them highly suitable for specific tasks. First, they exhibit efficiency by having fewer parameters compared to 2DCNNs, resulting in improved computational efficiency. Additionally, 1DCNNs are particularly effective for extracting local 1D temporal features, making them well-suited for sequenced data analysis. Moreover, 1DCNNs can handle variable-length input sequences, which is advantageous in NLP applications where input lengths can vary. These advantages highlight the strengths of 1DCNNs and their relevance in various domains.

1DCNNs find applications in diverse fields. In time series analysis, they prove valuable for tasks like forecasting and anomaly detection. In NLP, 1DCNNs can identify local dependencies between words and detect phrases when representing words as vectors. Moreover, in audio signal processing, such as speech recognition or music classification, 1DCNNs are employed, treating audio signals as 1D sequences. Additionally, 1DCNNs are relevant in genomic sequence analysis, where they can analyze DNA sequences represented as 1D sequences of nucleotide bases. Overall, 1DCNNs offer a powerful approach to analyzing temporal sequences and extracting meaningful features. Their efficiency and versatility have led to their widespread utilization across various domains dealing with sequence data. It is worth noting that the suitability of 1DCNNs also depends on the specific characteristics of the data and the problem at hand. For instance, combining CNNs and LSTM networks may yield superior results in scenarios involving long-term dependencies in time series data.

## 6.9 Generative AI

Generative AI is a branch of AI that focuses on creating new content or data based on the patterns and structures learned from existing data. The primary goal of generative AI models is to produce output that mimics human-generated content, such as text, images, audio, or video, in a coherent and contextually-relevant manner. Some of the most popular generative AI models are based on deep learning techniques, particularly neural networks such as generative adversarial networks (GANs), variational autoencoders (VAEs), transformers, and transformer-based models like OpenAI's generative pre-trained transformer (GPT) series. These models have found widespread application across an array of domains: in NLP, the power AI-driven text generation, translation, and summarization and serve as conversational agents; within computer vision, they're harnessed for image generation, style transfer, inpainting, and data augmentation; in the realm of audio and music, they're utilized to generate music, synthesize speech, and create sound effects; and in video, they're employed to generate video content, predict future frames, and facilitate video-to-video synthesis.

Despite their impressive capabilities, generative AI models face limitations and challenges, such as ensuring control over the generated content, mitigating biases, and addressing ethical concerns. Nevertheless, generative AI continues to evolve rapidly, with researchers and developers exploring new techniques and applications that can revolutionize how we interact with digital content.

Generative AI, exemplified by language models like GPT-4, has carved out a significant, multidimensional niche in our society. This cutting-edge AI technology has had a transformative impact on various sectors, making its presence felt in everyday life in myriad ways. It has revolutionized content creation by generating written material ranging from articles, blogs, and marketing copy to social media posts, proving indispensable for writers, journalists, and marketers. In the realm of art and design, it has pushed the envelope, generating visual art, music, and other creative pieces, providing artists with new avenues of exploration. Personalization and recommendation systems have been enhanced by AI's ability to generate content, products, and services tailored to individual preferences. Education has been enriched through AI's generation of custom learning materials, aiding teachers in formulating content that caters to unique learning styles. Generative AI's contribution extends to language translation and NLP, powering superior language translation services and applications for more effective cross-linguistic communication. Health care has benefited from AI's ability to draft personalized treatment plans, prognosticate disease progression, and assist in drug discovery, thereby elevating patient care and outcomes. The business world, spanning sectors like finance, retail, and manufacturing, employs generative AI for forecasting, trend analysis, and process optimization. Lastly, in research and development, AI facilitates researchers in ideation, pattern recognition, and making data-driven forecasts, accelerating the pace of scientific discovery and innovation.

## 6.10   Generative Adversarial Networks (GANs)

GANs are a class of ANN frameworks invented by Ian Goodfellow and his colleagues in 2014. GANs consist of two neural networks, a generator and a discriminator, that are trained together in a competitive process. The generator's goal is to create synthetic, or fake, data that resembles the real data as closely as possible by learning the underlying data distribution of the training set. The discriminator aims to distinguish between real data from the training set and fake data generated by the generator. During training, the generator tries to improve its generated data to fool the discriminator better, while the discriminator tries to improve its ability to identify real and fake data correctly. This adversarial process continues until an equilibrium is reached, where the generator produces data nearly indistinguishable from the real data and the discriminator can no longer differentiate between the two. GANs have shown impressive results in various applications, such as image synthesis, image-to-image translation, data augmentation, and style transfer.

The generator (G) is a function that takes a random noise vector (z) and maps it to data-space (G(z)). The purpose of the generator is to estimate the distribution that the real data comes from to generate new data from that same distribution. The discriminator (D) is a binary classification network that inputs data (x) and outputs a scalar (D(x)), representing the probability that x came from the real data rather than the generator.

The objective function of a GAN describes the competition between the generator and discriminator. It is formulated as a two-player minimax game with the following loss function: $\min_G \max_D V(D, G) = E_{x \sim p\_data(x)}[\log D(x)] + E_{z \sim p\_z(z)}[\log(1 - D(G(z)))]$.

Here, E represents the expectation, p_data(x) is the real data distribution, and p_z(z) is the distribution of the input noise vectors. The first term in the equation corresponds to the discriminator's ability to recognize real data, and the second term corresponds to its ability to recognize fake data. The generator aims to minimize this function, while the discriminator aims to maximize it.

In a real application, the sample generator is typically implemented as a neural network, often a deep CNN or deep FFN. The architecture and complexity of the generator network can vary depending on the specific application and complexity of the generated data. The discriminator network is also typically implemented as an ANN, often a deep CNN or a deep FFN, LSTM, or GRU. The training process involves both the generator and discriminator being trained simultaneously. The discriminator is trained by feeding it both real and fake data, and it updates its weights through backpropagation using the labels (real for real data, fake for data from the generator). The generator is then trained using the output of the discriminator. It wants the discriminator to believe its output is real, so it uses its predictions to update its weights.

During the training process, both networks improve by adjusting their internal parameters. This is done using gradient descent, a method of optimization that iteratively adjusts parameters in the direction that minimizes the loss function. The specific updates depend on the gradients of the loss function with respect to the parameters, which are computed using backpropagation.

## 6.11   Transformers

Transformers are a type of deep learning architecture introduced by Vaswani and others (2017) in the paper "Attention is All You Need." They have become the foundation for many state-of-the-art NLP models, including BERT, GPT, and T5. Transformers rely on self-attention mechanisms to process and generate sequences, making them well-suited for a wide range of NLP tasks. The self-attention mechanism allows the model to weigh the importance of each input token relative to other tokens in the sequence. This is achieved using scaled dot-product attention, which computes a weight matrix based on the query (Q), key (K), and value (V) matrices: Attention(Q, K, V) = softmax(QK^T / sqrt(d_k))V, where d_k is the dimension of the key vectors. The Q, K, and V matrices are obtained by linearly projecting the input embeddings.

Transformers use multihead attention to allow the model to simultaneously focus on different aspects of the input. Multihead attention computes multiple attention matrices in parallel and concatenates their results: MultiHead(Q, K, V) = Concat(head_1, ..., head_h)W^O, where head_i = Attention(QW^Q_i, KW^K_i, VW^V_i) and W^Q_i, W^K_i, W^V_i, W^O are learnable weight matrices.

Transformers use position-wise FFNs to process each token independently. The FFN consists of two linear layers with a nonlinear activation function (e.g., ReLU) in between: FFN(x) = max(0, xW_1 + b_1)W_2 + b_2, where W_1, W_2, b_1, and b_2 are learnable weights and biases.

Since transformers do not have any inherent notion of the position of tokens in a sequence, positional encodings are added to the input embeddings to provide information about the relative positions of tokens. Commonly used positional encodings are sine and cosine functions of different frequencies:

$$PE(pos, 2i) = \sin(pos / 10000^{(2i/d\_model)})$$
$$PE(pos, 2i+1) = \cos(pos / 10000^{(2i/d\_model)})$$

where pos is the position of a token in the sequence and d_model is the dimension of the input embeddings.

Transformers use layer normalization and residual connections to stabilize training and facilitate deeper architectures. Layer normalization normalizes the input across the feature dimension, while residual connections add the original input to the output of each sublayer (e.g., multihead attention or FFN).

A typical transformer model consists of an encoder and a decoder, each composed of multiple stacked layers. The encoder processes the input sequence; the decoder generates the output sequence. Both the encoder-decoder have multiple layers, each containing a multihead self-attention mechanism, position-wise FFN, layer normalization, and residual connections. The decoder also includes an additional encoder-decoder attention layer, allowing the decoder to focus on relevant parts of the input sequence when generating the output.

Transformers have gained recognition and succeeded in various domains, including time series analysis. The salient features that make the transformers well-suited for this particular task:

- Attention mechanism: Transformers utilize the attention mechanism, allowing them to capture dependencies between different time steps in a sequence effectively. This mechanism enables the model to focus on relevant information from distant time steps, making it well-suited for modeling long-range dependencies in time series data.

- Parallel computation: Unlike recurrent models like RNNs, transformers can process time series data in parallel rather than sequentially. This parallelization significantly accelerates the training and inference time, making them more efficient for large-scale time series analysis.

- Hierarchical representation: Transformers have multiple layers that can learn hierarchical representations of time series data. Lower layers capture local patterns, while higher layers integrate these patterns to capture more complex temporal dependencies. This hierarchical structure helps the model extract meaningful features at different levels of abstraction.

- Scalability: Transformers have demonstrated scalability in handling long sequences, which is crucial in time series analysis. They can process sequences of arbitrary lengths without suffering from the vanishing or exploding gradient problem that recurrent models often encounter.

- Flexibility: Transformers are highly flexible and can handle various types of time series data, including univariate and multivariate time series. They can accommodate irregular time intervals and missing values, making them adaptable to real-world time series data with diverse characteristics.

- Interpretability: Transformers offer interpretability by providing attention weights, indicating the importance of different time steps in the sequence. This transparency allows analysts to understand how the model makes predictions and provides insights into the underlying temporal relationships within the time series data.

- Transfer learning: Pretrained transformers, such as BERT and GPT, trained on large-scale language tasks, can be fine-tuned for time series analysis. This transfer learning approach provides a head start in modeling time series data, leveraging the knowledge and representations learned from extensive pretraining.

## 6.12  Variational Autoencoder (VAE)

Variational autoencoder (VAE), a generative model, was introduced in 2013 by Kingma and Welling, and they have since become a popular choice for generating and manipulating data, particularly images. A VAE consists of two main components: an encoder and a decoder. The encoder takes input data, such as images, and maps it to a lower-dimensional latent space, a continuous space representing the data's essential features. The decoder takes points from the latent space and reconstructs the original data, essentially reversing the encoding process. VAEs are trained using a combination of two loss functions: the reconstruction loss and the regularization loss. The reconstruction loss measures how well the decoder can reconstruct the original data from the latent space, while the regularization loss encourages the latent space to follow a specific distribution, usually a Gaussian distribution. This combination of loss functions allows VAEs to learn a smooth and meaningful latent space that can be easily sampled and manipulated to generate new data. VAEs have been used in various applications, such as generating images, audio, and text, as well as for tasks like data compression, dimensionality reduction, and data denoising.

The encoder is an inference model that takes an input data sample $(x)$ and maps it to a latent representation $(z)$ using a probabilistic function. The encoder approximates the true posterior distribution $(P(z|x))$ with a simpler distribution $(Q(z|x))$, usually a multivariate Gaussian with diagonal covariance: $Q(z|x) = N(z; \mu(x), \sigma^2(x)I)$, where $\mu(x)$ and $\sigma^2(x)$ are the mean and variance of the latent distribution, respectively, and the output of the encoder parametrizes them.

The decoder is a generative model that takes a latent representation $(z)$ as input and generates a reconstruction of the original data sample $(x')$. The decoder models the likelihood of the data given the latent representation $(P(x|z))$.

VAEs are trained by maximizing the evidence lower bound (ELBO), a lower bound on the log-likelihood of the data (log P(x)). The ELBO can be expressed as ELBO = E_Q(z|x)[log P(x|z)] − KL(Q(z|x) || P(z)), where E_Q(z|x) is the expectation under the approximate posterior distribution Q(z|x), KL(Q(z|x) || P(z)) is the Kullback-Leibler (KL) divergence between the approximate posterior and prior distribution P(z) (usually a standard normal distribution), and log P(x|z) is the log-likelihood of the data given the latent representation.

VAEs use the reparameterization trick to enable backpropagation through the encoder's sampling operation. Instead of directly sampling z from Q(z|x), a noise term $\varepsilon$ is sampled from a standard normal distribution: $\varepsilon \sim N(0, I)$.

Then the latent variable z can be computed as $z = \mu(x) + \sigma(x) \odot \varepsilon$

This reparameterization allows gradients to flow through $\mu(x)$ and $\sigma(x)$ during backpropagation, enabling end-to-end training of the VAE.

VAEs are trained by optimizing the ELBO using stochastic gradient descent or its variants. The objective is to maximize the ELBO, which can be seen as balancing the reconstruction loss (E_Q(z|x)[log P(x|z)]) and regularization term (KL(Q(z|x) || P(z))). The reconstruction loss encourages the model to generate samples similar to the input data. At the same time, the regularization term ensures the latent representations are distributed according to the prior distribution.

# 7
# Demystifying Reinforcement Learning (RL)

Reinforcement learning (RL) is a subfield of machine learning that focuses on teaching agents how to make a sequence of decisions in an environment to maximize a cumulative reward. It draws inspiration from behavioral psychology and operates based on trial and error. In RL, an agent interacts with an environment, and based on its actions, it receives feedback in the form of rewards or punishments. The agent's goal is to learn a policy, a mapping from states to actions, that maximizes the total expected reward over time. The key components of RL are listed below.

- Agent: The learner or decision-making entity that interacts with the environment. The agent takes actions based on its current state.

- Environment: The external context within which the agent operates. It provides the agent with observations, and based on the agent's actions, it generates rewards and transitions the agent to a new state.

- State: A representation of the environment at a given point in time. It captures relevant information required for decision-making.

- Action: The choices available to the agent in a particular state. The agent selects an action based on its policy.

- Policy: The strategy or set of rules that the agent follows to determine its actions in different states. The policy can be deterministic (i.e., mapping states to specific actions) or stochastic (i.e., mapping states to a probability distribution over actions).

- Reward: A scalar feedback signal that the agent receives from the environment after taking an action. The reward indicates the desirability of the agent's action in a specific state. The goal is to maximize the cumulative reward over time.

- Value function: An estimate of the expected future rewards that an agent will receive from a given state or state-action pair. The value function helps the agent evaluate the desirability of different states or state-action pairs.
- Model (optional): In some cases, a RL agent may use a model of the environment to simulate and plan future interactions. The model predicts the next state and reward based on the current state and action, allowing the agent to learn from simulated experiences.

RL algorithms typically use trial and error to improve the agent's policy iteratively. The agent explores the environment, receives rewards, and updates its policy based on the observed outcomes. RL has applications in various domains, including robotics, game-playing, recommendation systems, autonomous driving, and resource management. By providing a framework for learning through interaction with the environment, RL enables agents to adapt and optimize their behavior in complex and dynamic settings.

Nonlinearity is a critical component in RL as it facilitates modeling complex real-world problems, which are typically nonlinear. Consider, for instance, robotics or game-playing scenarios. Nonlinear equations of motion dictate the movements of a robot. Similarly, the rewards and penalties stemming from varying actions in a game may be unpredictable due to their nonlinear nature. RL algorithms usually employ nonlinear function approximators like neural networks to navigate these nonlinear environments. These approximators are adept at modeling the intricate, nonlinear relationships between system inputs and outputs.

Consequently, they empower the RL algorithm to make proficient decisions in such nonlinear circumstances. Furthermore, the applications of RL are wide-ranging. It is instrumental in optimizing control systems in manufacturing and energy production industries. From a public perspective, it can enhance traffic flow efficiency within transportation networks, including roads and airports.

## 7.1 Types of Reinforcement Learning (RL) Algorithms

RL can be divided into several types depending on the specific method used to learn the optimal policy. Each RL type has advantages and is suited for different problems. The choice of method depends on the specifics of the problem, such as the size of the state and action spaces, the availability of an expert to learn from, whether a model of the environment can be constructed, and so on.

## Model-Based Reinforcement Learning (RL)

In these methods, the agent builds a model of the environment. That is, it tries to understand the dynamics of the environment, including state transitions and rewards. It uses this model to plan and make decisions. These methods can be very simple and efficient but may struggle with inaccuracies in the model.

## Model-Free Reinforcement Learning (RL)

In contrast to model-based methods, model-free methods do not attempt to understand or model the environment's dynamics. Instead, they focus on learning directly from the rewards received. They can be further categorized into:

- Value-based methods: These methods try to learn a value function, which measures how good it is to be in a particular state (or to take a specific action from a state). The agent uses this information to select actions. Examples include Q-learning and Deep Q Networks (DQNs).

- Policy-based methods: Instead of learning a value function, these methods directly try to learn the policy, that is, the mapping from states to actions. They are instrumental when the action space is large or continuous. Examples include REINFORCE algorithm and policy gradient methods.

- Actor-critic methods: These hybrid methods combine value- and policy-based methods. They have two components: an actor (updates the policy similarly to policy-based methods) and a critic (estimates the value function, like value-based methods). Examples include advantage actor-critic (A2C), soft actor-critic, deep deterministic policy gradient (DDPG), and proximal policy optimization (PPO).

## Inverse Reinforcement Learning (RL)

In these methods, the agent learns from observing an expert. The goal is to infer the reward function that the expert seems to be optimizing, hence the name "inverse reinforcement learning."

**Multi-Agent Reinforcement Learning (RL)**

This is a type of RL where multiple learning agents interact or compete in a shared environment. These systems can be used to study complex adaptive behaviors but can be challenging due to the dynamics between the multiple agents.

## 7.2   Value-Based Methods

Value-based methods focus on learning the value function without maintaining an explicit policy. The value function measures how good it is for an agent to be in a particular state or how good it is to perform an individual action in a specific state. The goal of value-based methods is to learn an optimal value function, which, in turn, can be used to derive an optimal policy. This optimal policy directs the agent to choose the action that leads to the highest possible expected cumulative reward in every state.

Value-based methods can be further categorized into two types:

- Value iteration: In this method, the agent starts with a random value function and iteratively updates the value of each state based on the Bellman expectation equation until the value function converges to the optimal one. Once the optimal value function is found, the optimal policy can be derived by choosing the action that maximizes the expected value in each state.
- Q-learning: This is an extension of the value iteration method that works by learning the value of taking a particular action in a particular state, known as the Q-value. The algorithm updates the Q-value iteratively based on the Bellman optimality equation until the Q-function converges to the optimal one. The policy is then derived by choosing the action that maximizes the Q-value in each state.

## 7.3   Q-Learning

Q-learning is a model-free RL algorithm. It is used to learn a policy, which tells an agent what action to take under what circumstances. It does not require a model of the environment, and it can handle problems with stochastic transitions and rewards without requiring adaptations. The goal of Q-learning is to learn a policy, a way of choosing the action that will maximize the sum of future rewards based on the current state of the environment. It approximates the action-value function (Q(s, a)), which gives the expected utility (return) of taking a given action (an) in a given state (s) following a fixed policy.

The process begins with initializing the Q-values table (Q(s, a)) with arbitrary values. This table serves as a roadmap for the agent, directing it toward the optimal action in any given state. The agent then finds itself in a state (s), and based on the current Q-value estimates, it selects an action (a). This choice is predominantly made using the ε-greedy policy. This means that while most of the time, the agent selects the action with the highest Q-value in the current state, known as exploitation, it occasionally opts for a random action, known as exploration. Upon deciding on an action, the agent performs it, receiving a reward and transitioning to a new state. The Q-value for the state-action pair is then updated, influenced by the received reward and maximum Q-value for the new state, which represents the estimated optimal future value. This updated Q-value reflects the value of the action taken in the prior state. These steps are repeated for a large number of episodes until the Q-values converge.

The formula for updating the Q-value in Q-learning is $Q(s, a) = Q(s, a) + \alpha * [r + \gamma * \max Q(s', a') - Q(s, a)]$.

Here:
- s is the previous state,
- a is the action taken,
- r is the reward received for taking action (a) in state (s),
- s' is the new state,
- $\alpha$ (alpha) is the learning rate ($0 <= \alpha <= 1$), determining to what extent the newly acquired information will override the old information, and
- $\gamma$ (gamma) is the discount factor ($0 <= \gamma <= 1$), determining the importance of future rewards.

One of the advantages of Q-learning is that it allows the agent to learn from actions without needing to follow any sort of fixed policy. However, a downside is that it can be quite slow to converge, particularly in environments with a large number of states and actions. Nonetheless, it is a core technique in RL, and many more advanced techniques build upon it.

## 7.4 Deep Q Networks (DQNs)

Deep Q networks (DQNs) represent an innovative blend of Q-learning and deep neural networks, initially introduced by DeepMind scientists in 2015. This approach sets new standards in a range of Atari games, surpassing all earlier techniques. Traditional Q-learning encounters difficulties, particularly in dealing with expansive state spaces. This is due to its dependence on a tabular methodology, where every state-action pair requires a distinct Q-value. With an extremely large or continuous number of states, this approach becomes impractical because of memory constraints and the exploration time needed for each state-action pair. DQNs offer a solution to these problems by leveraging a neural network to approximate the Q-value function, enabling them to manage larger state spaces by generalizing across states. The deep neural network in DQNs processes the environmental state as an input and provides Q-values for each potential action as output.

The DQN algorithm utilizes the basic structure of Q-learning, as outlined below:

- Initialization of the Q-network: The weights of the Q-network are typically set randomly.
- Action selection: An action is selected based on the Q-network's current evaluations. This process is typically executed via an $\varepsilon$-greedy policy, similar to Q-learning.
- Action execution: The agent carries out the chosen action, obtains a reward, and observes the subsequent state.
- Transition storage in replay memory: This is a primary distinguishing factor between DQN and traditional Q-learning. Rather than updating the Q-network instantly, the agent stores the state, action, reward, and ensuing state (known as a transition) within a replay memory.
- Mini-batch sampling from replay memory: The agent randomly picks a set of transitions from the replay memory, a step that distinguishes DQN from Q-learning. This technique is designed to disrupt the correlations found in sequential state observations, thereby stabilizing the training process.
- Q-network update: Based on the sampled transitions, the agent updates the Q-network. Specifically, it performs a gradient descent step to minimize the discrepancy between the current Q-network's estimates and target Q-values, which are formulated on the basis of the received reward and highest estimated Q-value for the next state.
- Iteration of steps 2–6: These steps are reiterated for a large number of episodes. Periodically, the Q-network's weights are copied to a distinct target network, which is utilized to generate the target Q-values, further enhancing the stability of the learning process.

By combining Q-learning with deep neural networks, DQNs can learn complex policies over large state spaces, making them a powerful tool for a wide range of RL problems.

## 7.5   Policy-Based Methods

Policy-based methods are a subset of RL algorithms where the focus is on directly learning the policy function without learning a value function first. The policy function is a mapping from each state in the environment to an action, determining the action an agent should take in each state. This policy can be deterministic, where a specific state will always yield the same action, or it can be stochastic, where given a state, the policy outputs a probability distribution over the actions.

In policy-based methods, the primary concepts include policy optimization and policy gradient methods. Policy optimization aims to identify the optimal policy, maximizing the anticipated return from every state, typically achieved using gradient ascent, wherein the policy parameters are systematically updated to augment the expected return. Policy gradient methods, which fall under the umbrella of policy-based methods, also utilize gradient ascent to pinpoint the optimal policy. A basic policy gradient algorithm is REINFORCE, though it experiences considerable variance. More sophisticated policy gradient methods, such as actor-critic methods or proximal policy optimization (PPO), merge policy gradient methodologies with value-based approaches to mitigate this variance.

Policy-based methods come with a set of benefits and downsides. They excel in dealing with high-dimensional action spaces, learning stochastic policies, and offering theoretical convergence assurance. On the flip side, they often demonstrate slow convergence, and the optimal policy might only represent a local optimum. Unlike value-based methods, which aim to understand the value of being in a certain state or executing a particular action, policy-based methods focus on learning the specific action to be taken directly. These methods prove especially advantageous in environments with large or continuous action spaces or where a stochastic policy is required.

### 7.5.1   REINFORCE (Monte Carlo Policy Gradient)

REINFORCE, an acronym for "REward Increment = Nonnegative Factor x Offset Reinforcement x Characteristic Eligibility," is a policy gradient methodology utilized in RL. This algorithm, presented in a 1992 paper by Ronald J. Williams, is also referred to as the Monte Carlo policy gradient. Among the most straightforward policy gradient approaches, it employs the total return (accumulation of rewards) from an episode to calculate the policy gradient. The policy parameters are then adjusted in the direction of the gradient. Nevertheless, REINFORCE is prone to high variance as it doesn't incorporate a baseline or value function for variance reduction. Unlike value-based techniques, such as Q-learning and DQN, which strive to learn a value function subsequently used for action selection, policy-based methods like REINFORCE directly seek to optimize the policy function without needing an individual value function. The steps involved in REINFORCE algorithm are listed below.

- Initialize the policy: The policy is typically represented as a parameterized function, such as a neural network with weights ($\theta$). The policy, denoted $\pi(a|s; \theta)$, gives the probability of taking action (an) in the state (s) given the policy parameters ($\theta$).

- Generate an episode: Using the current policy, generate an episode, a sequence of state-action-reward tuples.

- For each step in the episode: For each time step t in the episode, perform the following update:

  - Compute the return ($G\_t$) from that time step until the end of the episode. The return is the total discounted reward from time step t.

  - Update the policy parameters ($\theta$) using gradient ascent. This update looks like $\theta \leftarrow \theta + \alpha * \nabla\theta \log \pi(At|St;\theta) * Gt$.

    Here,

    - $\alpha$ is the learning rate,

    - At is the action taken at time step t,

    - St is the state at time step t, and

    - Gt is the return at time step t.

$\nabla\theta \log \pi(At|St;\theta)$ is the gradient of the log probability of taking action, At, at state, St, with respect to the policy parameters, $\theta$.

This update rule essentially nudges the policy parameters in the direction that would make the taken action more probable in case of a positive return and less probable in case of a negative return.

The key concept of the REINFORCE algorithm is that it uses Monte Carlo sampling to estimate the expected return, which means it waits until the end of the episode to update the policy. This approach makes REINFORCE conceptually simple and easy to implement but can also lead to high variance in the updates, making the learning process slow and unstable. Various techniques, such as using a baseline to reduce the variance (leading to the actor-critic methods), or methods that reduce the variance of the gradient estimate (like TRPO or PPO) have been developed to address these issues.

## 7.6  Proximal Policy Optimization (PPO)

Proximal policy optimization (PPO) is a strategy for policy optimization employed in RL. Launched by OpenAI in 2017, PPO aims to resolve the computational challenges linked to earlier policy gradient strategies, notably the significant processing demands of trust region policy optimization (TRPO). Policy gradient methods traditionally involve updating the policy by introducing a change proportionate to the gradient of expected rewards. However, substantial updates can radically alter the policy and trigger instability in the learning journey. Conversely, minimal updates can excessively slow down the learning process. PPO's goal is to optimize the policy by taking the most significant improvement step while maintaining the new policy's consistency with the old one. Doing so merges the benefits of policy gradient methods with TRPO, facilitating good sample complexity while remaining easy to implement.

## 7.7  Trust Region Policy Optimization (TRPO)

Trust region policy optimization (TRPO) is an approach to policy optimization employed in RL. Introduced by John Schulman and team in 2015, TRPO's primary objective is to enhance the stability of the policy iteration procedure by setting a boundary on the extent to which each update can alter the existing policy. Introducing this trust region helps steer clear of situations where updates drastically downgrade performance. Essentially, TRPO secures the new policy within certain limits to avoid straying too far from the existing one, providing stability throughout the training process.

## 7.8  Actor-Critic Methods

Actor-critic methods in RL combine the advantages of policy gradient methods (actor) and value function estimation (critic). The actor updates the policy based on the feedback from the critic, which evaluates the new policy's value. These methods balance exploration and exploitation, allowing for efficient learning. They offer advantages in managing the variance of updates, leading to faster and more stable training.

## 7.9   Advantage Actor-Critic (A2C)

Advantage Actor-Critic (A2C) is a synchronous algorithm that runs parallel across multiple workers to improve training efficiency. It combines the advantages of both policy gradient and value function methods. As such, it maintains two separate neural networks, one to learn the policy and another to learn the state-value function. The policy network takes the current state as input and outputs a probability distribution over possible actions. The value network takes the current state as input and outputs an estimate of the expected reward from the current state.

During training, the agent interacts with the environment by selecting actions based on the policy and receiving rewards. The advantage function measures the advantage of taking a certain action over the average value of all actions in the current state. The policy is then optimized using the advantage function to update the policy parameters, and the value function is optimized using the mean squared error between the estimated value and actual reward. The advantage function measures how good a particular action is compared to the average action, and it is used to adjust the policy to favor more beneficial actions. By learning both the policy and value function, A2C can more efficiently update the policy based on environmental feedback.

## 7.10   Asynchronous Advantage Actor-Critic (A3C)

Asynchronous advantage actor-critic (A3C) is an extension of A2C. In A3C, multiple copies of the agent can run in parallel, each interacting with its instance of the environment. Each copy of the agent maintains its own set of model parameters, which are updated asynchronously by each worker based on its own experience. A3C allows for much faster training, as the agent can learn from multiple experiences in parallel. This is particularly useful for complex environments with large state spaces, as it can significantly reduce the time needed to explore and learn optimal policies. Due to the asynchronous nature of the algorithm, it can be more challenging to implement and may require careful tuning of hyperparameters.

## 7.11   Deep Deterministic Policy Gradient (DDPG)

Deep deterministic policy gradient (DDPG) extends the Q-learning algorithm to continuous action spaces. It is an actor-critic method that learns a policy function, the actor, and a value function, the critic. DDPG maintains two neural networks, one for the actor and one for the critic. The actor takes the current state as input and outputs a deterministic action. The critic takes the current state and action as input and outputs an estimate of the expected reward from the current state-action pair.

During training, the agent interacts with the environment by selecting actions based on the policy and receiving rewards. The critic is updated using the mean squared error between the estimated value and actual reward. The actor is then updated using the gradient of the Q-value with respect to the action. This allows the actor to learn a better policy that maximizes the expected reward. DDPG uses experience replay to store and sample past experiences and a target network to stabilize learning. The target network is a copy of the actor and critic networks used to compute the target values. It is updated periodically to reduce the variance of the Q-value estimates.

## 7.12   Twin Delayed Deep Deterministic Policy Gradient (TD3)

Twin delayed deep deterministic policy gradient (TD3) extends the deep deterministic policy gradient (DDPG) algorithm. TD3 is designed to reduce overestimation and improve the stability of learning. TD3 maintains two Q-value networks to reduce overestimation and a delayed policy update to stabilize learning further. The two Q-value networks estimate the Q-values, and the minimum Q-value is used as the target value for updating the critic. This helps to reduce the overestimation of Q-values that can occur in DDPG.

The delayed policy update stabilizes learning by reducing the correlation between the policy updates and Q-value estimates. The policy is updated only every n step, where n is a hyperparameter determining the delay. This helps reduce the Q-value estimates' variance and improve learning stability. TD3 uses experience replay to store and sample past experiences and a target network to stabilize learning. The target network is a copy of the actor and critic networks used to compute the target values. It is updated periodically to reduce the variance of the Q-value estimates.

## 7.13  Soft Actor-Critic (SAC)

Soft actor-critic (SAC) is designed to optimize the policy parameters using gradient descent directly. It is an actor-critic method that learns a policy function (the actor) and a value function (the critic). SAC maintains a stochastic policy and learns the policy's Q-function and entropy. The Q-function takes the current state and action as input and outputs an estimate of the expected reward from the current state-action pair. The entropy of the policy is a measure of the randomness of the actions selected by the policy. During training, the agent interacts with the environment by selecting actions based on the policy and receiving rewards. The critic is updated using the mean squared error between the estimated value and actual reward. The actor is updated using the gradient of the expected return with respect to the policy parameters, which includes a term that encourages exploration and improves the robustness of the learned policy. SAC uses experience replay to store and sample past experiences and a target network to stabilize learning. The target network is a copy of the actor and critic networks used to compute the target values. It is updated periodically to reduce the variance of the Q-value estimates.

The SAC, a RL algorithm, was used to build the model. The SAC aims to improve the reward signal by balancing exploration and exploitation, two critical aspects of RL. The algorithm is based on the actor-critic framework. It uses two separate neural networks: the actor network for learning the policy and the critic network for estimating the value of state-action pairs. SAC improves the reward signal and overall learning process by incorporating key features known as entropy regularization, soft value functions, off-policy learning, twin Q-networks, and delayed policy updates.

# 8

# Evaluating AI Model Accuracy:
# Unveiling Essential Metrics

In the context of AI, an accuracy metric evaluates an AI model's performance. It quantifies the degree to which the model's predictions match the actual values, helping to determine how well the model achieves its task. Different types of AI tasks, like classification, regression, and clustering, use their own suitable accuracy metrics to measure their performance. And within the type of task, the choice of accuracy metric depends on the specific problem, business context, and nature of the output.

## 8.1  Classification Accuracy Metrics

**Accuracy**

The accuracy metric measures the proportion of correct predictions made by the model over the total number of predictions. It is determined by comparing the model's predictions to the actual labels. The number of correct predictions is divided by the total number of predictions, resulting in a value between 0 and 1. An accuracy score of 1 signifies that the model accurately predicted all instances, while an accuracy of 0 indicates that none of the predictions were correct. Accuracy is a straightforward metric that provides an overall measure of how well the model performs in correctly classifying instances. However, it has limitations, especially when dealing with imbalanced datasets. In cases where the classes are not represented equally, accuracy may not accurately represent the model's performance. For instance, if a dataset contains 90 percent instances of class A and only 10 percent instances of class B, a model that always predicts class A would achieve an accuracy of 90 percent, even though it fails to capture the minority class accurately. In such cases, the other evaluation metrics, such as precision, recall, F1 score, or area under the receiver operating characteristic curve (AUC-ROC), are suitable depending on the specific requirements and characteristics of the classification problem.

**Precision**

Precision gives the percentage of positive predictions that are correct. It measures the proportion of correctly predicted positive observations from the total predicted positives. It is often used with recall to provide a more comprehensive overview of a model's performance. Precision is calculated using the following formula: Precision = True Positives / (True Positives + False Positives).

- True Positives (TP): These are the cases when the model predicted positive and the true label also was positive. In other words, the model correctly predicted the positive class.
- False Positives (FP): These are the cases when the model predicted positive but the true label was negative. Essentially, the model incorrectly predicted the positive class.

Let us consider a scenario where a model predicts whether an email is spam (positive class) or not spam (negative class). Out of one hundred predictions made by the model, let us assume it correctly identifies eighty emails as spam but erroneously labels twenty not-spam emails as spam. In this case, the precision of the model can be calculated as follows: Precision = 80 / (80 + 20) = 0.8, or 80 percent.

This indicates that when the model predicts an email as spam, it is correct 80 percent of the time. Precision addresses the question, "When the model predicts a positive result, how often is it correct?" This metric is particularly crucial when the cost of false positives (incorrectly identifying a non-spam email as spam) is high.

**Recall (Sensitivity)**

The percentage of actual positive instances that the model correctly identified. Recall, also known as sensitivity or true positive rate, is a metric that measures the proportion of actual positives that are correctly identified as such, Recall = True Positives / (True Positives + False Negatives).

- True positives (TPs): These are the cases in which the model predicted positive and the true label also was positive. In other words, the model correctly predicted the positive class.
- False negatives (FNs): These are the cases in which the model predicted negative but the true label was positive. Essentially, the model incorrectly predicted the positive class.

For example, consider a model that predicts whether a patient has a disease (positive) or not (negative). If out of one hundred actual disease cases, the model correctly identifies seventy as having the disease but misses thirty, then the recall of the model would be Recall = 70 / (70 + 30) = 0.7, or 70 percent.

This means the model correctly identifies 70 percent of all patients with the disease. Recall answers, "What proportion of actual positives was identified correctly?" It is particularly useful when the cost of false negatives is high.

## F1 Score

The relationship between recall and precision frequently represents a balancing act, where enhancing one can potentially diminish the other, a concept referred to as the precision-recall trade-off. The F1 score is typically employed as a comprehensive metric to encapsulate precision and recall harmoniously. As such, the F1 score combines precision and recall, giving harmonic mean to these two metrics. The F1 score is instrumental when there is uneven class distribution, as it seeks a balance between precision and recall.

F1-Score = 2 * (Precision * Recall) / (Precision + Recall)

Precision = True Positives / (True Positives + False Positives)

Recall = True Positives / (True Positives + False Negatives)

The F1 score ranges from 0 to 1, where 1 indicates perfect precision and recall, and 0 indicates that either the precision or the recall is zero.

In an illustration where precision is assigned a value of 0.75 and recall is given a value of 0.85, the calculation for the F1 score would be as follows: F1 Score = 2 * (0.75 * 0.85) / (0.75 + 0.85) = 0.795, or roughly 0.80.

The F1 score becomes an apt metric for looking at when equal importance is accorded to precision and recall. However, should precision or recall be considered of higher significance, these metrics might need to be evaluated independently, or other combined metrics, such as the F-beta score, might be employed. The F-beta score facilitates the assignment of extra weight to either precision or recall.

## ROC-AUC

ROC stands for "receiver operating characteristic." ROC-AUC is the area under the receiver operating characteristic curve. It provides an aggregate measure of performance across all possible classification thresholds. It is a method used in binary classification problems to understand the performance of a model by visualizing the trade-off between the true positive rate (TPR) and false positive rate (FPR, 1 - specificity). The ROC curve is created by plotting the TPR against the FPR at various threshold settings. The threshold in a binary classifier is the point that separates the probability outputs of the model into binary classes. The model's sensitivity to positive instances can be modified by adjusting this threshold, which subsequently changes the model's TPR and FPR. This results in a movement along the ROC curve.

The ideal point on the plot is found at the top-left corner, where the FPR is 0 and the TPR is 1. Although this position is not practically attainable, it symbolizes the most advantageous location. A classifier making predictions at random, comparable to flipping a coin, would have a ROC curve represented by a diagonal line extending from the bottom left to the top right. The model's proficiency is denoted by how much the curve exceeds this diagonal line.

AUC-ROC quantifies the capability of a parameter to differentiate between two distinct groups, such as patients with or without disease or emails being spam or not spam. An AUC of 0.5 implies an absence of discrimination, that is, an inability to differentiate between the classes. On the other hand, a perfect score of 1 indicates flawless discrimination, while a score of 0 reflects perfect discrimination but in an inverse relationship. The test's accuracy increases the more closely the curve adheres to the ROC space's left and top borders. Conversely, as the curve approaches the ROC space's 45-degree diagonal, the accuracy of the test diminishes. The ROC curve and AUC-ROC are extensively employed to demonstrate the balance between true and false positives and compare the performance of different classifiers.

**Log Loss**

This measures the performance of a classification model where the prediction input is a probability value between 0 and 1. Logarithmic loss, or log loss, measures a classification model's performance where the prediction output is a probability value between 0 and 1. Log loss increases as the predicted probability diverges from the actual label. The goal of machine learning models is to minimize this value.

The formula for log loss for binary classification where there are two classes, 0 and 1: Log Loss = - (1/N) * Σ [y * log(p) + (1 – y) * log(1 - p)].

Where:
- N is the total number of observations,
- Σ is the sum over all observations,
- y is the actual class label (either 0 or 1), and
- p is the predicted probability that the instance is in class 1.

A term is calculated for each instance based on whether it falls into class 0 or 1. The term becomes log(1 - p) if it is in class 0 and log(p) in class 1. These terms are then aggregated, taking the negative of this sum and normalizing it through division by the total number of instances. A perfectly confident and accurate prediction will yield a log loss of 0, as it mirrors reality flawlessly. Conversely, an incorrect yet confident prediction can escalate the log loss to infinity, making log loss a stringent metric capable of severely penalizing incorrect but confident models. Although log loss exhibits higher sensitivity to incorrect predictions than other metrics, such as accuracy, it carries the advantage of factoring in the probabilistic confidence of a prediction, a feature not present in metrics like the F1 score or accuracy.

## 8.2 Forecasting (Regression) Accuracy Metrics

Regression accuracy metrics critically evaluate models to predict continuous variables, like housing market values or stock prices. Key metrics include mean absolute error (MAE), which calculates the average absolute deviation from the true value; mean squared error (MSE), which measures the average of squared prediction errors; root mean squared error (RMSE), which delivers a heavier penalty for larger errors; mean absolute percentage error (MAPE), helpful in understanding prediction errors relative to true values in percentage terms; and R-squared ($R^2$), which quantifies the proportion of variance in the dependent variable that can be predicted from the independent variables.

**Mean Absolute Error (MAE)**

Mean absolute error (MAE) calculates the average discrepancy between predicted and actual values. In simpler terms, MAE quantifies the average mistake made by the model in the same units as the variable it is predicting. It is computed by determining the absolute differences between predicted and real values, adding up these differences, and then taking their average. This makes it a clear and simple way to understand the average size of the model's errors.

For n observations, if $y\_i$ represents the actual value and $yhat\_i$ represents the predicted value for the ith observation, then MAE = (1/n) * $\Sigma$|$y\_i$ - $yhat\_i$|.

Where:
- n is the total number of observations or instances,
- $\Sigma$ signifies summation (adding up all the values produced by the absolute difference operation), and
- |$y\_i$ - $yhat\_i$| is the absolute error of the prediction for the i-th observation (the absolute value of the difference between the actual value ($y\_i$) and the predicted value ($yhat\_i$).

The absolute value is used to avoid cancellations between positive and negative errors. This way, MAE represents the average magnitude of the error, regardless of direction. A smaller MAE indicates a better model fit to the data. However, because the absolute value of the residuals is taken into account, MAE can be influenced significantly by outliers. To put it another way, the MAE can be drastically affected by extremely large or small errors. Therefore, other metrics, such as MSE or RMSE, are preferable if the specific task contains many outliers.

## Mean Squared Error (MSE)

Mean squared error (MSE) is the average of the squares between the predicted and actual values. This metric gives a higher penalty for large errors. The MSE is another common metric used to evaluate the performance of regression models. Unlike MAE, which calculates the absolute difference, MSE squares the difference between the predicted and actual values. The main advantage of MSE over MAE is that MSE penalizes large errors more due to the squared term. This makes it more sensitive to outliers compared to MAE. However, because the errors are squared before averaged, the MSE gives a relatively high weight to large errors. This means the MSE should be more useful when large errors are particularly undesirable.

$$MSE = (1/n) * \Sigma(y\_i - yhat\_i)^2$$

Where:

- n is the total number of observations or instances,
- $\Sigma$ signifies summation (adding up all the values produced by the square difference operation), and
- $(y\_i - yhat\_i)^2$ is the squared error of the prediction for the i-th observation (the square of the difference between the actual value ($y\_i$) and the predicted value ($yhat\_i$).

## Root Mean Squared Error (RMSE)

The root mean squared error (RMSE) is the square root of the MSE. It possesses a higher sensitivity to larger errors when compared to the MAE. By square-rooting the MSE, the error metric is returned to the same unit as the output variable, enhancing its interpretability. Like MSE, a smaller RMSE signifies a superior model fit, with an RMSE of 0 denoting a perfect fit to the data. Large errors are allocated a relatively high weight in the RMSE as errors are squared prior to averaging. This makes RMSE more applicable in situations where large errors are highly undesirable. The principal distinction, therefore, is that the RMSE, being in the same units as the target variable, penalizes larger errors more heavily than the MSE due to the squaring operation. This feature proves beneficial when large errors are especially unwelcome or when comparison is required across different units or scales.

**R-Squared (Coefficient of Determination)**

R-squared, also known as the coefficient of determination, assesses the goodness of fit of a model. It represents the proportion of the variance for a dependent variable explained by an independent variable or variables in a regression model. In other words, R-squared measures how well the observed outcomes are replicated by the model, based on the proportion of total variation of outcomes explained by the model. The value of R-squared lies between 0 and 1, where 1 indicates the model perfectly predicts the target variable and 0 indicates the model does not explain any of the variance in the target variable.

$$R^2 = 1 - (SSR / SST)$$

Sum of squared residuals (SSR) is the sum of the squared differences between the actual and predicted values. It represents the error of our model.

$$SSR = \Sigma(y\_i - yhat\_i)^2$$

Total sum of squares (SST) is the sum of the squared differences between the actual values and the mean of actual values ($\bar{y}$). It represents the total variance in the data.

$$SST = \Sigma(y\_i - \bar{y})^2$$

In these formulas, $y\_i$ represents the actual values, $yhat\_i$ represents the predicted values, and $\bar{y}$ (y-bar) represents the mean of the actual values.

An R-squared of 100 percent indicates that all changes in the dependent variable are completely explained by changes in the independent variable(s).

**Mean Absolute Percentage Error (MAPE)**

Mean absolute percentage error (MAPE) determines the accuracy of a forecasting model in statistics, specifically in trend estimation. It expresses accuracy as a percentage, providing an understanding of error in terms of the actual values' scale. Since it expresses accuracy as a percentage, it helps understand the scale of the prediction errors relative to predicted values. This can make it more interpretable than other metrics.

$$MAPE = (100/n) * \Sigma (|\ (y\_i - yhat\_i) / y\_i\ |)$$

Where:

- n is the total number of observations,
- $\Sigma$ represents the summation operator,
- y_i is the actual value for the i-th observation,
- yhat_i is the predicted value for the i-th observation, and
- | (y_i - yhat_i) / y_i | is the absolute percentage error for each individual observation.

This formula essentially calculates the absolute difference between the actual and predicted value for each data point, expresses it as a percentage of the actual value, and then takes the average of all these percentage error values. Since MAPE is a percentage, it is unitless, thus allowing for comparing forecasting errors across different datasets and units.

## Mean Squared Logarithmic Error (MSLE)

Mean squared logarithmic error (MSLE) can be used when targets have exponential growth, such as population counts, average sales of a commodity over a span of years, and so forth. MSLE measures the error between predicted and actual values in a regression problem. It is calculated as the mean of the squared differences between the predicted values' logarithms and the actual values' logarithms.

$$MSLE = 1/n * sum((log(y\_hat) - log(y))\text{\^{}}2)$$

Where:

- n is the number of data points,
- y_hat is the predicted value for a data point, and
- y is the actual value for a data point.

MSLE is a more resilient error measurement than MSE, notably when predicted and actual values can drastically differ. The key reason is that MSLE considers the logarithmic scale of values, something that MSE overlooks. MSLE proves helpful in regression problems where anticipated and actual values can greatly vary. It is more sensitive to changes in predicted values, enabling it to detect minor alterations that MSE might miss. Furthermore, MSLE, a percentage, is easier to interpret and communicate, making it a more user-friendly metric than MSE.

## 8.3   Clustering Accuracy Metrics

Evaluation of clustering algorithms typically involves using different metrics, as the focus is on determining the algorithm's efficacy in assembling similar instances and segregating dissimilar ones instead of predicting a target value. Some frequently used clustering evaluation metrics include silhouette coefficient, Davies-Bouldin index, and Rand index.

**Silhouette Coefficient**

The silhouette coefficient evaluates the quality of clusters a clustering algorithm produces. It provides a way to assess how close each data point in one cluster is to the points in the neighboring clusters, thus indicating the separation between the formed clusters.

The silhouette coefficient is calculated for each sample in the dataset and takes values in the range of -1 to 1. For a given sample, a silhouette coefficient close to 1 indicates the sample is well-matched to its own cluster and poorly matched to neighboring clusters. The clustering configuration is appropriate if most samples have a high silhouette coefficient. If many points have a low or negative silhouette coefficient, the clustering configuration may have too many or too few clusters.

The calculation of the silhouette coefficient for a set of data points is carried out in a sequential manner. For each data point, the first step involves determining the average distance from all other points within the same cluster, which is termed as the average dissimilarity, or a. Next, the average distance from all points in the nearest cluster is computed for that identical data point, known as the average dissimilarity of the closest cluster, or b. The silhouette coefficient for that particular point is then established using the formula (b - a) / max(a, b). This step-by-step process results in the silhouette coefficient, offering a means to quantify the quality of clusters created by a clustering algorithm.

## Davies-Bouldin Index (DBI)

The Davies-Bouldin index (DBI) is a popular metric for evaluating the quality of a clustering algorithm. The index helps determine the similarity between clusters, where lower values indicate better clustering performance. The DBI is based on a ratio of within-cluster and between-cluster distances. For each cluster, it calculates a measure (R) of that cluster's average similarity with all other clusters. Here, similarity compares the distance between clusters with the size of the clusters.

$$R(i, j) = (S(i) + S(j)) / D(i, j)$$

Here:

- S(i) is the average distance of all elements in cluster i to the centroid of cluster I,
- S(j) is the average distance of all elements in cluster j to the centroid of cluster j, and
- D(i, j) is the distance between the centroids of clusters i and j.

After calculating the R-value for each cluster with all other clusters, the maximum R-value is selected. The DBI is the average of all maximum R-values across all clusters. The goal is to have a lower DBI value, as it signifies that clusters are compact (small S(i)) and far from each other (large D(i, j)). In other words, a lower DBI means the clustering algorithm has performed well in grouping similar instances together and separating dissimilar ones.

## Calinski-Harabasz Index

The Calinski-Harabasz index (CHI), also known as the variance ratio criterion, is another criterion used for assessing the quality of a clustering algorithm. It is an internal evaluation scheme where higher values indicate better clustering. The CHI measures the dispersion within clusters and between clusters. It is defined as the ratio of the sum of between-cluster dispersion and the sum of within-cluster dispersion. The between-cluster dispersion is the sum of squared distances between each cluster center and center of all data points. The within-cluster dispersion is the sum of squared distances between each data point and its cluster center.

$$CHI = [(B / (K - 1)) / (W / (N - K))]$$

Where:

- B is the between-group dispersion matrix (sum of squared distances from the cluster centroids to the overall data centroid),
- W is the within-cluster dispersion matrix (sum of squared distances from each data point to its cluster centroid),
- K is the number of clusters, and
- N is the total number of data points.

The higher CHI value indicates a better model. A high CHI means the between-cluster dispersion is large and the within-cluster dispersion is small, indicating well-separated and tight clusters. It is especially useful when comparing the performance of different clustering algorithms or choosing the optimal number of clusters.

## Rand Index (RI)

The Rand index (RI) evaluates the similarity between two data clustering, often used to assess the performance of clustering algorithms. This metric ranges from 0 to 1, with 0 indicating that the two data clustering do not agree on any pair of points and 1 indicating the data clustering are exactly the same. More specifically, given a set of n elements and two partitions of these elements into clusters, the RI computes the percentage of decisions that are agreed upon by both partitions. Decisions in this context are whether a pair of elements should be in the same cluster or different clusters. For each pair of elements, there are two types of decisions: $RI = (TP + TN) / (TP + FP + FN + TN)$.

The pair of elements belong to the same cluster in both partitions (true positives, TPs, and true negatives, TNs). The pair of elements belong to different clusters in both partitions (false positives, FPs, and false negatives, FNs).

An adjusted form of the RI, the adjusted Rand index (ARI), corrects the RI by the expected similarity of all pairings of clusters. ARI has a maximum value of 1, and its expected value is 0 when random clusters are input. Negative values indicate the result of the clustering algorithm is not as good as a random assignment.

Both RI and ARI are symmetric, meaning swapping the label assignments does not change the score, and they can be used to compare different clustering methods or the same method with different numbers of clusters.

## Mutual Information-Based Scores

Mutual information-based scores, often used in evaluating clustering algorithms, measure the agreement between two assignments, such as the actual and predicted clusters. These scores quantify the amount of shared information between the two assignments, how much knowing one of these variables reduces uncertainty about the other. In a clustering context, the mutual information score computes the mutual dependence between the true labels and ones assigned by the clustering algorithm. A high mutual information score indicates a high agreement between the two clustering, whereas a score of 0 means the clustering are independent and share no information.

Two commonly used mutual information-based scores in clustering evaluation are normalized mutual information (NMI) and adjusted mutual information (AMI). NMI is a normalization of the mutual information (MI) score to scale the results between 0 (no mutual information) and 1 (perfect correlation). In other words, 0 means dissimilar, and 1 means a perfect match.

Conversely, AMI is an adjustment of the MI score to account for chance. It corrects the agreement's effect solely due to random chance between clustering, which is especially significant when the number of clusters is large. AMI has a maximum value of 1, and its expected value is 0 when random clusters are input. Negative values are highly unlikely.

Both NMI and AMI provide more reliable results than the raw MI score, particularly in situations with a large number of clusters and when comparing clustering algorithms or determining the optimal number of clusters.

# 9
# Hyperparameter Tuning: Techniques for Improving Model Outcomes

Adjusting algorithmic settings to optimize performance in AI models constitutes hyperparameter tuning. These settings, termed hyperparameters, act like dials or switches that individuals involved in the process can manipulate to alter the algorithm's behavior. For instance, while training a deep neural network, the aspects subject to alteration might comprise the learning rate, the network's layer count, unit quantity per layer, and dropout rate. Contrasting with a model's parameters, hyperparameters differ in that they are preset before the commencement of training rather than data-derived during the learning phase. Hyperparameters impact the model's performance but do not derive from the data. These must be preset before initiating the learning process. This hyperparameter fine-tuning is often deemed necessary given the absence of a universal hyperparameter set that suits all datasets. The most optimal settings usually vary, hinging on factors such as the dataset's size and characteristics, the problem's complexity that needs resolution, and the computational resources at hand. As such, hyperparameter tuning becomes a critical part of model construction.

## 9.1  Optimizing Machine Learning Models

Hyperparameter tuning is a vital component of the machine learning process, regardless of the model being utilized. Contrasting with model parameters acquired during training, hyperparameters act as configuration variables. These are established before training and directly govern the structure or training method of the model. For instance, when a decision tree is being trained, its depth, or the maximum number of levels it can possess, is regarded as a hyperparameter. Similarly, in training a support vector machine, the regularization parameter (C) is identified as a hyperparameter. Numerous machine learning models can exhibit a considerable sensitivity to hyperparameter choices. Consequently, selecting suitable hyperparameters can facilitate a significant improvement in a model's performance.

The random forest algorithm has several key hyperparameters that often need tuning to optimize performance.

## Number of Trees (n_estimators)

This refers to the desired quantity of trees to be constructed before resorting to maximum voting or averages of predictions. A larger number of trees improves performance, although it results in slower code execution. The "number of trees" denotes the count of individual decision trees comprising the forest. Each tree is independently trained on varying bootstrapped subsets of the data, contributing a vote to the ultimate prediction.

Commonly, the variance of predictions is diminished by the presence of more trees, resulting in a more stable, robust model, and exhibits enhanced generalization performance. The model becomes less susceptible to overfitting as predictions are averaged over numerous trees, each trained on a distinct dataset. Nonetheless, the need for more computational resources and increased training time is a consequence of having more trees. Additionally, there are diminishing returns in prediction improvement after a certain threshold of tree numbers.

Contrarily, the necessity for fewer computational resources and reduced training time is associated with a smaller number of trees. However, increased model variance and reduced accuracy may result from fewer trees. The optimal tree count varies depending on the problem and dataset size. A good number for the problem at hand, balancing computational efficiency and model performance, can be determined through cross-validation.

While adding more trees generally improves the performance of a random forest, there is a point of diminishing returns beyond which adding more trees does not significantly improve the model's performance, and it might just be wasting computational resources. So it is crucial to experiment and find a sweet spot appropriate for the specific use case.

## Max Features (max_features)

Max features represent the upper limit on the number of features that random forest can consider per individual tree. This parameter allows various settings like auto, sqrt, log2, none, or a specific integer, which signifies the number of features. If auto or none is chosen, all features will be assessed when constructing each tree in the forest. On the other hand, choosing sqrt or log2 implies the square root or log2 of the total feature count will be utilized, respectively. The max features hyperparameter in the random forest algorithm determines the maximum quantity of features that should be evaluated when seeking the optimal split at each node within an individual decision tree.

In the scikit-learn's random forest algorithm, options to set the max features parameter include an integer (an exact feature count), a float (a fraction of the total features), sqrt (considering sqrt(n_features)), log2 (considering log2(n_features) features), or auto (equivalent to sqrt). Like other hyperparameters, the ideal max features value relies on the specific problem and dataset. It is typically identified via trial and error, often employing techniques like cross-validation. This ensures the chosen value achieves a beneficial trade-off between bias and variance, thus aiding the model in effectively generalizing to unobserved data.

## Minimum Samples Split (min_samples_split)

This figure indicates the least number of samples necessary for an internal node split. It can range from needing a single sample at each node to requiring all samples at each node. The tree becomes more restricted when this parameter is increased, as more samples are needed at each node. Minimum samples split is a critical hyperparameter in building trees in random forests and other tree-based algorithms. It establishes the least number of samples necessary for an internal node split. An internal node is a decision point that splits into other nodes in the decision tree based on an input feature condition. When the condition is met, the data at that node is divided into two or more child nodes.

Assigning a high value to this parameter makes the model more cautious. It reduces overfitting as the model needs more samples at a node to warrant the complexity brought by the split. However, setting it excessively high can oversimplify the model, potentially leading to underfitting the data and may prevent the creation of essential splits for accurate data classification or prediction. On the other hand, lower values permit the model to create splits even with fewer samples at the node. This makes the model more complex and can help it detect detailed patterns in the data; if set too low (like 2), the model might become overly complex, potentially leading to overfitting. It might capture noise and outliers in the training data and, thus, perform poorly on new, unseen data.

This hyperparameter's value is usually determined through trial and error, ideally employing techniques like cross-validation to ensure the chosen value results in a model that generalizes well to new data. Striking a balance between underfitting and overfitting is essential when choosing this hyperparameter.

## Minimum Samples Leaf (min_samples_leaf)

The minimum number of samples that must be present at a leaf node is represented by this parameter. Similar to min_samples_splits, this parameter describes the minimum number of samples at the leaf nodes, the tree's base. The minimum samples leaf serves as another hyperparameter in random forests and other tree-based methods. The requirement for the minimum number of samples to be present at a leaf node is specified by it. Leaf nodes, the endpoints of a decision tree, are where predictions are made. Allowing a smaller number of samples at a leaf node can capture fine details and complex patterns in the data.

However, if the model's minimum sample requirement at a leaf node is set too small, noise and outliers might be captured in the training data, leading to possible overfitting. This could result in poor generalization performance on unseen data. On the other hand, setting a larger minimum number of samples at a leaf node can prevent overfitting by ensuring the model is not overly complex and each leaf node generalizes well across multiple samples. But if set too high, the model might become overly simple and fail to capture important patterns in the data, which may lead to underfitting.

The specific dataset and problem determine the optimal value for the minimum samples leaf parameter. It must often be identified through experimentation and model validation techniques like cross-validation. In practice, setting a reasonable minimum number of samples at a leaf node can assist in balancing the trade-off between underfitting and overfitting, thereby enhancing the robustness and generalization ability of the random forest model.

## Maximum Depth (max_depth)

This parameter regulates the tree's maximum depth. If set to none, nodes expand until all leaves become pure or until every leaf contains fewer than min_samples_split samples. The maximum depth of a tree within a random forest is a hyperparameter that controls the growth limit of the tree to a maximum number of levels. Each tree level is correlated with a decision point that utilizes one of the dataset's features to create a split.

At level 0 is the tree's root, with its children at level 1, the grandchildren at level 2, and so on. A tree with a maximum depth of n can possess up to n levels. The model is simplified, and overfitting is avoided with the help of this parameter, making the model more generalized and preventing it from learning the noise within the data. If the maximum depth is excessively small, the model may become too simplistic to capture the data's underlying pattern, resulting in underfitting. This parameter can increase the model's complexity. This could be beneficial if a simple model cannot capture complex underlying patterns in the data. However, if the maximum depth is too large, the model could become overly complex and begin to overfit the data. This might lead to good performance on the training data but poor performance on new, unseen data.

Due to its ensemble nature, random forest is less susceptible to overfitting compared to individual decision trees, even with a large maximum depth. This is because it averages the predictions of multiple trees, each trained on different bootstrap samples and considering different feature subsets, thus reducing the overall variance. Nonetheless, setting a reasonable maximum depth can still significantly control the model's complexity, reduce training time, and potentially enhance performance. Techniques such as cross-validation may be required to determine the optimal value for the maximum depth, which often involves experimentation.

## Bootstrap

This parameter decides the use of bootstrap samples when constructing trees. When set to false, the entire dataset is employed to construct each tree. A fundamental operation in the random forest algorithm, bootstrap sampling, or bootstrapping, is a resampling method utilized in statistics. In relation to random forests, bootstrapping is applied to generate different sets of training data. A bootstrapped dataset, created by randomly selecting instances from the original dataset with replacement, is used for each tree in the forest. The term "with replacement" implies the same instance can be chosen more than once for the same bootstrap sample.

Consider a training dataset with five instances (A, B, C, D, E). A bootstrapped dataset might resemble (A, B, A, B, C). Note that instances from the original data (D, E) may not appear, and instances (A, B) may appear multiple times. This is the result of random "with replacement" sampling. This process is replicated for each decision tree in the random forest, which means each decision tree in the random forest is likely trained on a slightly different dataset. This helps ensure the individual trees are not correlated and reduces the final model's variance, potentially leading to improved prediction performance.

After all, the trees have been trained, and predictions from individual trees are combined, usually through a majority vote for classification or averaging for regression, to generate the final prediction of the random forest model. Since each tree is trained on slightly different data, they will likely produce different predictions for the same input. By amalgamating their predictions, the model can often generate more accurate predictions than any individual tree. Bootstrap sampling is just one aspect that makes random forests effective. The other key aspect is feature randomness, where each tree in the forest only considers a random subset of features when making splits, further increasing the diversity among the trees in the forest.

### 9.1.2 Hyperparameter Tuning for XGBoost

The important XGBoost hyperparameters that require tuning are listed below:
- n_estimators: This is the number of gradient-boosted trees. Too many can lead to overfitting.
- max_depth: This is the maximum tree depth for base learners. This defines how deep each tree can grow during any boosting round.
- learning_rate: This shrinks the feature weights to make the boosting process more conservative. Lower values make the model robust to the specific characteristics of each individual tree but requires more trees in the model.

- subsample: This is the subsample ratio of the training instance. This prevents overfitting, but setting it too low could lead to underfitting issues.
- colsample_bytree / colsample_bylevel / colsample_bynode: These parameters can be used for subsampling of columns. The first one is for subsampling before creating a tree, the second one is for subsampling for each split in a level, and the third one is for each split in a node.
- gamma: This is the minimum loss reduction required to make a further partition on a leaf node of the tree. The larger, the more conservative the algorithm will be.
- reg_alpha and reg_lambda: These are regularization parameters. The first is L1 regularization term on weights (analogous to lasso regression); the second is L2 regularization term on weights (analogous to ridge regression).

## 9.2   Optimizing Deep Learning Models

Hyperparameter tuning for deep learning models involves adjusting various parameters that control the structure and training process of the models.

**Learning Rate**

The training of an ANN or any model that uses gradient-based optimization methods is significantly influenced by the learning rate, one of the most important hyperparameters. The degree to which the weights of the network are adjusted concerning the loss gradient is governed by it. During gradient descent, the process through which ANNs learn from data, the update to the network's weights happens in the direction opposite to the gradient of the loss function, which measures the model's error. The learning rate dictates the size of these steps. A slower convergence toward the minimum of the loss function is observed when the learning rate is smaller, meaning the weights are updated more slowly. A more rapid weight update, which could potentially hasten convergence but might also cause the learning process to miss the minimum and fail to converge or even diverge, is caused by a larger learning rate. Between speed and accuracy, a balance is sought in the learning rate. Faster learning can be achieved with a higher learning rate, but it might miss the optimal point.

On the other hand, more accurate learning can be achieved with a lower learning rate, but it will require more epochs to train, which will make the process slower. It is common practice to begin with a larger learning rate to expedite the initial learning process and then decrease it gradually to facilitate more precise learning, an approach known as learning rate scheduling or learning rate decay.

The tuning of the learning rate is a pivotal part of neural network training. If the learning rate is set too high, the model might fail to learn, and if set too low, the learning might be either too slow or get stuck at a suboptimal solution. Determining the optimal learning rate can depend on the specific dataset, the model architecture, and other hyperparameters, thereby making it necessary, quite often, to test out different learning rates to find the most suitable one. This is where techniques like grid search, random search, or learning rate decay schedules may prove helpful. Several factors can influence the choice of the learning rate. Due to their more intricate optimization landscape, deeper networks and other more complex models might necessitate smaller learning rates. The batch size can impact the optimal learning rate, with larger batch sizes offering a more precise estimate of the gradient and possibly allowing for larger learning rates. Conversely, smaller batch sizes introduce noise into the gradient estimate, which might act as an implicit form of regularization, potentially necessitating smaller learning rates.

The characteristics of the data itself can also affect the optimal learning rate. A smaller learning rate might be necessary for noisy data or data with many outliers because larger steps, influenced by such data, could potentially misdirect the optimization process. Different optimizers may require different learning rates. While careful tuning of the learning rate might be necessary for optimizers like stochastic gradient descent (SGD), others like adaptive moment estimation (Adam) feature an adaptive learning rate that can self-adjust during training. However, even when it comes to adaptive optimizers, the initial learning rate can still serve as an important hyperparameter.

SGD is an optimization algorithm commonly used to train ANN. Unlike traditional gradient descent, which updates model weights based on the loss function calculated over the entire dataset, SGD updates weights using the gradient of the loss function for a single, randomly-selected training example. This frequent updating, though noisy, can help escape local minima, potentially leading to better solutions. The process begins with a model defined with random weights and then, in iterations, calculates the gradient of the loss function for one instance, updating the weights in the direction opposite to the gradient. This continues until a stopping condition, like a maximum number of epochs or a threshold of improvement in loss, is met. Variants of SGD, like mini-batch SGD, use a small randomly-selected subset of the data for each update, providing a balance between computational efficiency and accurate gradient estimation. In practice, SGD often uses a learning rate decay schedule, enabling larger adjustments early in training and smaller, fine-tuning adjustments later. Despite its effectiveness, especially with large-scale data, SGD may require careful hyperparameter tuning, such as learning rate and batch size.

Adam, short for adaptive moment estimation, is another optimization algorithm commonly used in training ANN. Preferred over traditional methods like SGD, Adam uniquely combines the benefits of AdaGrad, which optimizes per-parameter learning rates enhancing performance on sparse gradient problems, and RMSProp, which adapts learning rates based on recent gradient magnitudes, making it effective for noisy and nonstationary problems. This versatile and robust optimizer, known for being easy to implement, computationally efficient, and memory conservative, is invariant to diagonal rescaling of gradients, making it suitable for large-scale, nonstationary problems and those with noisy or sparse gradients. One of Adam's significant strengths lies in its intuitively interpretable hyperparameters that typically require minimal tuning, making it a default choice for training deep learning models.

An interaction between the learning rate and regularization term might occur if regularization methods like L1 or L2 are used. A smaller learning rate might be needed in case of stronger regularization. The learning rate can also be affected if features vary significantly in scale. Before training, normalizing or standardizing input features is often advisable, as it can assist in the choice of learning rate.

These factors imply that various variables linked to the specific dataset can influence the optimal learning rate, model architecture, and training configuration. As a result, it is often deemed necessary to employ techniques such as grid search or random search, combined with cross-validation, to pinpoint the best learning rate for a specific scenario. The balance between training speed and accuracy is also managed by some practitioners using learning rate schedules, which commence with a larger learning rate and reduce it over time.

**Number of Layers**

This defines the architecture of the neural network. Deeper networks, possessing more layers, can model more complex functions, but they are more susceptible to overfitting and can be more demanding computationally. It refers to the count of neuron layers sandwiched between the input and output layer, and these are referred to as hidden layers. A neural network, for instance, that features one hidden layer populated with several neurons is categorized as a shallow neural network. Conversely, a deep neural network, or deep learning model, is characterized by multiple hidden layers. Adding more layers facilitates the learning of more complex representations by the model, but it also increases the difficulty in training the network and makes it more susceptible to overfitting. A key aspect of model design is selecting the optimal number of layers in an ANN, which can substantially impact model performance. However, there is not a universally correct number of layers to select, as the optimal count can depend on the problem's specifics, including the task's complexity and amount of data available.

Several strategies can be considered when choosing the number of layers in a neural network. Starting small is often beneficial, beginning with a simple network such as one with a single hidden layer or a basic multilayer perceptron (MLP) with two hidden layers. If the model has difficulty learning, more layers can be progressively added to enhance its capabilities. The complexity of the problem can also guide the choice of layers. More intricate tasks like image or speech recognition might necessitate numerous layers, while simpler tasks like binary classification or regression could be adequately addressed with fewer layers. The amount of training data available can further impact the optimal number of layers. If the dataset is small, a model with excessive layers might overfit, meaning it learns the training data too well but performs poorly with new data.

Conversely, with a larger dataset, employing a more complex model with additional layers might be feasible. Utilizing a validation set to fine-tune the number of layers can be another effective approach. This involves training models with different layer configurations on the training data and then selecting the one that achieves the best performance on the validation set. Much of this process involves experimentation and learning, with trial and error playing a significant role. Over time, dealing with similar problems and network architectures helps build experience. Lastly, automated approaches such as neural architecture search (NAS), which leverages machine learning to determine the best structure automatically, can be considered a more advanced technique.

It is not always beneficial to add more layers to a neural network. Deep networks pose increased challenges in training due to issues such as vanishing gradients and are more susceptible to overfitting, particularly when the available training data is limited. Additionally, deeper networks demand greater computational resources. Thus, balancing model complexity and performance is crucial to ensuring an efficient and effective network.

**Neurons Per Layer**

In an ANN, a neuron, or node or unit, is a basic part of the network. While inspired by brain neurons, these are not exactly the same. In an ANN, a neuron generally does two things. First, it works out a total of the input features, each multiplied by a certain weight, and adds a bias term. The weights and biases can be learned and adjusted to reduce the network's prediction error. Next, the neuron applies an activation function to the total. This function adds complexity, enabling the network to learn intricate patterns. Common activation functions include ReLU, sigmoid, and tanh.

An ANN is made up of layers of neurons. The first layer (input) gets the raw input features. The last layer (output) makes the network's predictions. The middle layers (hidden) change the input features into a format that helps the network predict accurately. How neurons are linked, their activation functions, and how their weights and biases are adjusted during training can change. This depends on the types of ANNs (like feedforward, CNNs, or RNNs) and the training methods used (like SGD or backpropagation).

It is deemed crucial to determine the right number of neurons in an ANN, a decision contingent on the problem, size of the input data, and complexity of data features. A conventional approach posits that the number of hidden neurons ought to fall between the sizes of the input and output layers, while some suggest it should equal two-thirds of the input layer size plus the output layer size. It is frequently suggested to commence with a smaller number and gradually augment it until the network begins to overfit, defined as the stage when the network memorizes the training data and has difficulties with new data. The problem's complexity can serve as an indication of the requisite number of neurons, implying that more complex problems might demand more neurons and layers, while simpler problems might require fewer.

A word of caution is often given to prevent overfitting when adding an excessive number of neurons, particularly with limited training data. A balance between bias and variance is advocated for, highlighting that an increase in neurons can decrease bias but heighten variance, potentially resulting in overfitting and the inverse. Models with varying neuron counts can be trained, and the best performing one on validation data can be selected through methods like grid search or random search. Advanced techniques like neural architecture search (NAS) can also be employed to automatically pinpoint the optimal structure using machine learning.

**Dropout Rate**

Dropout is a regularization technique that prevents overfitting in ANN, which is particularly beneficial in deep learning models. It randomly ignores a proportion of neurons during each training iteration, reducing the risk of overfitting. The dropout rate dictates the proportion of neurons to drop. For instance, a rate of 0.5 means approximately half of the neurons in a layer are temporarily turned off during each training pass. Their contribution to the next layer is removed on the forward pass, and weight updates are not applied on the backward pass.

The reduction of overfitting is facilitated by dropout through the random omission of neurons, effectively creating a less complex model with each training iteration. Each pass of the data during training uses a different thinned version of the original network, which can be interpreted as averaging multiple diverse network architectures due to dropout. Additionally, the prevention of excessive co-adaptation of neurons is promoted by dropout. The random dropout of neurons compels other neurons to adapt and take over the representation necessary for making predictions in place of the missing neurons. This contributes to developing a more robust model that can make accurate predictions with less dependence on any particular neuron.

The setting of the dropout rate, typically between 0.2 and 0.5, is contingent on the complexity of the model and volume of training data. The optimal rate is often found by attempting various values or tuning it systematically. The dropout is typically utilized solely during training. When testing or using the model, all neurons are active, and their outputs are adjusted to account for dropouts during training. The ideal dropout rate depends on a multitude of factors. Networks of larger size, prone to overfitting, may necessitate a higher dropout rate, while smaller networks might require a lower rate. It is often observed that a larger dataset diminishes the likelihood of model overfitting; hence, a high dropout rate may not be essential. Conversely, a higher dropout rate could be beneficial for smaller datasets that could overfit with ease. If the dataset has a considerable amount of noise, a higher dropout rate could prevent the model from overfitting the noise. The dropout rate might also influence other parameters, such as the learning rate and batch size, suggesting these might need adjustment based on the dropout rate. Lastly, it is noted that high dropout rates can decelerate training since they effectively reduce the network's size. Concerns about training time would necessitate a balancing act between the dropout rate and training time.

## Activation Functions

Activation functions are considered a fundamental component of ANNs. They determine the output of a neural network, add nonlinearity to the network by them, and enable the network to learn and perform more complex tasks. Several factors must be considered when tuning activation functions in ANN models. The most appropriate activation function can be dictated by the nature of the problem. For binary classification problems, the sigmoid or softmax function could be chosen for the output layer. A tanh or ReLU function might be opted for if it is a forecasting problem, due to their efficiency.

Vanishing or exploding gradients during backpropagation can be caused by certain activation functions like sigmoid and tanh. This problem occurs when gradients become excessively large or small, making the network more difficult to train. This problem is mitigated by the design of the ReLU activation function and its variants like leaky ReLU and parametric ReLU. Some activation functions are more computationally intensive than others. For example, more complex calculations are involved in the sigmoid function than the ReLU function. An activation function that is less computationally expensive might need to be chosen if a very large network is being worked with or if computational resources are limited.

Some form of nonlinearity is introduced into the network by most activation functions. This allows the network to capture and learn complex patterns from the data. In some scenarios, the form of nonlinearity can make a difference. Sigmoid and tanh functions can saturate the regions far from zero. During backpropagation, little or no learning can occur when an activation function's output approaches its upper or lower asymptote, and its gradient nearly vanishes. ReLU and its variants can mitigate this issue.

In the case of ReLU, the problem of dead neurons, where certain parts of the model cease to respond to variations in error/input, should be kept in mind. This is due to the fact that for inputs less than 0, the ReLU function returns 0, which results in the weights not being updated during backpropagation. Variants of ReLU, such as leaky ReLU and parametric ReLU, can be helpful in such scenarios, as they allow small negative values when the input is less than zero. Some advanced activation functions, such as the Swish function or self-normalizing neural networks (SELU), add an element of stochasticity, which can sometimes improve performance.

## Weight Initialization

Weight initialization in an ANN involves setting the initial values of the weights (parameters) before training commences. The significance of proper weight initialization lies in its considerable impact on the training process. If weights are poorly initialized, the network's learning process may be slowed down or even inhibited. Weight initialization operates as a form of hyperparameter tuning since the strategy used to initialize the weights is decided before training and not a characteristic learned from the data. The chosen strategy can greatly influence the model's final performance.

The most common strategies for weight initialization include zero initialization, random initialization, Xavier/Glorot initialization, and He initialization. Zero initialization is a basic form where all weights are set to zero, but this prevents the network from learning, as it causes all neurons to become symmetric and learn the same features during training. With random initialization, weights are set to small random values, which help to break the symmetry. Still, if weights are too small or large, they could result in issues like vanishing gradients or exploding gradients problems. Xavier/Glorot initialization uses values from a normal distribution with 0 mean and variance of $1/n$, where $n$ is the number of inputs to the neuron, to counter the problems of vanishing and exploding gradients, particularly in deep networks. He initialization is similar but uses a variance of $2/n$ and typically used with ReLU activation functions and their variants. The best method for weight initialization may depend on specific network architecture, the activation function used, and the data itself, and experimenting with different methods often proves beneficial for optimal model performance.

## Optimizer

Optimizers are crucial tools in training neural networks, tasked with adjusting network parameters such as weights and learning rate to minimize the loss function. The loss function quantifies the discrepancy between the network's prediction and actual value for given input data, and optimizers aim to diminish this difference by fine-tuning the weights and biases. The parameter space can be complex and multidimensional, with many layers and nodes in a neural network. Optimizers aid in efficiently navigating this space to find the optimal parameter combination that results in a minimal loss.

There are a variety of optimizers, each offering unique ways of adjusting parameters, which can greatly influence the speed and efficiency of training. For instance, SGD makes small, consistent adjustments. In contrast, optimizers like Adam or RMSprop employ advanced techniques such as momentum or adaptive learning rates to accelerate training and evade local minima. Certain optimizers can also help counter overfitting and underfitting through regularization terms or methods. During the training of deep neural networks, issues like vanishing and exploding gradients can arise, complicating the training process. However, optimizers with adaptive learning rates, such as Adam, RMSprop, and Adagrad, can assist in alleviating these problems.

The optimizer selected can substantially impact the rate of learning and the final model's performance. Below are some common optimizers:

- Gradient descent (batch gradient descent): This basic optimization algorithm employs the full training set to compute the cost function's gradient for each training algorithm iteration. Despite its effectiveness, it can be slow with larger datasets as it performs only one update after computing the gradients for the entire dataset.
- Stochastic gradient descent (SGD): SGD enhances computational efficiency by using a single sample (a batch of size 1) per iteration for the updates instead of processing the entire dataset. This approach can hasten the learning process but may introduce substantial noise during training.

- Mini-batch gradient descent: A variant of SGD, this method uses a mini-batch of n samples per iteration for updates. It establishes a balance between SGD's computational efficiency and stability of batch gradient descent, introducing mini-batch size as an additional hyperparameter.

- Momentum: Momentum aims to quicken SGD in the pertinent direction and dampen oscillations. It accomplishes this by adding a fraction of the past time step's update vector to the current one.

- Adagrad: Adagrad is a gradient-based optimization algorithm that adjusts the learning rate to the parameters. It performs smaller updates for parameters tied to frequently occurring features and larger updates for infrequently occurring features.

- Root mean square propagation (RMSProp): Proposed by Geoff Hinton, RMSProp is an adaptive learning rate optimization algorithm. It attempts to fix Adagrad's drastically decreasing learning rates by utilizing a MA of the squared gradient.

- Adaptive moment estimation (Adam): Adam integrates the concepts of momentum and RMSprop, computing adaptive learning rates for each parameter. It is a highly favored optimization algorithm, often delivering good results with default settings.

- AdamW: This Adam variant separates the weight decay from the optimization steps.

**Regularization Techniques**

The use of regularization in the training of ANN is undertaken to avoid the occurrence of overfitting. Overfitting is the phenomenon wherein a network adapts too well to the training data, resulting in subpar performance when confronted with unseen data. Regularization dissuades the network from learning an overly complicated or flexible model by adding a penalty to the network's complexity, thereby mitigating overfitting.

Several regularization techniques, such as L1 and L2 regularization, dropout, early stopping, noise Injection, and batch normalization, are typically employed. L1 and L2 regularization penalizes the loss function according to the size of the model weights, encouraging the model to prefer smaller weights. In the case of L1 regularization, this penalty is in direct proportion to the absolute value of the weights, leading to a sparse weight matrix, while in L2 regularization, the penalty is tied to the square of the weights, causing the weight values to distribute more evenly.

Dropout, a technique exclusive to neural networks, randomly deactivates a subset of neurons in a layer during a single gradient step in training. This discourages the model from depending excessively on a single neuron, fostering the learning of redundant representations and thus enhancing generalization. Early stopping refers to ceasing the training process before the model crosses into overfitting. Typically, this is achieved by monitoring the model's performance on a validation set during training and halting the process as performance begins to wane. Noise injection, on the other hand, adds a minor amount of noise to the input data or the hidden layer's activations, enhancing the model's robustness and curtailing overfitting. Although primarily an optimization technique for deep networks, batch normalization has a regularizing effect and can diminish the necessity for dropout or L1/L2 regularization.

The tuning of regularization methods requires the adjustment of their hyperparameters. For instance, L1 and L2 regularization need a lambda parameter that decides the strength of the regularization term, while dropout necessitates deciding the proportion of neurons to deactivate. Grid search, random search, or more advanced techniques such as Bayesian optimization can be employed to tune these hyperparameters. Typically, a separate validation set is used for this purpose. The goal is to discover a value that achieves a balance between underfitting and overfitting, ensuring the model learns effectively from the training data while also generalizing successfully to new, unseen data.

## Epochs

Epoch is the total number of complete passes through the entire dataset. Underfitting can result from insufficient epochs, whereas overfitting can result from excessive epochs. In training an ANN, an epoch signifies one full pass through the training dataset. Following each epoch, updates are made to the weights and biases of the network.

Determining the appropriate number of epochs for training a model, that is, the number of complete passes through the training data, constitutes a crucial aspect of model configuration and significantly influences model performance. Underfitting the data may result from training with too few epochs, implying the model does not adequately learn the inherent patterns. Overfitting the data, on the other hand, may result from training with too many epochs, implying the model learns the noise in the training data, leading to a subpar performance on unseen data.

Certain strategies to decide on the number of epochs include manual selection, early stopping, learning curves, and automated hyperparameter tuning. The simplest method, manual selection, involves deciding the number of epochs. A lower number, such as 10 or 50, could be the starting point, after which the number of epochs increases until the performance on a validation set ceases to improve or even deteriorates, indicating overfitting. A more advanced method, early stopping, involves observing the model's performance on a validation set following each epoch. Training is halted if performance ceases to improve for a specified number of epochs, known as the patience parameter, allowing automatic training for the optimal number of epochs.

Learning curves, another strategy, involves plotting curves that display the model's performance on the training and validation set over each epoch. This enables visual identification of the point at which the model stops improving or starts overfitting. Automated hyperparameter tuning involves advanced techniques like grid search, random search, or Bayesian optimization to select the ideal number of epochs automatically. These techniques entail training and evaluating models with various epochs and selecting the number that yields the best validation set performance. The optimal number of epochs are also influenced by other hyperparameters, such as the learning rate and batch size, and attributes of the data, like its size and complexity. Thus, returning the number of epochs might be required if these elements of the model or data are altered.

## Batch Size

Batch size refers to the quantity of samples propagated through the network at a single instance. The potential for better model generalization is associated with a smaller batch size, albeit at a slower training rate. A larger batch size may quicken training and result in inferior generalization. For instance, if there are one thousand training examples, and a batch size of one hundred is selected, each epoch will comprise ten iterations.

Several impacts on the training process can be attributed to batch sizes, such as computational efficiency, noise in estimates, and memory usage. Enhanced use of parallel computing resources is possible with larger batch sizes since many examples can be processed simultaneously. This can quicken each iteration. However, as larger batches provide a more accurate gradient estimate, convergence may require fewer iterations. Smaller batch sizes introduce noise to the gradient estimate, which can have a regularizing effect and facilitate better model generalization. However, this noise may also render the learning process unstable. Larger batch sizes demand more memory to store the inputs, outputs, and intermediate values for each example in the batch, which, if memory is constrained, limits the maximum usable batch size.

The batch size selection forms part of the model configuration and can significantly impact model performance and training time. Some strategies for selecting batch size include memory constraints, empirical tuning, and automated hyperparameter tuning. A simple strategy is to choose the largest batch size that fits into memory, maximizing the use of computing resources. However, this does not consider the potential regularizing effect of smaller batch sizes. Another strategy, empirical tuning, involves testing various batch sizes and selecting the best performance on a validation set. Starting with small batch sizes, such as 32, followed by incrementally larger sizes like 64, 128, 256, and so on, could be an approach.

More sophisticated techniques such as grid search, random search, or Bayesian optimization can be used to automatically select the best batch size under the automated hyperparameter tuning strategy. These techniques involve training and evaluating models with different batch sizes and choosing the size that results in the best performance. Ultimately, the optimal batch size can depend on numerous factors, including the specific model architecture, the optimizer in use, the nature of the data, and available computing resources. Consequently, experimentation might be necessary to determine the best value.

## 9.3  Optimizing Reinforcement Learning (RL)

The complexity of hyperparameter tuning in RL arises from the interplay among the environment, agent, policy, and value function. The commonly adjusted hyperparameters when training a RL model include learning rate ($\alpha$), discount factor ($\gamma$), exploration vs. exploitation ($\epsilon$), policy parameters, update frequency, batch size, memory size, initialization parameters, reward scaling, number of episodes or iterations, and network architecture parameters.

The learning rate ($\alpha$) dictates the extent of the agent's Q-values updates at each step. A high learning rate allows the agent to forget past experiences quickly, while a low learning rate slows down the agent's learning process. The discount factor (γ) calculates the total expected future reward. Its value determines the significance of future rewards. A value of 0 renders the agent shortsighted, considering only immediate rewards, while a value closer to 1 encourages the agent to prioritize long-term rewards. The equilibrium between investigating fresh actions to comprehend their implications, also known as exploration, and choosing the optimum activity derived from existing understanding, known as exploitation, is frequently governed by a specific parameter in ε-greedy policies. This parameter is referred to as exploration vs. exploitation, symbolized by ε.

If function approximation is employed for policy, the policy's weights and biases are also hyperparameters that must be learned. The update frequency, a critical component of methods such as Q-learning, determines the frequency of action-value function or policy update. For actor-critic methods, it might also dictate the frequency of critic updates relative to actor updates. In methods utilizing experience replay or other forms of batch updates, the batch size signifies the number of experiences used in each update. The memory size in methods that use experience replay indicates the number of past experiences stored. The initialization parameters, or the initial values of the policy or action-value function, can often impact learning, especially in nonstationary environments. In some instances, reward scaling might be required to simplify learning. This involves scaling or transforming the rewards. The model's performance can be dramatically affected by the number of episodes/iterations and number of training loops the agent undergoes.

When deep RL algorithms like deep Q-network or actor-critic methods are employed, the neural network's architecture, including parameters like the number of layers, the number of nodes in each layer, and the type of activation function used, can be tuned. It is important to remember that RL is highly sensitive to the choice of hyperparameters, and what proves effective for one problem may not work for another. Hence, experimenting with different configurations and validating the model's performance using techniques such as cross-validation is always beneficial.

## 9.4   Approaches for Hyperparameter Tuning
There are a plethora of strategies to employ hyperparameter tuning, and these methods range from hands-on experimental techniques to more mechanized procedures. Some commonly-utilized techniques encompass trial and error methods, grid search, random search, and even

advanced procedures such as Bayesian optimization. The primary objective of this intricate process is to discover the set of hyperparameters that can produce the most efficient results on a validation dataset, all the while avoiding the trap of overfitting on the training dataset.

**Grid Search**

Grid search is an elementary yet commonly used method for hyperparameter tuning. The process starts with defining a grid or a range of possible values for each hyperparameter involved in the machine learning model. For instance, for tuning a support vector machine, the grid might include various values for C or the penalty parameter and gamma or the kernel coefficient. Once the grid is established, the algorithm iterates over all possible combinations of hyperparameters. This equates to running the learning algorithm once for each hyperparameter combination on the grid. For example, if there are two hyperparameters each with ten possible values, it would run the learning algorithm one hundred times.

After the runs are completed, the performance of each model is evaluated using a validation dataset. The set of hyperparameters that results in the highest model performance is then determined to be the optimal set. The grid search is appreciated for its simplicity and effectiveness, attributes that contribute to it being a commonly-chosen method for hyperparameter tuning. However, it does not come without disadvantages. It can demand extensive resources and be time-consuming, especially when the quantity of hyperparameters increases or the range of potential values for each hyperparameter expands. This curse of dimensionality, as it is often referred to, is a familiar issue in grid search since it requires comprehensive exploration of the hyperparameter space, frequently leading to steep computational expenses.

**Random Search**

Random search is another method employed for hyperparameter optimization to optimize a machine learning model. The technique works by randomly selecting points from a predefined hyperparameter space for model evaluation and training, hence its name, "random search." This is in contrast to the exhaustive exploration of the entire hyperparameter space that characterizes grid search. Random search takes the approach of evaluating randomly chosen points within the hyperparameter space, making it notably more efficient, especially when only a few hyperparameters significantly influence the model's performance. This method generally proves to be quicker and less resource-intensive than grid search, particularly when dealing with a large number of hyperparameters or when performance checks are costly. Although it may not pinpoint the perfect set of hyperparameters, it can typically find a satisfactory set faster than a comprehensive grid search.

The process of random search optimization includes several steps. First, the possible settings for each hyperparameter must be defined. For instance, in the case of a random forest model, the number of trees to include in the forest, such as ten, one hundred, or five hundred, must be decided, along with how deep these trees could potentially be, like five, ten, or twenty. The next step is deciding how to sample from the set of options. This stage is similar to picking names out of a hat. Not every possible combination of hyperparameters is used; rather a random selection is made from the available options. The manner of this selection can be completely random or follow a certain pattern, depending on the specific requirements and type of hyperparameters involved. Then, for each set of randomly selected hyperparameters, the model is trained, and its performance is evaluated using a specific measure, such as accuracy for classification tasks or MSE for predicting values. This process is repeated a specific number of times or until the model's performance reaches the desired level. Finally, after enough iterations, the set of hyperparameters that results in the best model performance is chosen.

## Bayesian Optimization

Bayesian optimization is a sophisticated technique that creates a probability model of the function to be optimized, utilizing previous evaluation results. This model is then harnessed to pinpoint the most promising hyperparameters for evaluation. When handling high-dimensional hyperparameter spaces, this method can be more efficient than either random or grid search. The optimization process involves the creation of a function distribution, known as the surrogate function, that best represents the function to be optimized. This is particularly useful when the objective function, typically our model's performance based on a specific set of hyperparameters, is expensive to assess. After each evaluation of the objective function, the surrogate probability model is updated, continually fine-tuning the hyperparameter selection. This continual refinement is at the heart of how Bayesian optimization operates.

Diving deeper into the mechanism of Bayesian optimization, the process begins by defining a surrogate function, also termed a probability model. This function, usually a Gaussian process, is a distribution over functions that predicts the likely values of the objective function based on current observations, offering a measure of uncertainty that aids in determining the next sampling point. Following this, an acquisition function is selected, which helps identify the next query point in the hyperparameter space. By choosing points where the surrogate function anticipates high performance or where uncertainty is elevated, it maintains a balance between exploration and exploitation. Common choices for acquisition functions include expected improvement (EI), probability of improvement (PI), and upper confidence bound (UCB). The point with the highest acquisition function value is then chosen as the next sampling point, the point most likely, as per the surrogate and acquisition functions, to boost the model's performance. After sampling a new point by evaluating the objective function, the surrogate function is updated to include the new data. Steps three and four are repeated until a stopping criterion is met, such as a maximum number of iterations, a maximum time limit, or a performance improvement below a certain threshold. After all iterations, the set of hyperparameters that yields the best-performing model is selected. Owing to its ability to utilize past evaluations when selecting the next set of hyperparameters for evaluation, Bayesian optimization is often more efficient than random or grid search, particularly for high-dimensional hyperparameter spaces and expensive objective functions. By learning from data gathered in previous steps, it can often discover superior hyperparameters in fewer iterations.

**Gradient-Based Optimization**

Gradient-based optimization hinges on calculating the gradient of hyperparameters and using this information to adjust the hyperparameters with the aim of improving the objective function. This method is typically applied when the hyperparameters can be differentiated with respect to the objective function. Frequently employed in the context of neural networks, gradient-based optimization strives to optimize machine learning models' hyperparameters. Its distinguishing factor lies in leveraging gradient data to pinpoint the optimal set of hyperparameters. The fundamental idea is to estimate the gradient of the validation performance in relation to the hyperparameters and use this data to modify the hyperparameters, similar to how gradients are utilized to adjust parameters (like weights and biases in a neural network) during the training phase. However, the calculation of these gradients is intricate, as the validation performance is a complex function of the hyperparameters. This function is often non-differentiable and stochastic, causing gradient-based hyperparameter optimization to frequently depend on some form of approximation or indirect computation to estimate these gradients.

Delving into the specifics of gradient-based hyperparameter tuning, the process commences by defining a space of hyperparameters, akin to other forms of hyperparameter tuning. However, in gradient-based tuning, the hyperparameters are usually real-valued (continuous) to facilitate the computation of meaningful gradients. Initial values for the hyperparameters are then selected, either randomly or based on existing knowledge. Subsequently, the model is trained on the training set using the current hyperparameters, and the validation performance (the loss or error on a separate validation set) is computed. The gradients of the validation performance with respect to the hyperparameters are then calculated or estimated using methods like backpropagation through the training process, also known as hypergradient, or approximate methods. Using the computed gradients, the hyperparameters are updated through gradient descent or a similar method. Steps three to five are iterated until a stopping criterion, such as a maximum number of iterations, a maximum time limit, or a validation performance improvement below a certain threshold, is reached. While gradient-based optimization can be remarkably efficient when viable and precise gradient calculations are possible, it also presents challenges, including managing noisy gradients and choosing an appropriate learning rate for the hyperparameters. A prominent example of gradient-based hyperparameter optimization is learning rate schedules, where the learning rate is gradually reduced during training, informed by gradient data.

## Other Methods

Evolutionary optimization is a strategy that emulates natural selection processes, deploying techniques like genetic algorithms to mutate and refine hyperparameters until an optimum solution is found. The tree-structured Parzen estimator (TPE) is a type of Bayesian optimization technique that models $P(x|y)$ and $P(y)$, where $x$ denotes hyperparameters and $y$ represents the objective function. TPE has been incorporated into the Hyperopt library. Moreover, tools and libraries like AutoML, Keras Tuner, and Hyperopt can help to assist in automating the hyperparameter tuning process, employing diverse strategies to do so.

# 10

# The AI Transformation: New Dimensions in Time Series Analysis

Real-world time series analysis is characterized by a complex matrix of numerical sequences, where each subsequent data point reveals a new layer of complexity. Here, data weaves an intricate ballet, one where conventional mathematical and statistical models often find it challenging to keep pace. The tapestry of reality is intricately interwoven with intricate patterns in time series data, akin to enigmatic pieces of a sophisticated puzzle, harboring the power to decode enlightening forecasts. What are the architects of these labyrinthine patterns? The influences are diverse and multilayered, each instilling its unique degree of complication. Let us momentarily demystify these intricacies.

Nonlinearity, a connection among variables that eschews linear predictability, engenders these elaborate patterns, occasionally triggering unpredictable behavior. Nonstationarity, another elusive entity, ceaselessly modifies statistical properties such as trends or seasonality. Simultaneously, volatility clustering engenders epochs of intense fluctuations, contributing to the multifaceted rise and fall of variability. Introducing yet another layer of complexity is the notion of long memory or dependence, a phenomenon where antecedent values persistently impact current values, even over substantial temporal intervals. We also encounter asymmetry, an expression of imbalance in the statistical properties of the series over time. This creates unique challenges that vary across different levels or phases. Complexity takes on a new dimension when we encounter stochastic processes, which, despite their random nature, can still weave patterns so intricate they're hard to predict. These threads of stochastic complexity are indeed challenging to untangle. However, we are not without the tools to navigate this labyrinth.

In such a maze of intricacies, AI, with its self-learning and predictive capabilities, provides a remarkable alternative to traditional techniques, decoding and learning from these complexities to generate accurate and insightful predictions. AI-based time series models excel at handling intricate patterns within time series data. These models leverage the power of AI theory, utilizing historical observations and neural-like elements to perceive, analyze, synthesize, and store information. These models facilitate learning, training, reasoning, systematizing, and classifying information by harnessing this capability. They can identify connections, patterns, and distinctions within the data, generating signals to predict future values. The advantages of AI-based time series models lie in their ability to effectively capture the complexities inherent in time series data and provide valuable insights for forecasting.

AI has the potential to revolutionize the analysis and prediction of time series data. AI-based time series models are especially suited to dealing with complex patterns in time series data. Traditional statistical models like ARIMA or exponential smoothing often struggle with the complexities of time series data, particularly nonlinear relationships, abrupt changes, and high-dimensional contexts. These traditional models are also limited by their assumptions about the underlying data.

AI models, particularly deep learning models, do not have these limitations. They can learn complex nonlinear relationships, adapt to changes, and handle high-dimensional data effectively. Deep learning models are a subset of AI that mimics how the human brain works, using layers of artificial neurons, or nodes, to process information. These models, like LSTMs, can understand historical data observations, including the order of these observations, a crucial aspect of time series prediction. They analyze and store information, and over time, they can learn the patterns within the data, enabling them to reason and predict future values accurately.

The learning process involves training, where the model is exposed to historical data and learns to predict the next value based on previous values. Through systematizing the learning process, the models can classify the information; identify the relationships, patterns, and anomalies within the data; and generate signals that can be used to predict future values. The advantages of AI-based time series models are numerous. They can effectively capture complex, nonlinear relationships; they are adaptive and can handle abrupt changes in the data; they can process high-dimensional data effectively; they can learn from the historical data, reason, and make accurate predictions.

Moreover, these models provide valuable insights that can be used for forecasting. These insights could be about patterns and trends in the data, the influence of certain features on the target variable, and many others. These insights can be used to make informed business decisions, manage risks, and identify opportunities. In a nutshell, AI-based time series models have great potential in various applications, including financial forecasting, weather prediction, energy demand forecasting, sales prediction, and many others. They leverage the power of AI to handle the complexities of time series data effectively and provide valuable insights for forecasting.

Time series analysis, though applicable to numerous domains, was specifically employed for stock price forecasting in this case due to the ease of data accessibility. The required data was gathered from Yahoo Finance, which provides a wealth of financial details including stock quotes, analyses, press releases, and financial reports. The stock data sourced from Yahoo Finance offers a historical overview of data recorded over a particular period, with each time point corresponding to transaction-specific variables. In the historical stock price dataset, elements like opening price, closing price, highest price, lowest price, and trading volume are attached to each trading day.

Multivariate time series analysis involves more than one time-dependent variable, each reliant not just on its past values, but also somewhat dependent on other variables. This interdependency is instrumental in forecasting future values. Specifically, for predicting stock closing prices, multivariate time series analysis was taken into account the attributes of a single stock such as closing price, opening price, highest price, and lowest price to predict a future closing price.

The next chapter mentioned utilizes specific machine learning models such as random forest and XGBoost. Random forest is an ensemble learning method that combines multiple decision trees to make predictions, while XGBoost is another ensemble learning algorithm that sequentially trains weak models and combines their predictions.

Raghurami Reddy Etukuru, the author, pioneered the concept of 'Complexity-Conscious Prediction and Decision-Making.' The innovative method, known as 'Complexity-Conscious Prediction,' recognizes and incorporates the inherent complexity in data. It involves assessing the complexity of input data and developing models that are specifically designed to manage this complexity. The aim is to significantly enhance the accuracy of predictions, a factor that is particularly vital in situations where data demonstrates complex patterns and behaviors not adequately addressed by simpler predictive models. Furthermore, Raghurami Reddy Etukuru extended this concept to include decision-making processes, moving beyond just forecasting. By harnessing AI, the decision-making processes that depend on these predictions can be substantially improved.

Raghurami Reddy Etukuru, the author, defines 'Complexity-Conscious Prediction and Decision-Making' as a method that integrates the inherent complexity in data and designs models to improve predictions and decision-making. This approach involves assessing complex data patterns and developing specialized models to manage this complexity, thereby enhancing prediction accuracy and aiding AI-driven decision-making processes.

Complexity-conscious prediction and decision-making, in the context of time series forecasting, represents a sophisticated, nuanced approach to understanding and predicting temporal patterns. This approach acknowledges the inherent complexity within time series data, which includes nonlinearity, nonstationarity, long-term memory, asymmetry, and stochasticity and the influence of these factors. Rather than using simple linear models that assume independence among observations, complexity-conscious methods seek to capture these intricate, often nonlinear, interrelationships. Techniques such as machine learning methods or even complex deep learning architectures, like LSTMs, GRUs, and GANs, are part of such a complexity-conscious toolkit. The goal is to provide more accurate forecasts by fully acknowledging and integrating the underlying complexity of the data into the predictive model. The aforementioned approach to time series forecasting doesn't just stop at making accurate predictions. Informed by these forecasts, decision-making processes can be enhanced using RL.

Therefore, the subsequent chapter explores and employs deep learning models for time series forecasting. These models include LSTM, a type of RNN capable of capturing long-term dependencies in sequential data. BiLSTM is an extension of LSTM that processes the input sequence in both forward and backward directions, enhancing its ability to capture context from both past and future. 1DCNN apply convolutional operations to one-dimensional data, effectively learning local patterns and dependencies. Hybrid models, such as 1DCNN-LSTM and 1DCNN-BiLSTM, combine the strengths of CNNs and LSTMs. GRU is another type of RNN similar to LSTM but with a simpler architecture. GAN is a framework involving two neural networks, a generator and a discriminator, which are trained adversarially to generate realistic samples.

Moving beyond these chapters, the subsequent chapter employs an RL model called the soft actor-critic model. RL is a branch of machine learning where an agent learns to take actions in an environment to maximize a reward signal. The soft actor-critic algorithm is a specific approach that combines RL with maximum entropy RL, which encourages exploration and robustness.

The data set was divided into two sets; the first part was used to optimize the model, and the second data set was used to test the model on an 80:20 basis. The first part is the training dataset, and the second is the test dataset. In cases where there is no dependence from one observation to another, the data can be randomly split on an 80:20 basis. Since in time series data, one observation can influence the following observation, then the data cannot be divided randomly. Therefore, the values at the frontal 80 percent of the time series were used for optimization, and the rear 20 percent were used for testing. The data was normalized before using the time series data in the models.

The data normalization method produces high-quality data that improves the effectiveness of the learning algorithm. The min-max normalization method was used to normalize the time series data. The min-max normalization method scales a variable in the sample set to [-1, 1] or [0, 1]. The frontal part of the dataset was fed into the model. The model then learns to relate the input to the output and optimizes it. The model was then provided with the second part of the dataset. The model generated the outcome based on the input in the dataset. The output generated by the model was compared against the output contained in the second dataset.

# 11

# Machine Learning Approaches for Time Series Modeling

To showcase the efficacy of machine learning in time series forecasting, the book used two key algorithms as points of reference, specifically, random forest and XGBoost.

## 11.1   Random Forest

Random forest is a robust machine learning algorithm for classification and regression analysis. It operates by constructing a forest of decision trees, forming an ensemble model. This approach enables the algorithm to uncover intricate relationships among the input variables and derive the underlying rules governing these relationships. The technique involves dividing the dataset into subsets and training numerous decision trees on these subsets. This ensures that each tree is unique and offers distinct predictions. By combining the individual predictions, the random forest produces a more accurate and robust overall prediction. When presented with new data, each tree in the forest generates a prediction, and the final prediction is determined by aggregating the outputs of all the trees. This aggregation is typically performed for regression tasks by computing the average of the predictions, while for classification tasks, the majority vote is taken into account.

One of the main advantages of using a random forest is its ability to theoretically reduce overfitting and mitigate the impact of noise or outliers, which are common challenges in decision tree models. In a random forest, each tree is constructed using a subset of samples, and predictions are recorded. By employing voting, the random forest selects the most appropriate tree. This approach enhances the accuracy of decision trees by leveraging multiple trees and averaging their predictions. As a result, biases are minimized, addressing the overfitting issue. Another advantage of the random forest technique is its unbiased selection of suitable trees during voting.

Let us implement the random forest model to forecast the stock prices for the CREG ticker. The figure below visualizes the time series data for the CREG stock from January 2, 2008, to February 10, 2023.

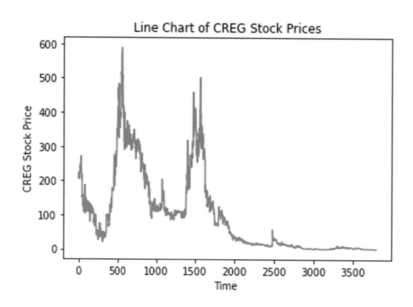

Figure 8: Actual Time Series of the Combined Training Set
and Test Set for the CREG Stock.

For the time series data of the CREG ticker, the statistical measures of four key characteristics—nonstationarity, nonlinearity, long memory or dependence, and asymmetry—have been produced as provided below.

- Nonstationarity: The ADF test tests the null hypothesis that a unit root is present in a time series sample. The alternative hypothesis differs depending on the test version but is usually stationarity or trend-stationarity. A p-value of 0.31 from the ADF test indicates the null hypothesis of a unit root cannot be rejected at conventional levels of statistical significance (0.05). Hence, the time series appears nonstationary, implying the mean, variance, and covariance are not constant over time for the CREG stock.

- Nonlinearity: The Lyapunov exponent is a measure that characterizes the rate of separation of infinitesimally close trajectories in a dynamical system. A positive Lyapunov exponent (0.0019) indicates a chaotic system with sensitive dependence on initial conditions, which suggests a high degree of nonlinearity in the price dynamics of CREG stock.

- Long memory or dependence: The DFA Hurst exponent measures the autocorrelation of a time series. It quantifies the relative tendency of a time series either to regress strongly to the mean or to cluster in a direction. A Hurst exponent value above 0.5 (in this case, 1.53) suggests a long memory process, indicating its past values significantly influence future values of the CREG stock price series.

- Asymmetry: Skewness measures the asymmetry of the probability distribution of a real-valued random variable about its mean. Positive skewness indicates the tail on the right side of the probability density function is longer or fatter than the left. A skewness value of 1.36 indicates a relatively significant right-skewness of the CREG stock returns, which implies that large positive returns occur more frequently than large negative returns.

- Stochasticity: An entropy value of 6.42 was computed for the time series data of CREG, a figure exceeding 90 percent of the maximum possible entropy. This maximum entropy was determined as the logarithm of the number of unique elements within the time series data, that is, log(len(np.unique(time_series_data))). The resulting entropy reveals the significant unpredictability of the time series, likely suggesting a pronounced level of stochasticity.

A time series model predicated on random forest has been employed to project stock prices for CREG, manifesting the aforementioned complex patterns. Comprehensive code for the application of the fandom forest model to forecast stock prices is presented in this section, momentarily. Nevertheless, the excerpt provided below only represents a portion of the complete code set. This code snippet is intended to function as a blueprint for the development and training of a random forest model, subsequently applied to stock price prediction.

```
Model = RandomForestRegressor(n_estimators=60, random_state=42, min_samples_split=4, min_samples_leaf=1, max_depth=35, bootstrap=True)
model.fit(X_train, np.ravel(y_train,order='C'))
yhat = model.predict(X_test)
```

The model was constructed using multiple bootstrapped samples derived from the training data. By setting the parameter bootstrap = True in random forest, each decision tree in the forest was trained on a distinct bootstrap sample extracted from the original data. This deliberate randomization during training helps to mitigate overfitting to some extent. By generating numerous bootstrapped datasets and training individual decision trees on each one, the random forest becomes adept at generalizing well to unseen data.

In this particular case, the number of estimators was set to 60. The number of estimators is a hyperparameter in the random forest algorithm, determining the quantity of decision trees in the forest. The random forest algorithm guarantees that each decision tree is trained on a different subset of the training data and features. Subsequently, the predictions of all the trees are aggregated to generate a final prediction. The number of estimators influences the model's bias and variance. The optimal value for the number of estimators was carefully selected to achieve a lower mean absolute percentage error (MAPE) across a larger number of stocks.

For consistency and reproducibility, a random state value of 42 was assigned. This random state value helps control the randomization process and ensures consistent results across multiple runs. By using the same random state value each time the algorithm is executed, identical outcomes can be obtained consistently. The random forest model was configured with a minimum number of splits set to four. This parameter plays a role in regularization by controlling the complexity of the decision trees. A lower value for the number of splits allows the trees to have more nodes, enabling them to match the training data closely.

Similarly, the minimum sample leaves parameter was specified as one. Like the minimum number of splits, this parameter contributes to regularization by regulating the complexity of the decision trees. With a lower value for minimum sample leaves, the trees can have more leaves, facilitating a closer fit to the training data. To prevent overfitting, the maximum depth parameter was set to 35. This parameter helps limit the trees' depth, ensuring they do not become excessively complex and overly specialized to the training data. The model becomes more generalizable and less prone to overfitting by controlling the maximum depth.

```
Import numpy as np
import pandas as pd
import os
```

```python
import math

import matplotlib.pyplot as plt

from datetime import datetime

from sklearn.preprocessing import MinMaxScaler, StandardScaler

from sklearn.model_selection import train_test_split

import tensorflow as tf

from keras.losses import mean_squared_error

from sklearn.ensemble import RandomForestRegressor

from sklearn.model_selection import RandomizedSearchCV


ticker = 'CREG'

df = pd.read_csv(ticker + '.csv')

datetime_series = pd.to_datetime(df['Date'])

datetime_index = pd.DatetimeIndex(datetime_series.values)

df = df.set_index(datetime_index)

df = df.sort_values(by='Date')

df = df.drop(columns='Date')


X_value = pd.DataFrame(df.iloc[:, 0:4])

y_value = pd.DataFrame(df.iloc[:, 3])


X_scaler = MinMaxScaler(feature_range=(0, 1))

y_scaler = MinMaxScaler(feature_range=(0, 1))

X_scaler.fit(X_value)

y_scaler.fit(y_value)


X_scale_dataset = X_scaler.fit_transform(X_value)

y_scale_dataset = y_scaler.fit_transform(y_value)


def split_train_test(data):

train_size = round(len(data) * 0.8)
```

```python
    data_train = data[0:train_size]
    data_test = data[train_size:]
    return data_train, data_test


X_train, X_test, = split_train_test(X_scale_dataset)
y_train, y_test, = split_train_test(y_scale_dataset)


model = RandomForestRegressor(n_estimators=60, random_state=42, min_samples_split=4,
min_samples_leaf=1, max_depth=35, bootstrap=True)


model.fit(X_train, np.ravel(y_train,order='C'))


yhat = model.predict(X_test)
yhat = yhat.reshape(-1,1)
actual_prices = y_scaler.inverse_transform(y_test)
predicted_prices = y_scaler.inverse_transform(yhat)


mse = tf.keras.losses.mean_squared_error(actual_prices[:,0], predicted_prices[:,0]).numpy()
rmse = math.sqrt(mse)
print('RMSE', rmse)
mape = tf.keras.losses.mean_absolute_percentage_error(actual_prices[:,0], predicted_prices
[:,0]).numpy()
print('MAPE', mape)


plt.plot(actual_prices, color='green', label=f"Actual {ticker} price")
plt.plot(predicted_prices, color= 'red', label=f"predicted {ticker} price")
plt.title(f"{ticker} Stock Prices – Actual Vs. Predicted")
plt.xlabel("time")
plt.ylabel(f"{ticker} Stock Price")
plt.legend()
plt.show()
```

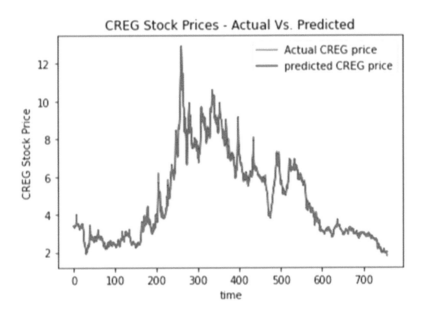

Figure 9: Actual Time Series and Random Forest-Predicted Time Series
for the CREG Stock.

The chart above shows the comparison of actual time series from the test set and predicted time series. The model produced an RMSE of 0.09. Since the RMSE is a relative measure of the underlying values, the MAPE is best suited to interpret the model's accuracy. The model produced a MAPE of 1.15, indicating there is a 1.15 percent of error in prediction. The lower MAPE indicates the random forest algorithm is capable of forecasting the stock prices when the time series data exhibits complex patterns mentioned earlier.

## 11.2  XGBoost

XGBoost operates on the principle of boosting, combining multiple weak learners, typically decision trees, into a robust learner by sequentially adding new models to rectify the errors made by the existing ensemble. It implements the gradient boosting framework, which utilizes gradient descent to minimize the loss as new models are integrated. Whenever a new tree is added, it identifies the optimal splits in the data to minimize the loss, that is, the difference between the actual and predicted values.

Let us implement the XGBoost model to forecast the stock prices for the RILY ticker. The figure below visualizes the time series data for the RILY stock from January 2, 2008, to February 10, 2023.

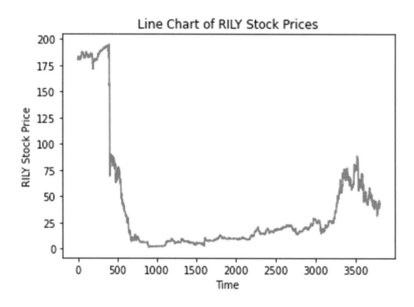

Figure 10: Actual Time Series of the Combined Training Set
and Test Set for the RILY Stock.

The statistical measures for the RILY stock ticker highlight critical characteristics of the time series data.

- Nonstationarity: The ADF test's p-value is 0.078, above the standard 0.05 threshold. This suggests the time series is nonstationary, implying that the mean and variance might change over time.

- Nonlinearity: The Lyapunov exponent is 0.0001, a positive value. A positive Lyapunov exponent indicates a certain level of chaos in the system, suggesting nonlinearity.

- Long memory or dependence: The DFA Hurst Exponent is 1.64, significantly higher than 0.5. This suggests a strong long-term memory or dependence on the time series, meaning that future values depend heavily on past values.

- Asymmetry: The skewness value of 1.96 suggests a right-skewed distribution, meaning the returns distribution has a longer right tail. This indicates the positive returns are more extreme than negative ones for the RILY stock, hinting at asymmetric return distribution.

- Stochasticity: An entropy value of 6.48 was computed for the time series data of RILY, a figure exceeding 50 percent but below 90 percent of the maximum possible entropy. This maximum entropy was determined as the logarithm of the number of unique elements within the time series data, that is, log(len(np.unique(time_series_data))). The resulting entropy reveals the time series is moderately unpredictable, suggesting a mix of stochastic and deterministic behavior.

The XGBoost-driven time series forecasting model was developed to anticipate the RILY stock prices, accounting for the intricate patterns outlined earlier. This section momentarily details the full programming sequence for deploying the XGBoost model for stock price prediction. However, the excerpt below is a fraction of the entire code. The given code segment serves as a blueprint for building and training an XGBoost model designed for stock price prediction.

```
Model = XGBRegressor(objective='reg:squarederror')
```

```
param_grid = {
'n_estimators': [50, 100, 150, 200],
'learning_rate': [0.01, 0.05, 0.1],
'max_depth': [3, 4, 5, 6, 7],
'colsample_bytree': [0.6, 0.7, 0.8, 0.9, 1],
'gamma': [0.0, 0.1, 0.2]
}
```

```
# Instantiate the grid search model
grid_search = GridSearchCV(estimator = model, param_grid = param_grid,
cv = 3, n_jobs = -1, verbose = 2)
grid_search.fit(X_train, np.ravel(y_train,order='C'))
best_params = grid_search.best_params_
print(best_params)
best_model = grid_search.best_estimator_
yhat = best_model.predict(X_test)
```

The provided script uses the XGBoost regressor model for a machine learning task, leveraging the GridSearchCV function from the Scikit-Learn library for hyperparameter tuning. The model is initially defined with the reg:squarederror objective, using a squared error loss function. A dictionary of potential hyperparameters is specified for grid search, including options for n_estimators, learning_rate, max_depth, colsample_bytree, and gamma.

The GridSearchCV function executes an exhaustive search over the defined parameter grid, utilizing a three-fold cross-validation strategy. The grid search is conducted in parallel, using all available cores, thanks to n_jobs = -1. After fitting the grid search to the training data, the script extracts and displays the optimal parameters and retrains the model with these. The tuned model is subsequently used to predict the test dataset.

GridSearch is a powerful tool in machine learning for hyperparameter tuning. It systematically works through multiple combinations of parameter tunes, cross-validates each, and determines the best performance. The primary advantage is that it can optimize model performance by selecting the most appropriate parameters, saving time and computational cost compared to manually tuning each parameter. However, it can be computationally expensive for large datasets or complex models, as it effectively performs a model training process for each unique combination of parameters.

```
Import numpy as np
import pandas as pd
import os
import math
import matplotlib.pyplot as plt
from datetime import datetime
from sklearn.preprocessing import MinMaxScaler, StandardScaler
from sklearn.model_selection import train_test_split
import tensorflow as tf
from keras.losses import mean_squared_error
from xgboost import XGBRegressor
from sklearn.model_selection import GridSearchCV
ticker = 'RILY'
df = pd.read_csv(ticker + '.csv')
datetime_series = pd.to_datetime(df['Date'])
datetime_index = pd.DatetimeIndex(datetime_series.values)
df = df.set_index(datetime_index)
```

```
df = df.sort_values(by='Date')
df = df.drop(columns='Date')
X_value = pd.DataFrame(df.iloc[:, 0:4])
y_value = pd.DataFrame(df.iloc[:, 3])
X_scaler = MinMaxScaler(feature_range=(0, 1))
y_scaler = MinMaxScaler(feature_range=(0, 1))
X_scaler.fit(X_value)
y_scaler.fit(y_value)
X_scale_dataset = X_scaler.fit_transform(X_value)
y_scale_dataset = y_scaler.fit_transform(y_value)
def split_train_test(data):
train_size = round(len(data) * 0.8)
data_train = data[0:train_size]
data_test = data[train_size:]
return data_train, data_test
X_train, X_test, = split_train_test(X_scale_dataset)
y_train, y_test, = split_train_test(y_scale_dataset)
model = XGBRegressor(objective='reg:squarederror')
param_grid = {
'n_estimators': [50, 100, 150, 200],
'learning_rate': [0.01, 0.05, 0.1],
'max_depth': [3, 4, 5, 6, 7],
'colsample_bytree': [0.6, 0.7, 0.8, 0.9, 1],
'gamma': [0.0, 0.1, 0.2]
}
grid_search = GridSearchCV(estimator = model, param_grid = param_grid,
cv = 3, n_jobs = -1, verbose = 2)
grid_search.fit(X_train, np.ravel(y_train,order='C'))
best_params = grid_search.best_params_
print(best_params)
best_model = grid_search.best_estimator_
yhat = best_model.predict(X_test)
```

161

```
yhat = yhat.reshape(-1,1)

actual_prices = y_scaler.inverse_transform(y_test)

predicted_prices = y_scaler.inverse_transform(yhat)

mse = tf.keras.losses.mean_squared_error(actual_prices[:,0], predicted_prices[:,0]).numpy()

rmse = math.sqrt(mse)

print('RMSE', rmse)

mape = tf.keras.losses.mean_absolute_percentage_error(actual_prices[:,0], predicted_prices[:,0]).numpy()

print('MAPE', mape)

plt.plot(actual_prices, color='green', label=f"Actual {ticker} price")

plt.plot(predicted_prices, color= 'red', label=f"predicted {ticker} price")

plt.title(f"{ticker} Stock Prices – Actual Vs. Predicted")

plt.xlabel("time")

plt.ylabel(f"{ticker} Stock Price")

plt.legend()

plt.show()
```

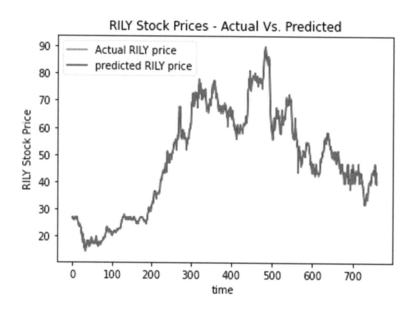

Figure 11: Actual Time Series and XGBoost Predicted Time Series for the RILY Stock.

The chart above shows the comparison of actual time series from the test set and the predicted time series of RILY. The model produced an RMSE of 0.80. Since the RMSE is a relative measure of the underlying values, the MAPE is best suited to interpret the model's accuracy. The model produced a MAPE of 1.25, indicating there is a 1.25 percent of error in prediction. The lower MAPE indicates the XGBoost algorithm is capable of forecasting the stock prices when the time series data exhibits complex patterns mentioned earlier.

# 12

# Deep Learning for Time Series Modeling

Deep learning models, such as LSTMs and 1DCNNs, have shown promising effectiveness in time series forecasting. For example, LSTMs, a specialized type of RNN, can learn and remember over long sequences and can thereby overcome the problem of vanishing and exploding gradients that RNNs can suffer from. They do this by using a system of gates that allow more precise control over the information flow in the network. In this chapter, we delve into the utilization of several models, including LSTM, BiLSTM, 1DCNN, 1DCNN-LSTM, 1DCNN-BiLSTM, GRU, and GAN in forecasting time series data.

## 12.1   Long Short-Term Memory (LSTM)

One of the limitations intrinsic to traditional time series models is their lack of memory capability. To address this deficiency, RNNs incorporate cyclic connections within their hidden layers, which allows them to retain some degree of memory. However, since this memory tends to be short term, the RNNs can retain information briefly but struggle to maintain it over extended durations. This issue arises from what's known as the vanishing gradient problem, a limitation that hampers RNNs' ability to learn long-range dependencies.

The vanishing gradient problem occurs when the value being multiplied during the training process is a small fraction less than one. In RNNs, the backpropagation process involves deriving the gradient of earlier layers by multiplying the gradients of later layers. When the gradients of the later layers are smaller than one, their product diminishes quickly. This rapidly vanishes the gradient, preventing the network from effectively learning from distant past information.

Contrary to RNNs, LSTM models augment the memory capabilities of neural networks, enabling them to remember and learn long-term dependencies within inputs. As a specialized type of RNN, LSTMs excel at capturing temporal sequences and long-range dependencies more effectively than RNNs. In LSTM architectures, using activation functions within their recurrent components helps maintain stored values as constant, preventing the gradient from vanishing during training. LSTMs are structured in blocks, each featuring several gates, specifically input, forget, and output gates. These gates manage the flow of information using the logistic function. This mechanism enables LSTM networks to retain valuable information in memory cells while discarding unnecessary data. By employing feedback connections and preserving state information in purposefully-designed memory cells, LSTM networks are capable of learning long-term dependencies. As a result, LSTMs generally outperform traditional RNNs in time series analysis tasks. Another advantage of the LSTM network is that it can model the spikes of unknown size between unknown duration intervals.

An LSTM unit comprises a cell (commonly called the memory cell) and three gates: an input gate, an output gate, and a forget gate. The memory cell retains values over time, essentially serving as the model's memory. These three gates function similarly to traditional artificial neurons in a MLP. They compute an activation of a weighted sum, regulating the flow of values through the LSTM network, hence the term "gates." Connections are formed between these gates and the memory cell, allowing the LSTM to regulate and manage information flows efficiently. One of the significant features of an LSTM is its ability to sustain short-term memories for prolonged periods. This capability makes LSTMs particularly effective at predicting time series data, especially in scenarios where there are unpredictable fluctuations in size and duration. To adapt a dataset for LSTM use, it will be converted into a supervised learning format by normalizing variables. This essentially transforms the task into a supervised learning problem, where the objective is to predict the next expected observation based on previous time series data. The forecast horizon can be set according to specific needs.

The dataset is usually split into randomly chosen parts for research utilizing machine learning or deep learning models on non-time series data. One portion serves to uncover underlying relationships or patterns, while the other is used to validate these discovered relationships or patterns. However, this approach of random partitioning isn't feasible for time series data due to its sequential nature. Instead, an approach based on chronological order is adopted. Typically, the initial segment of the time series data is employed to identify patterns, and the latter part is used for validation purposes. The figure below visualizes the time series data for the SO stock from January 2, 2008, to February 10, 2023.

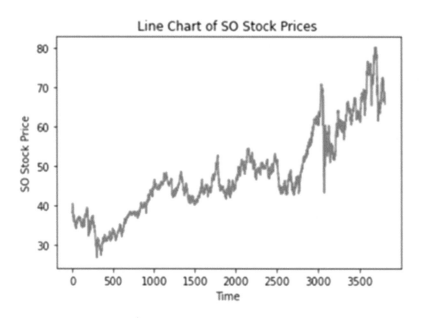

Figure 12: Actual Time Series of the Combined Training Set
and Test Set for the SO Stock.

The statistical measures are generated to assess the complexity of the above time series data. Listed below are detailed descriptions of the statistical measures for the SO ticker:

- ADF p-value (0.54) refers to the p-value obtained from the ADF test. The ADF test is a statistical procedure used to determine whether a time series is stationary or not. A high p-value of 0.54 (>0.05) suggests the null hypothesis of the ADF test (the time series is nonstationary) cannot be rejected. In this case, a p-value of 0.54 indicates the SO time series data is nonstationary, suggesting it has some time-dependent structure.

- DFA Hurst exponent (1.45): The Hurst exponent is a statistical measure that classifies time series data. The time series is considered mean-reverting if the Hurst exponent is less than 0.5. If it is 0.5, the time series is a geometric Brownian motion (a random walk). If it is greater than 0.5, the time series is trending or persistent. A Hurst exponent of 1.45 indicates the SO time series data is highly persistent or trending, indicating long-term memory or dependency.

- Lyapunov exponent (0.0047): The Lyapunov exponent measures the rate of separation of infinitesimally-close trajectories, a key quantity to understanding the chaotic dynamics in a system. A positive Lyapunov exponent typically indicates chaos. In this case, a value close to zero (0.0047) suggests the time series data is chaotic though with lesser severity and small changes will lead to significantly different trajectories. In other words, the time series data of SO stock exhibits nonlinearity.

- Skewness (0.66): Skewness measures the asymmetry of the probability distribution of a real-valued random variable about its mean. A positive skewness value indicates the tail on the probability density function's right side (positive side) is longer or fatter than the left side. A skewness of 0.66 for the SO time series data suggests a positively skewed distribution, indicating relatively more unusually high values than low ones.

- Stochasticity: An entropy value of 7.59 was computed for the time series data of SO, a figure exceeding 90 percent of the maximum possible entropy. This maximum entropy was determined as the logarithm of the number of unique elements within the time series data, that is, log(len(np.unique(time_series_data))). The resulting entropy reveals the time series is highly unpredictable, likely indicating a high degree of stochasticity.

The LSTM-based time series model has been implemented to forecast the stock prices for the SO, exhibiting the complex patterns described above. The complete code for implementing the LSTM model to predict stock prices is demonstrated momentarily in this section. However, the snippet below is part of the entire code set. The code provided serves as a guide to constructing and training an LSTM-based deep learning model, which is used for predicting stock prices.

```
model = Sequential()
model.add(LSTM(units = 512, return_sequences = True, activation = 'tanh', input_shape =
(input_dim, feature_size)))
model.add(Dropout(0.2))
model.add(LSTM(units = 384, activation = 'tanh'))
model.add(Dense(64))
model.add(Dense(units=1))
model.compile(optimizer='adam', loss='mse')
model.fit(X_train, y_train, epochs=25, batch_size = 25)
```

A sequential model is created, acting as a foundation upon which different neural network layers are sequentially built. The first layer added is an LSTM layer with 512 units. Its distinctive feature, the return_sequences parameter, is set to true, which allows the layer to generate an output at every timestep, not solely at the end. The activation function applied is tanh, shaping the input data in a specific format defined by input_dim and feature_size.

Following the LSTM layer, a dropout layer is incorporated, introducing a dropout rate of 20 percent. This layer safeguards against overfitting by randomly neglecting certain neurons during training. The model is then extended by adding another LSTM layer equipped with 384 units. Unlike its predecessor, this layer only produces output for the final timestep. Subsequently, a dense layer consisting of 64 neurons is added, fully connected to the preceding layer.

In the final construction stage, a dense layer with a single neuron is added, serving as the model's output layer. This layer generates a single value output, such as a predicted stock price. Once the model's architecture is completed, the model is compiled using the Adam optimizer and the MSE loss function. Adam, known for its adaptive learning rate optimization, works well with deep learning models, while MSE is frequently used for regression problems such as predicting stock prices. Finally, the model is trained using the dataset, divided into X_train and y_train, over 25 epochs with a batch size of 25. In this stage, each epoch represents a complete pass through the entire training dataset, with the model updating its learning after processing each batch of samples.

The LSTM network's multilayered structure was crucial in attaining superior accuracy levels. Furthermore, the inclusion of a dropout mechanism served to curtail overfitting. The tanh activation function also assisted the model, which facilitated the comprehension of the dataset's intricacies, thereby enhancing forecast precision. The LSTM's two-layered design boosted the neural network model's performance in several significant ways. First, it enabled the model to identify longer-term dependencies, an essential aspect of tasks demanding an in-depth understanding of the data. Second, the supplementary layer augmented the model's capacity to discern more complicated relationships between input and output. Finally, the additional layer endowed the model with a heightened resilience to noise, improving its generalizability to unfamiliar data.

Incorporating a dropout function between the layers served as a regularization tool, safeguarding the model against overfitting. A dropout value of 0.2 ensured the random exclusion of 20 percent of the inputs before their transfer to the succeeding layer during the training phase. This selective elimination of connections between layers prevented the model from excessively relying on a specific set of features, thereby averting overdependency. Essentially, the dropout function regulated the model by injecting noise into the training procedure, mitigating the risk of overfitting.

The network's inaugural layer specified a configuration of 512 memory cells. Each cell functions as an independent processing entity, capable of retaining information over a duration and modifying its internal state based on the interplay with other network cells. The quantity of memory cells determines the model's sophistication and learning capacity. While a greater number of units might equip the model to decipher intricate patterns in the data, it simultaneously heightens the risk of overfitting. This is because the model could lean toward rote learning of the training data rather than generalizing from unseen data. However, through extensive experimentation, it was concluded that 512 units constituted the optimal number. In the second layer, the number of memory cells was curtailed to 384. This strategic reduction compelled the model to retain only the most crucial information from the first layer. It served as a measure to dissuade the model from merely memorizing the training data, thereby guiding it toward discerning more generalizable patterns transferable to novel data.

The tanh activation function was employed in the network to incorporate nonlinearity and to modulate the information flow through the memory cells. This nonlinear function adeptly transfigures the input data into a more manageable scope. Tanh proves useful in averting values from inflating or evaporating as they traverse multiple layers, thereby enabling the LSTM network to grasp and preserve the nonlinearities and long-term dependencies inherent in sequential data.

A pair of dense layers were implemented to formulate predictions based on the output derived from the LSTM layers. The initial dense layer offered a nonlinear mapping of the LSTM output to a higher-dimensional space, facilitating the recognition of pertinent patterns for prediction. The secondary dense layer reduced the dimensionality of the output by mapping it to the output space, which conventionally has a significantly lower dimensionality.

Adam was employed to refine the neural network weights throughout the training phase. Adam calculates individual adaptive learning rates for distinct parameters as an adaptive learning rate optimization algorithm. This calculation is derived from estimates of the first and second moments of the gradients. Utilizing Adam facilitated an enhancement in the network's convergence speed and its ability to generalize. By adapting the learning rate for each weight based on their gradient magnitudes and previous gradients, Adam proficiently maintains a balance between speedy convergence and avoiding getting trapped in local minima.

The MSE served as the chosen loss function. MSE calculates the average of the squared disparities between the forecasted and actual values, so the model is guided to minimize the overall squared difference between these values. This process aids in obtaining a more precise prediction. The full code for the implementation is provided below.

```
import numpy as np
import pandas as pd
import matplotlib.pyplot as plt
from datetime import datetime
import math
from sklearn.preprocessing import MinMaxScaler
from sklearn.model_selection import train_test_split
import tensorflow as tf
from tensorflow.keras.callbacks import ModelCheckpoint, EarlyStopping
from keras.losses import mean_squared_error
from tensorflow.keras.models import Sequential
from tensorflow.keras.layers import LSTM, Dense, Dropout


ticker = 'SO'
df = pd.read_csv(ticker + '.csv')
datetime_series = pd.to_datetime(df['Date'])
datetime_index = pd.DatetimeIndex(datetime_series.values)
df = df.set_index(datetime_index)
```

```
df = df.sort_values(by='Date')
df = df.drop(columns='Date')


X_value = pd.DataFrame(df.iloc[:, 0:4])
y_value = pd.DataFrame(df.iloc[:, 3])


X_scaler = MinMaxScaler(feature_range=(0, 1))
y_scaler = MinMaxScaler(feature_range=(0, 1))
X_scaler.fit(X_value)
y_scaler.fit(y_value)


X_scaile_dataset = X_scaler.fit_transform(X_value)
y_scale_dataset = y_scaler.fit_transform(y_value)
y_scale_dataset_inv = y_scaler.inverse_transform(y_scale_dataset)


n_steps_in = 10
n_features = X_value.shape[1]
n_steps_out = 1


X = []
y = []


length = len(X_scale_dataset)
for i in range(0, length, 1):
X_val = X_scale_dataset[i: i + n_steps_in][:, :]
y_val = y_scale_dataset[i + n_steps_in: i + (n_steps_in + n_steps_out)][:, 0]
if len(X_val) == n_steps_in and len(y_val) == n_steps_out:
X.append(X_val)
y.append(y_val)
```

```python
X = np.array(X)
y = np.array(y)


def train_test_split(data):
train_size = round(len(data) * 0.8)
data_train = data[0:train_size]
data_test = data[train_size:]
return data_train, data_test


X_train, X_test = train_test_split(X)
y_train, y_test = train_test_split(y)


input_dim = X_train.shape[1]
feature_size = X_train.shape[2]
output_dim = y_train.shape[1]


model = Sequential()
model.add(LSTM(units = 512, return_sequences = True, activation = 'tanh', input_shape =
(input_dim, feature_size)))
model.add(Dropout(0.2))
model.add(LSTM(units = 384, activation = 'tanh'))
model.add(Dense(64))
model.add(Dense(units=1))


model.compile(optimizer='adam', loss='mse')


model.fit(X_train, y_train, epochs=25, batch_size = 25)


yhat = model.predict(X_test, verbose=0)
```

```
actual_prices = y_scaler.inverse_transform(y_test)
predicted_prices = y_scaler.inverse_transform(yhat)


mse = tf.keras.losses.mean_squared_error(actual_prices[:,0], predicted_prices[:,0]).numpy()
rmse = math.sqrt(mse)
print('RMSE', rmse)
mape = tf.keras.losses.mean_absolute_percentage_error(actual_prices[:,0], predicted_
prices[:,0]).numpy()
print('MAPE', mape)


plt.plot(actual_prices, color='green', label=f"Actual {ticker} price")
plt.plot(predicted_prices, color= 'red', label=f"predicted {ticker} price")
plt.title(f"{ticker} Stock Prices–- Actual Vs. Predicted")
plt.xlabel("time")
plt.ylabel(f"{ticker} Stock Price")
plt.legend()
plt.show()
```

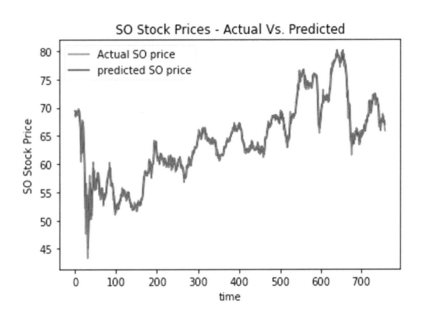

Figure 13: Actual Time Series and LSTM-Predicted Time Series for the SO Stock.

The chart above compares the actual time series from the test set and predicted time series. The model produced an RMSE of 1.24. Since the RMSE is a relative measure of the underlying values, the MAPE is best suited to interpret the model's accuracy. The model produced a MAPE of 1.35, indicating there is a 1.35 percent of error in prediction. The lower MAPE indicates the LSTM network is capable of forecasting the stock prices when the time series data exhibits complex patterns mentioned earlier.

## 12.2   Bidirectional Long Short-Term Memory (BiLSTM)

BiLSTM networks, a specialized version of RNNs, were developed to enhance the standard LSTM architecture, specifically to combat the vanishing gradients often seen in conventional RNNs. BiLSTMs can process data in both forward and reverse directions. The BiLSTM network comprises two LSTM layers: one layer analyzes the input sequence in a forward sequence, while the other analyzes it in reverse. This architecture's ability to assimilate past and future contexts proves particularly beneficial for tasks such as time series analysis, NLP, and speech recognition.

While training a BiLSTM network, the forward and backward LSTM layers are trained independently, but at the inference stage, the outputs from both layers are merged to generate the final prediction. Multiple methods exist to accomplish this merge, such as combining the output vectors or applying element-wise maximum or average operations. BiLSTM networks have shown efficacy in a range of sequence modeling tasks, including time series forecasting. Their performance can be further enhanced when combined with other deep learning methods, like attention mechanisms.

Let us implement BiLSTM to forecast the stock prices for the MO ticker. The figure below visualizes the time series data for the MO stock from January 2, 2008, to February 10, 2023.

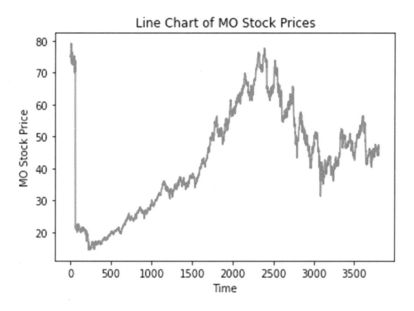

Figure 14: Actual Time Series of the Combined Training Set
and Test Set for the MO Stock.

The statistical measures are generated to assess the complexity of the above time series data. Listed below are detailed descriptions of the statistical measures for the ticker MO:

- ADF p-value (0.13) refers to the p-value obtained from the ADF test. The ADF test is a statistical procedure used to determine whether a time series is stationary or not. A high p-value (> 0.05) suggests the null hypothesis of the ADF test (the time series is nonstationary) cannot be rejected. In this case, a p-value of 0.13 indicates the MO time series data is nonstationary.

- DFA Hurst exponent (1.56): The Hurst exponent is a statistical measure that classifies time series data. The time series is considered mean-reverting if the Hurst exponent is less than 0.5. If it is 0.5, the time series is a geometric Brownian motion (a random walk). If it is greater than 0.5, the time series is trending or persistent. A Hurst exponent of 1.56 indicates the MO time series data is highly persistent or trending, revealing long-term memory or dependency.

- Lyapunov exponent (0.002): The Lyapunov exponent measures the rate of separation of infinitesimally close trajectories, a key quantity to understanding the chaotic dynamics in a system. A positive Lyapunov exponent typically indicates chaos. In this case, a value of 0.002 suggests the time series data is chaotic with low severity and small changes will lead to significantly different trajectories. In other words, the time series data of MO exhibits nonlinearity.

- Skewness (0.10): Skewness measures the asymmetry of the probability distribution of a real-valued random variable about its mean. A positive skewness value indicates the tail on the probability density function's right side (positive side) is longer or fatter than the left side. A skewness of 0.10 for the MO time series data suggests a positively skewed distribution, indicating relatively more unusually high values than low ones.

- Stochasticity: An entropy value of 5.22 was computed for the time series data of MO, a figure exceeding 50 percent but below 90 percent of the maximum possible entropy. This maximum entropy was determined as the logarithm of the number of unique elements within the time series data, that is, log(len(np.unique(time_series_data))). The resulting entropy reveals the time series is moderately unpredictable, suggesting a mix of stochastic and deterministic behavior.

The BiLSTM-based time series model has been implemented to forecast the stock prices for the MO stock, exhibiting the complex patterns described above. The complete code for implementing the BiLSTM model to predict stock prices is demonstrated momentarily in this section. However, the snippet below is just a part of the entire code set. The code provided serves as a guide to constructing and training a BiLSTM-based deep learning model, which is used for predicting stock prices.

```
model = Sequential()
model.add(Bidirectional(LSTM(units= 512, return_sequences = True, activation = 'tanh'),
input_shape=(input_dim, feature_size)))
model.add(Bidirectional(LSTM(units= 256, activation = 'tanh')))
model.add(Dense(units=output_dim))
model.compile(optimizer='adam', loss='mse')
model.fit(X_train, y_train, epochs=25, batch_size = 25)
```

This code defines and trains a BiLSTM model using Keras. The BiLSTM network interprets the input sequence bidirectionally, hence, assimilating information from both prior and subsequent contexts. This dual-context capture allows the BiLSTM to learn more robust representations of the input sequence, consequently enhancing the precision of predictions. Similar to the LSTM structure, the BiLSTM network employs two layers. The first layer is a BiLSTM layer with 512 units, and it returns sequences, meaning it provides its full sequence of outputs as input to the next layer. This layer uses the tanh activation function and receives an input with a shape corresponding to input_dim timesteps and feature_size features per timestep. Using the tanh activation function, as in traditional LSTM, aids in deciphering nonlinear patterns present within the time series data. The second layer is also a BiLSTM layer but with 256 units. It does not return sequences and uses tanh as the activation function. The final layer is a dense (fully-connected) layer with output_dim units for output prediction.

The model is compiled with the Adam optimizer and the MSE loss function, common choices for regression tasks. Finally, the model is trained on the provided training data (X_train and y_train) for 25 epochs with a batch size 25. This means the model's weights are updated after every 25 training examples and the entire training process is repeated 25 times.

```
import numpy as np
import pandas as pd
import math
import matplotlib.pyplot as plt
from sklearn.preprocessing import MinMaxScaler
from sklearn.model_selection import train_test_split
import tensorflow as tf
from tensorflow.keras.callbacks import ModelCheckpoint, EarlyStopping
from keras.losses import mean_squared_error
from tensorflow.keras.models import Sequential
from tensorflow.keras.layers import Dense, Dropout, LSTM, Bidirectional
ticker = 'MO'
df = pd.read_csv(ticker + '.csv')
datetime_series = pd.to_datetime(df['Date'])
datetime_index = pd.DatetimeIndex(datetime_series.values)
df = df.set_index(datetime_index)
df = df.sort_values(by='Date')
```

```python
df = df.drop(columns='Date')

X_value = pd.DataFrame(df.iloc[:, 0:4])

y_value = pd.DataFrame(df.iloc[:, 3])

X_scaler = MinMaxScaler(feature_range=(0, 1))

y_scaler = MinMaxScaler(feature_range=(0, 1))

X_scaler.fit(X_value)

y_scaler.fit(y_value)

X_scale_dataset = X_scaler.fit_transform(X_value)

y_scale_dataset = y_scaler.fit_transform(y_value)

y_scale_dataset_inv = y_scaler.inverse_transform(y_scale_dataset)


n_steps_in = 10

n_features = X_value.shape[1]

n_steps_out = 1

X = []

y = []

length = len(X_scale_dataset)

for i in range(0, length, 1):

X_val = X_scale_dataset[i: i + n_steps_in][:, :]

y_val = y_scale_dataset[i + n_steps_in: i + (n_steps_in + n_steps_out)][:, 0]

if len(X_val) == n_steps_in and len(y_val) == n_steps_out:

X.append(X_val)

y.append(y_val)

X = np.array(X)

y = np.array(y)

def train_test_split(data):

train_size = round(len(data) * 0.8)

data_train = data[0:train_size]

data_test = data[train_size:]

return data_train, data_test

X_train, X_test = train_test_split(X)

y_train, y_test = train_test_split(y)
```

```python
input_dim = X_train.shape[1]
feature_size = X_train.shape[2]
output_dim = y_train.shape[1]
model = Sequential()
model.add(Bidirectional(LSTM(units= 512, return_sequences = True, activation = 'tanh'),
input_shape=(input_dim, feature_size)))
model.add(Bidirectional(LSTM(units= 256, activation = 'tanh')))
model.add(Dense(units=output_dim))
model.compile(optimizer='adam', loss='mse')
model.fit(X_train, y_train, epochs=25, batch_size = 25)
yhat = model.predict(X_test, verbose=0)
actual_prices = y_scaler.inverse_transform(y_test)
predicted_prices = y_scaler.inverse_transform(yhat)
mse = tf.keras.losses.mean_squared_error(actual_prices[:,0], predicted_prices[:,0]).numpy()
rmse = math.sqrt(mse)
print('RMSE', rmse)
mape = tf.keras.losses.mean_absolute_percentage_error(actual_prices[:,0], predicted_prices
[:,0]).numpy()
print('MAPE', mape)
plt.plot(actual_prices, color='green', label=f"Actual {ticker} price")
plt.plot(predicted_prices, color= 'red', label=f"predicted {ticker} price")
plt.title(f"{ticker} Stock Prices–- Actual Vs. Predicted")
plt.xlabel("time")
plt.ylabel(f"{ticker} Stock Price")
plt.legend()
plt.show()
```

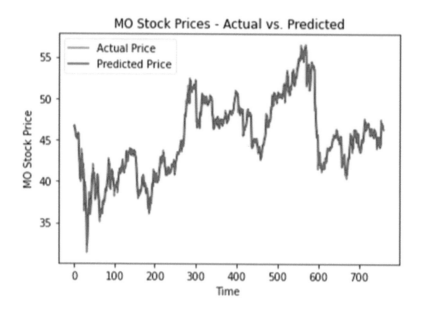

Figure 15: Actual Time Series and BiLSTM-Predicted Time Series
for the MO Stock.

The chart above compares the actual time series from the test set and predicted time series. The model produced an RMSE of 0.84. Since the RMSE is a relative measure of the underlying values, the MAPE is best suited to interpret the model's accuracy. The model produced a MAPE of 1.33, indicating there is a 1.33 percent of error in prediction. The lower MAPE indicates the BiLSTM network is capable of forecasting the stock prices when the time series data exhibits complex patterns mentioned earlier.

## 12.3   One-Dimensional Convolutional Neural Network (1DCNN)

Traditional CNNs are biologically-inspired, feedforward ANNs that model the mammalian visual cortex in two dimensions. They can learn directly from minimal data sets. While CNNs are well known for detecting patterns in images to recognize objects, they also perform well in analyzing non-image data like time series and signal data. The CNN algorithm allocates weights and biases to various image elements in image recognition, enabling differentiation between diverse images. Even though basic attributes are typically hand-engineered, ConvNets can master more complex features through training. The one-dimensional CNN, also known as 1DCNN, is a streamlined variant of the 2DCNN.

The 1DCNNs are beneficial when dealing with datasets that feature limited labeled data and significant signal variations, a common situation when data is procured from multiple sources. Hence, the 1DCNN is highly effective in extracting useful features from shorter segments of the overall dataset, particularly when the feature within a given segment is not pertinent.

1DCNNs are frequently employed for tasks like time series analysis, NLP, and speech recognition, all of which involve data with a sequential or time-oriented structure. These networks excel at such tasks as they can discern local patterns and relationships within the data and manage sequences of varying lengths. This function is especially beneficial when analyzing time series data, where the series is divided into numerous segments.

Let us implement 1DCNN to forecast the stock prices for the HSTM ticker. The figure below visualizes the time series data for the HSTM stock from January 2, 2008, to February 10, 2023.

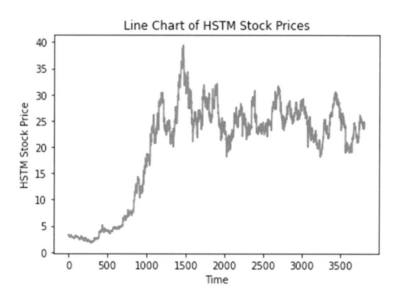

Figure 16: Actual Time Series of the Combined Training Set
and Test Set for the HSTM Stock.

The statistical measures are generated to assess the complexity of the above time series data. Listed below are detailed descriptions of the statistical measures for the ticker HSTM:

- ADF p-value (0.31) refers to the p-value obtained from the ADF test. The ADF test is a statistical procedure used to determine whether a time series is stationary or not. A high p-value (> 0.05) suggests the null hypothesis of the ADF test (the time series is nonstationary) cannot be rejected. In this case, a p-value of 0.31 indicates the HSTM time series data is likely nonstationary, suggesting it has some time-dependent structure.

- DFA Hurst exponent (1.50): The Hurst exponent is a statistical measure that classifies time series data. The time series is considered mean-reverting if the Hurst exponent is less than 0.5. If it is 0.5, the time series is a geometric Brownian motion (a random walk). If it is greater than 0.5, the time series is trending or persistent. A Hurst exponent of 1.50 indicates the HSTM time series data is highly persistent or trending revealing long-term memory or dependency.

- Lyapunov exponent (0.001): The Lyapunov exponent measures the rate of separation of infinitesimally close trajectories, a key quantity to understanding the chaotic dynamics in a system. A positive Lyapunov exponent typically indicates chaos. In this case, a value of 0.001 suggests the time series data is chaotic and small changes will lead to significantly different trajectories. In other words, the time series data of stock HSTM exhibits nonlinearity.

- Skewness (-0.84): Skewness measures the asymmetry of the probability distribution of a real-valued random variable about its mean. A negative skewness value indicates the tail on the probability density function's left side (negative side) is longer or fatter than the right side. A skewness of -0.84 for the HSTM time series data suggests a negatively skewed distribution, indicating relatively more unusually low values than high ones.

- Stochasticity: An entropy value of 8.2 was computed for the time series data of HSTM, a figure exceeding 90 percent of the maximum possible entropy. This maximum entropy was determined as the logarithm of the number of unique elements within the time series data, that is, log(len(np.unique(time_series_data))). The resulting entropy reveals the time series is highly unpredictable, likely indicating a high degree of stochasticity.

The 1DCNN-based time series model has been implemented to forecast the stock prices for the HSTM stock, exhibiting the complex patterns described above. The complete code for implementing the 1DCNN model to predict stock prices is demonstrated momentarily in this section. However, the snippet below is part of the entire code set. The code provided serves as a guide to constructing and training a 1DCNN-based deep learning model, which is used for predicting stock prices.

```
model = Sequential()
model.add(Conv1D(filters=64, kernel_size=5, activation='tanh', input_shape = (input_
dim,feature_size)))
model.add(Conv1D(filters=64, kernel_size=5, activation='tanh'))
model.add(MaxPooling1D(pool_size=2))
model.add(Flatten())
model.add(Dense(1))
model.compile(optimizer='adam', loss='mse')
model.fit(X_train, y_train, epochs=25, batch_size = 25)
```

The given code defines and trains a 1DCNN using Keras. The model is structured sequentially and consists of two convolutional layers, each with 64 filters and a tanh activation function. A max-pooling layer is incorporated to reduce dimensionality, and the data is then flattened before being fed into a dense layer with a single unit suitable for a regression task. The model uses Adam as the optimizer and MSE as the loss function. Training is conducted on the dataset (X_train, y_train) for 25 epochs with a batch size of 25.

A kernel, a filter, is a collection of trainable parameters employed to extract features from the input data. The kernel operates as a small-weighted window that moves across the input data. At each placement, it executes a dot product operation with the input values within its scope, resulting in a single output value. The dimensions of the kernel dictate the receptive field of the convolution operation, which represents the quantity of input values assessed at each point. For instance, a kernel size of 3 implies the convolution operation contemplates three input values at a time.

The network comprises several layers: convolutional, pooling, and fully connected. The convolutional layers apply filters to the input data in a 1DCNN to distill local features, resulting in a feature map. Following this, the pooling layers downsample this feature map to decrease the data's dimensions, thereby reducing the network's computational complexity. Pooling plays a significant role in 1DCNNs, enabling the network to understand spatial hierarchies, emphasize the most relevant features, and reduce data dimensionality. Furthermore, pooling aids in mitigating overfitting and enhancing network performance. Typically, pooling is utilized after one or several convolutional layers to summarize their outputs and extract the most salient features from the data.

Three primary pooling techniques can be implemented in 1DCNN: max pooling, average pooling, and sum pooling. Max pooling selects the highest value from a set of contiguous input values as the output, thus lowering data dimensionality while retaining only the most critical values. Average pooling computes the mean of a group of neighboring input values to produce the output, thereby reducing data dimensionality by evening out the values and eliminating noise. Sum pooling generates the output by summing up a cluster of adjacent input values, thus decreasing the data's dimensionality by accentuating the total magnitude of the values. Ultimately, the fully-connected layers fuse the features extracted by the convolutional and pooling layers to deliver a final prediction.

1DCNNs are typically proficient at processing sequential data like time series, as they can capture local patterns and short-term dependencies. However, to enhance the capability of identifying more complex sequence patterns, a multilayer structure of CNNs is employed. Here, two 1DCNNs are stacked together, each layer discerning progressively complex features, including long-term dependencies.

Setting the kernel size to 5 in the 1DCNN aids in recognizing longer-term patterns in the input sequence. Using 64 filters in each layer further contributes to identifying complex patterns and long-term dependencies. Filters play a crucial role in detecting patterns relevant to predicting the target output, and they propagate this information across various network layers. As the input sequence interacts with the filters in the 1DCNN, each filter detects a particular feature or pattern. Filters designed to identify long-term dependencies can recognize patterns spread across multiple time steps in the sequence. By processing the input sequence with these filters, the 1DCNN can recognize these long-term dependencies, leading to more accurate predictions.

The tanh activation function incorporates nonlinearity in the network and manages the information flow through memory cells. A max-pooling size of 2 is implemented to decrease the network's parameters by diminishing the spatial dimensionality of the feature maps, the outputs of the convolutional layers. This makes the network more computationally efficient and reduces overfitting.

The flatten function is used before passing the feature maps to the fully connected layers, which expect one-dimensional input. By transforming the feature maps into a one-dimensional vector, the network is enabled to perform high-level classification or regression tasks based on the extracted features. Lastly, Adam optimizer enhances the network's convergence speed and generalization ability. The complete code for the implementation is provided below.

```python
import numpy as np
import pandas as pd
import os
import math
import matplotlib.pyplot as plt
from datetime import datetime
from sklearn.preprocessing import MinMaxScaler
from sklearn.model_selection import train_test_split
import tensorflow as tf
from tensorflow.keras.callbacks import ModelCheckpoint, EarlyStopping
from keras.losses import mean_squared_error
from tensorflow.keras.models import Sequential
from tensorflow.keras.layers import Conv1D, Dense, MaxPooling1D, Flatten, Dropout


ticker = 'HSTM'
df = pd.read_csv(ticker + '.csv')


datetime_series = pd.to_datetime(df['Date'])
datetime_index = pd.DatetimeIndex(datetime_series.values)
df = df.set_index(datetime_index)
df = df.sort_values(by='Date')
df = df.drop(columns='Date')


X_value = pd.DataFrame(df.iloc[:, 0:4])
y_value = pd.DataFrame(df.iloc[:, 3])
```

```
X_scaler = MinMaxScaler(feature_range=(0, 1))
y_scaler = MinMaxScaler(feature_range=(0, 1))
X_scaler.fit(X_value)
y_scaler.fit(y_value)


X_scale_dataset = X_scaler.fit_transform(X_value)
y_scale_dataset = y_scaler.fit_transform(y_value)
y_scale_dataset_inv = y_scaler.inverse_transform(y_scale_dataset)


n_steps_in = 10
n_features = X_value.shape[1]
n_steps_out = 1


X = []
y = []


length = len(X_scale_dataset)
for i in range(0, length, 1):
X_val = X_scale_dataset[i: i + n_steps_in][:, :]
y_val = y_scale_dataset[i + n_steps_in: i + (n_steps_in + n_steps_out)][:, 0]
if len(X_val) == n_steps_in and len(y_val) == n_steps_out:
X.append(X_val)
y.append(y_val)


X = np.array(X)
y = np.array(y)


def train_test_split(data):
train_size = round(len(data) * 0.8)
data_train = data[0:train_size]
```

```
data_test = data[train_size:]
return data_train, data_test


X_train, X_test = train_test_split(X)
y_train, y_test = train_test_split(y)


input_dim = X_train.shape[1]
feature_size = X_train.shape[2]
output_dim = y_train.shape[1]


model = Sequential()
model.add(Conv1D(filters=64, kernel_size=5, activation='tanh', input_shape = (input_dim,feature_size)))
model.add(Conv1D(filters=64, kernel_size=5, activation='tanh'))
model.add(MaxPooling1D(pool_size=2))
model.add(Flatten())
model.add(Dense(1))
model.compile(optimizer='adam', loss='mse')
model.fit(X_train, y_train, epochs=25, batch_size = 25)


yhat = model.predict(X_test, verbose=0)


actual_prices = y_scaler.inverse_transform(y_test)
predicted_prices = y_scaler.inverse_transform(yhat)


mse = tf.keras.losses.mean_squared_error(actual_prices[:,0], predicted_prices[:,0]).numpy()
rmse = math.sqrt(mse)
print('RMSE', rmse)
mape = tf.keras.losses.mean_absolute_percentage_error(actual_prices[:,0], predicted_prices[:,0]).numpy()
```

```
print('MAPE', mape)


plt.plot(actual_prices, color='green', label=f"Actual {ticker} price")

plt.plot(predicted_prices, color= 'red', label=f"predicted {ticker} price")

plt.title(f"{ticker} Stock Prices–- Actual Vs. Predicted")

plt.xlabel("time")

plt.ylabel(f"{ticker} Stock Price")

plt.legend()

plt.show()
```

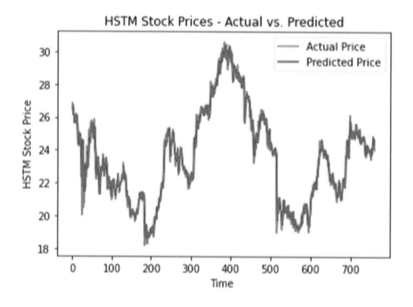

Figure 17: Actual Time Series and 1DCNN-Predicted Time Series
for the HSTM Stock.

The chart above compares the actual time series from the test set and predicted time series. The model produced an RMSE of 0.55. Since the RMSE is a relative measure of the underlying values, the MAPE is best suited to interpret the model's accuracy. The model produced a MAPE of 1.65, indicating there is a 1.65 percent of error in prediction. The lower MAPE indicates the 1DCNN is capable of forecasting the stock prices when the time series data exhibits complex patterns mentioned earlier.

## 12.4 1DCNN-LSTM

As previously noted, convolutional layers can extract valuable insights and learn the internal representation of time series data. LSTM networks excel at recognizing short- and long-term dependencies. A combination of CNN and LSTM can amalgamate the strengths of both these systems. This joint architecture consists of two components. The convolutional layers conduct mathematical operations to generate features from the input data. Specifically, these layers yield new feature values by performing a convolution operation between the raw input data and convolution kernels. In a CNN-LSTM structure, the output of the 1DCNN is fed into the LSTM. A nonlinear activation function and pooling layer are utilized following the convolutional layers. This implies the activation function is applied to the outputs of the CNN and LSTM layers. The pooling layer, a subsampling technique, extracts specific values from the convolved features, resulting in a matrix with reduced dimensions. This new matrix can be viewed as a summarization of the convolved features generated by the convolutional layer.

In a CNN-LSTM hybrid architecture, the convolutional layers typically serve the role of feature extraction from the input data. Subsequently, the LSTM layers are utilized to learn the data's temporal dependencies, capturing long-term dependencies. The network's final layers, usually fully connected, make the ultimate predictions based on the output of the LSTM layers.

Although 1DCNNs are proficient in processing data sequences, such as time series, and identifying short-term dependencies within a sequence, they fail to capture long-term dependencies. To tackle this limitation, in contrast to the 1DCNN model where stacked 1DCNN layers were used, an LSTM is introduced as the second layer in the 1DCNN-LSTM model precisely to capture these long-term dependencies. The fusion of 1DCNN and LSTM boosts accuracy and generalization, harnessing the strengths of both architectures.

Let us explore the 1DCNN-LSTM to forecast the stock prices for the YORW ticker. The figure below visualizes the time series data for the YORW stock from January 2, 2008, to February 10, 2023.

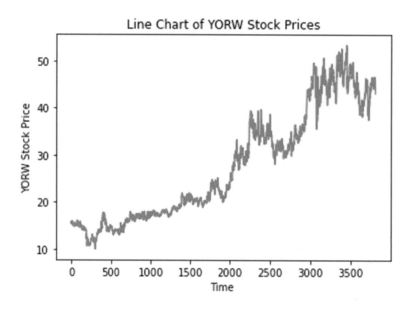

Figure 18: Actual Time Series of the Combined Training Set
and Test Set for the YORW Stock.

The statistical measures are generated to assess the complexity of the above time series data. Listed below are detailed descriptions of the statistical measures for the YORW ticker:

- ADF p-value (0.81) refers to the p-value obtained from the ADF test. The ADF test is a statistical procedure used to determine whether a time series is stationary or not. A high p-value 0.81 (>0.05) suggests the null hypothesis of the ADF test (the time series is nonstationary) cannot be rejected. In this case, a p-value of 0.81 indicates the YORW time series data is nonstationary, suggesting it has some time-dependent structure.

- DFA Hurst exponent (1.39): The Hurst exponent is a statistical measure that classifies time series data. The time series is considered mean-reverting if the Hurst exponent is less than 0.5. If it is 0.5, the time series is a geometric Brownian motion (a random walk). If it is greater than 0.5, the time series is trending or persistent. A Hurst exponent of 1.39 indicates the YORW time series data is highly persistent or trending, indicating long-term memory or dependency.

- Lyapunov exponent (0.0029): The Lyapunov exponent measures the rate of separation of infinitesimally close trajectories, a key quantity to understanding the chaotic dynamics in a system. A positive Lyapunov exponent typically indicates chaos. In this case, a value close to zero (0.0029) suggests the time series data is chaotic though with lesser severity and small changes will lead to significantly different trajectories. In other words, the time series data of YORW stock exhibits nonlinearity.

- Skewness (0.45): Skewness measures the asymmetry of the probability distribution of a real-valued random variable about its mean. A positive skewness value indicates the tail on the probability density function's right side (positive side) is longer or fatter than the left side. A skewness of 0.45 for the YORW time series data suggests a positively skewed distribution, indicating relatively more unusually high values than low ones.
- Stochasticity: An entropy value of 7.39 was computed for the time series data of YORW, a figure exceeding 90 percent of the maximum possible entropy. This maximum entropy was determined as the logarithm of the number of unique elements within the time series data, that is, log(len(np.unique(time_series_data))). The resulting entropy reveals the time series is highly unpredictable, likely indicating a high degree of stochasticity.

The 1DCNN-LSTM-based time series model has been implemented to forecast the stock prices for the YORW, exhibiting the complex patterns described above. The complete code for implementing the 1DCNN-LSTM model to predict stock prices is demonstrated momentarily in this section. However, the snippet below is part of the entire code set. The code provided serves as a guide to constructing and training a 1DCNN-LSTM-based deep learning model, which is used for predicting stock prices.

```
model = Sequential()
model.add(Conv1D(filters=32, kernel_size=5, activation='tanh', input_shape = (input_dim, feature_size)))
model.add(LSTM(units=512, activation='tanh'))
model.add(Dense(1))
model.compile(optimizer='adam', loss='mse')
model.fit(X_train, y_train, epochs=25, batch_size = 25)
```

This code defines and trains a sequential model in Keras that combines a 1DCNN and LSTM layer. First, a 1DCNN layer with 32 filters, a kernel size of 5, and a hyperbolic tangent (tanh) activation function is added. This layer will extract features from the input data, which is assumed to have a shape defined by the variables input_dim and feature_size. Next, an LSTM layer with 512 units and a tanh activation function is added. This layer will learn the temporal dependencies in the data, capturing both short- and long-term dependencies. Then, a dense layer with a single unit is added to produce the network's final output, which suggests it is a regression problem. The model is then compiled with the Adam optimizer and MSE as the loss function, indicating a regression task. Finally, the model is fitted to the training data (X_train and y_train) over 25 epochs with a batch size of 25. The number of epochs is the number of times the learning algorithm will work through the entire training dataset. The batch size is a subset of the training dataset that the model uses to compute the error gradient during training.

This methodology has adjusted the 1DCNN layer to utilize 32 filters instead of the previously used 64. A kernel size of 5 is retained to recognize intricate patterns within the input sequence. To manage the transfer of information through the network's memory cells and introduce an element of nonlinearity, the hyperbolic tangent (tanh) function is utilized as the activation function. The LSTM layer of the model contains 512 memory units. Each of these memory units functions as an independent processing entity, capable of maintaining information over time and updating its internal state based on inputs and outputs from other cells within the network. The total number of these units impacts the model's capacity and complexity. While increasing the number of units can enhance the model's capability to learn complex patterns in the data, it could also raise the risk of overfitting. Overfitting occurs when the model becomes too attuned to the training data, limiting its ability to generalize to new and unseen data effectively. After several trials, 64 was the optimal number of units. The optimizer used in the model, Adam, aids in accelerating the speed of convergence while enhancing the ability of the model to generalize. The complete code is provided below.

```
import numpy as np
import pandas as pd
import os
import math
import matplotlib.pyplot as plt
from datetime import datetime
from sklearn.preprocessing import MinMaxScaler
from sklearn.model_selection import train_test_split
import tensorflow as tf
```

```python
from tensorflow.keras.callbacks import ModelCheckpoint, EarlyStopping
from keras.losses import mean_squared_error
from tensorflow.keras.models import Sequential
from tensorflow.keras.layers import LSTM, Conv1D, Dense, MaxPooling1D, Flatten, Dropout


ticker = 'YORW'
df = pd.read_csv(ticker + '.csv')


datetime_series = pd.to_datetime(df['Date'])
datetime_index = pd.DatetimeIndex(datetime_series.values)
df = df.set_index(datetime_index)
df = df.sort_values(by='Date')
df = df.drop(columns='Date')


X_value = pd.DataFrame(df.iloc[:, 0:4])
y_value = pd.DataFrame(df.iloc[:, 3])


X_scaler = MinMaxScaler(feature_range=(0, 1))
y_scaler = MinMaxScaler(feature_range=(0, 1))
X_scaler.fit(X_value)
y_scaler.fit(y_value)


X_scale_dataset = X_scaler.fit_transform(X_value)
y_scale_dataset = y_scaler.fit_transform(y_value)
y_scale_dataset_inv = y_scaler.inverse_transform(y_scale_dataset)


n_steps_in = 10
n_features = X_value.shape[1]
n_steps_out = 1
```

```python
X = []
y = []


length = len(X_scale_dataset)
for i in range(0, length, 1):
X_val = X_scale_dataset[i: i + n_steps_in][:, :]
y_val = y_scale_dataset[i + n_steps_in: i + (n_steps_in + n_steps_out)][:, 0]
if len(X_val) == n_steps_in and len(y_val) == n_steps_out:
X.append(X_val)
y.append(y_val)


X = np.array(X)
y = np.array(y)


def train_test_split(data):
train_size = round(len(data) * 0.8)
data_train = data[0:train_size]
data_test = data[train_size:]
return data_train, data_test


X_train, X_test = train_test_split(X)
y_train, y_test = train_test_split(y)


input_dim = X_train.shape[1]
feature_size = X_train.shape[2]
output_dim = y_train.shape[1]


model = Sequential()
model.add(Conv1D(filters=32, kernel_size=5, activation='tanh', input_shape = (input_dim,
feature_size)))
```

```
model.add(LSTM(units=512, activation='tanh'))
model.add(Dense(1))
model.compile(optimizer='adam', loss='mse')
model.fit(X_train, y_train, epochs=25, batch_size = 25)


yhat = model.predict(X_test, verbose=0)


actual_prices = y_scaler.inverse_transform(y_test)
predicted_prices = y_scaler.inverse_transform(yhat)


rmse = math.sqrt(tf.keras.losses.mean_squared_error(actual_prices[:,0], predicted_prices[:,0]).
numpy())
print('RMSE', rmse)
mape = tf.keras.losses.mean_absolute_percentage_error(actual_prices[:,0], predicted_
prices[:,0]).numpy()
print('MAPE', mape)


plt.plot(actual_prices, color='green', label=f"Actual {ticker} price")
plt.plot(predicted_prices, color= 'red', label=f"predicted {ticker} price")
plt.title(f"{ticker} Stock Prices–- Actual Vs. Predicted")
plt.xlabel("time")
plt.ylabel(f"{ticker} Stock Price")
plt.legend()
plt.show()
```

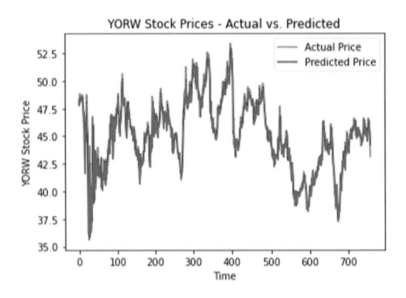

Figure 19: Actual Time Series and 1DCNN-LSTM Predicted Time Series
for the YORW Stock.

The chart above compares the actual time series from the test set and predicted time series. The model produced an RMSE of 1.03. Since the RMSE is a relative measure of the underlying values, the MAPE is best suitable to interpret the model's accuracy. The model produced a MAPE of 1.58, indicating there is a 1.58 percent of error in prediction. The lower MAPE indicates the 1DCNN-LSTM is capable of forecasting the stock prices when the time series data exhibits complex patterns mentioned earlier.

## 12.5   1DCNN-BiLSTM

The 1DConvolutional Bidirectional Long Short-Term Memory (1DCNN-BiLSTM) networks amalgamate the advantages of both CNNs and BiLSTM networks, forming a hybrid deep learning architecture. Primarily designed for processing sequential data, such as time series or textual data, 1DCNN-BiLSTM networks find their applications in a variety of tasks like speech recognition, NLP, and medical diagnosis. In a 1DCNN-BiLSTM network, the process starts with the input sequence being transmitted through a 1D convolutional layer. This layer utilizes filters to extract pertinent features from the input sequence. The subsequent feature maps are then directed to a BiLSTM layer that deals with these maps in both forward and backward directions to encapsulate temporal dependencies.

Throughout the training phase, the weights associated with the 1D convolutional and BiLSTM layers undergo modifications using backpropagation. In the inference phase, predictions are made based on the output of the BiLSTM layer. The 1DCNN-BiLSTM architecture has multiple benefits. First, it allows the 1D convolutional layer to learn local patterns within the input sequence, which can augment the network's performance. Second, by capturing both past and future contexts through the BiLSTM layer, the network gains a comprehensive understanding of the input sequence. Lastly, this hybrid architecture can decrease the parameter count within the network, contributing to improved computational efficiency.

Let us explore the 1DCNN-BiLSTM to forecast the stock prices for the TRV ticker. The figure below visualizes the time series data for the TRV stock from January 2, 2008, to February 10, 2023.

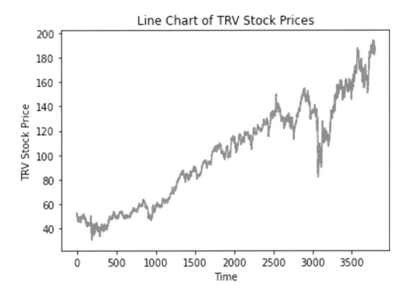

Figure 20: Actual Time Series of the Combined Training Set
and Test Set for the TRV Stock.

The statistical measures are generated to assess the complexity of the above time series data. Listed below are detailed descriptions of the statistical measures for the TRV ticker:

- ADF p-value (0.92) refers to the p-value obtained from the ADF test. The ADF test is a statistical procedure used to determine whether a time series is stationary or not. A high p-value 0.92 (>0.05) suggests the null hypothesis of the ADF test (the time series is

197

nonstationary) cannot be rejected. In this case, a p-value of 0.92 indicates the TRV time series data is nonstationary, suggesting it has some time-dependent structure.

- DFA Hurst Exponent (1.47): The Hurst exponent is a statistical measure that classifies time series data. The time series is considered mean-reverting if the Hurst exponent is less than 0.5. If it is 0.5, the time series is a geometric Brownian motion (a random walk). If it is greater than 0.5, the time series is trending or persistent. A Hurst exponent of 1.47 indicates the TRV time series data is highly persistent or trending, indicating long-term memory or dependency.

- Lyapunov exponent (0.0019): The Lyapunov exponent measures the rate of separation of infinitesimally close trajectories, a key quantity to understanding the chaotic dynamics in a system. A positive Lyapunov exponent typically indicates chaos. In this case, a value close to zero (0.0019) suggests the time series data is chaotic though with lesser severity and small changes will lead to significantly different trajectories. In other words, the time series data of TRV stock exhibits nonlinearity.

- Skewness (0.14): Skewness measures the asymmetry of the probability distribution of a real-valued random variable about its mean. A positive skewness value indicates the tail on the probability density function's right side (positive side) is longer or fatter than the left side. A skewness of 0.14 for the TRV time series data suggests a positively skewed distribution, indicating relatively more unusually high values than low ones.

- Stochasticity: An entropy value of 8.01 was computed for the time series data of TRV, a figure exceeding 90 percent of the maximum possible entropy. This maximum entropy was determined as the logarithm of the number of unique elements within the time series data, that is, log(len(np.unique(time_series_data))). The resulting entropy reveals the time series is highly unpredictable, likely indicating a high degree of stochasticity.

The 1DCNN-BiLSTM-based time series model has been implemented to forecast the stock prices for the TRV stock, which exhibits the complex patterns as described above. The complete code for implementing the 1DCNN-BiLSTM model to predict stock prices is demonstrated momentarily in this section. However, the snippet provided below is just a part of the entire code set. The code provided serves as a guide to constructing and training an 1DCNN-BiLSTM-based deep learning model, which is used for predicting stock prices.

```
model = Sequential()
model.add(Conv1D(filters=32, kernel_size=5, activation='tanh', input_shape = (input_dim,
feature_size)))
model.add(Bidirectional(LSTM(units=512, activation='tanh')))
model.add(Dense(1))
model.compile(optimizer='adam', loss='mse')
model.fit(X_train, y_train, epochs=25, batch_size = 25)
```

The provided code represents the creation, compilation, and training of a 1D Convolutional Bidirectional Long Short-Term Memory (1D Conv-BiLSTM) neural network model. The model is initiated with a Conv1D layer having 32 filters, each with a kernel size of 5 and utilizing a tanh activation function. This convolutional layer is designed to extract relevant features from the input data, specified by input_dim and feature_size. Next, a bidirectional LSTM layer is added with 512 memory units, again using the tanh activation function. The bidirectionality of this layer allows the model to understand the context from both past and future data points. The network concludes with a dense layer with a single output unit, which serves to make final predictions based on the processed data. The model is compiled with the Adam optimization algorithm and MSE as the loss function, indicating the model is likely dealing with a regression task. Finally, the model is trained on the provided training data (X_train, y_train) for 25 epochs with a batch size of 25, optimizing the weights of the model to minimize the loss over these iterations.

While 1DCNNs are efficient at analyzing sequential data like time series and identifying short-term relationships within the data, they struggle to capture long-term dependencies. To address this limitation, the 1DCNN-BiLSTM model is introduced, similar to the 1DCNN-LSTM model, but uses BiLSTM instead to account for long-term relationships in the data. The fusion of 1DCNN and BiLSTM enhances the model's overall accuracy and generalization capabilities.

```
import numpy as np
import pandas as pd
import os
import math
```

```python
import matplotlib.pyplot as plt
from datetime import datetime
import pandas_datareader.data as web
from sklearn.preprocessing import MinMaxScaler
from sklearn.model_selection import train_test_split
import tensorflow as tf
from tensorflow.keras.callbacks import ModelCheckpoint, EarlyStopping
from keras.losses import mean_squared_error
from tensorflow.keras.models import Sequential
from tensorflow.keras.layers import LSTM, Conv1D, Dense, MaxPooling1D, Flatten, Dropout,
Bidirectional


ticker = 'TRV'
df = pd.read_csv(ticker + '.csv')


datetime_series = pd.to_datetime(df['Date'])
datetime_index = pd.DatetimeIndex(datetime_series.values)
df = df.set_index(datetime_index)
df = df.sort_values(by='Date')
df = df.drop(columns='Date')


X_value = pd.DataFrame(df.iloc[:, 0:4])
y_value = pd.DataFrame(df.iloc[:, 3])


X_scaler = MinMaxScaler(feature_range=(0, 1))
y_scaler = MinMaxScaler(feature_range=(0, 1))
X_scaler.fit(X_value)
y_scaler.fit(y_value)
```

```python
X_scale_dataset = X_scaler.fit_transform(X_value)
y_scale_dataset = y_scaler.fit_transform(y_value)
y_scale_dataset_inv = y_scaler.inverse_transform(y_scale_dataset)


n_steps_in = 10
n_features = X_value.shape[1]
n_steps_out = 1


X = []
y = []


length = len(X_scale_dataset)
for i in range(0, length, 1):
X_val = X_scale_dataset[i: i + n_steps_in][:, :]
y_val = y_scale_dataset[i + n_steps_in: i + (n_steps_in + n_steps_out)][:, 0]
if len(X_val) == n_steps_in and len(y_val) == n_steps_out:
X.append(X_val)
y.append(y_val)


X = np.array(X)
y = np.array(y)


def train_test_split(data):
train_size = round(len(data) * 0.8)
data_train = data[0:train_size]
data_test = data[train_size:]
return data_train, data_test


X_train, X_test = train_test_split(X)
y_train, y_test = train_test_split(y)
```

```python
input_dim = X_train.shape[1]
feature_size = X_train.shape[2]
output_dim = y_train.shape[1]


model = Sequential()
model.add(Conv1D(filters=32, kernel_size=5, activation='tanh', input_shape = (input_dim,
feature_size)))
model.add(Bidirectional(LSTM(units=512, activation='tanh')))
model.add(Dense(1))


model.compile(optimizer='adam', loss='mse')


model.fit(X_train, y_train, epochs=25, batch_size = 25)


yhat = model.predict(X_test, verbose=0)


actual_prices = y_scaler.inverse_transform(y_test)
predicted_prices = y_scaler.inverse_transform(yhat)


rmse = math.sqrt(tf.keras.losses.mean_squared_error(actual_prices[:,0], predicted_prices[:,0]).
numpy())
print('RMSE', rmse)
mape = tf.keras.losses.mean_absolute_percentage_error(actual_prices[:,0], predicted_
prices[:,0]).numpy()
print('MAPE', mape)


plt.plot(actual_prices, color='green', label=f"Actual {ticker} price")
plt.plot(predicted_prices, color= 'red', label=f"predicted {ticker} price")
plt.title(f"{ticker} Stock Prices-- Actual Vs. Predicted")
plt.xlabel("time")
```

```
plt.ylabel(f"{ticker} Stock Price")
plt.legend()
plt.show()
```

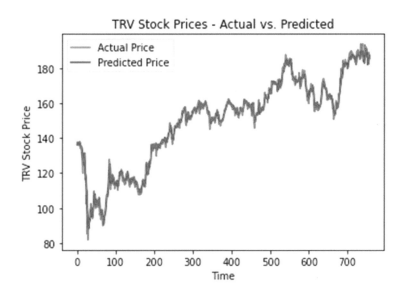

Figure 21: Actual Time Series and 1DCNN-BiLSTM-Predicted Time Series
for the TRV Stock.

The chart above shows the comparison of actual time series from the test set and predicted time series. The model produced RMSE of 3.09. Since the RMSE is a relative measure to the underlying values, the MAPE is best suited to interpret the accuracy of the model. The model produced MAPE of 1.61, indicating there is 1.61 percent of error in prediction. The lower MAPE indicates the 1DCNN-BiLSTM is capable of forecasting the stock prices when the time series data exhibits complex patterns mentioned earlier.

## 12.6   Gated Recurrent Unit (GRU)

GRU networks represent a type of RNN, initially developed as a streamlined alternative to the comparatively intricate LSTM networks. Both GRUs and LSTMs were conceived to counteract the vanishing gradient problem that often surfaces in conventional RNNs. Within a GRU network, each unit features a gating mechanism that governs the information flow within the unit. This mechanism comprises two distinct gates: an update gate and a reset gate. The update gate ascertains the degree to which the previous state is retained, whereas the reset gate establishes the extent to which new input should be incorporated into the current state. Throughout the training phase, the weights within the GRU network undergo adjustments via backpropagation through time. In the inference stage, the network can anticipate the next element in a sequence or generate fresh sequences based on a learned distribution.

GRU networks have several advantages over traditional RNNs and LSTMs. First, they are computationally more efficient, with fewer parameters than LSTMs. Second, they can be trained more efficiently, with fewer gates to tune. GRUs have been shown to perform well on various sequence modeling tasks related to heart sound analysis.

Let us explore the GRU to forecast the stock prices for the NI ticker. The figure below visualizes the time series data for the stock NI from January 2, 2008, to February 10, 2023.

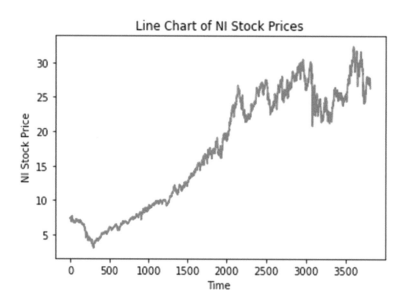

Figure 22: Actual Time Series of the Combined Training Set
and Test Set for the NI Stock.

The statistical measures are generated to assess the complexity of the above time series data. Listed below are detailed descriptions of the statistical measures for the ticker NI:

- ADF p-value (0.78) refers to the p-value obtained from the ADF test. The ADF test is a statistical procedure used to determine whether a time series is stationary or not. A high p-value (> 0.05) suggests the null hypothesis of the ADF test (the time series is nonstationary) cannot be rejected. In this case, a p-value of 0.78 indicates the NI time series data is likely nonstationary, suggesting it has some time-dependent structure.

- DFA Hurst exponent (1.48): The Hurst exponent is a statistical measure that classifies time series data. The time series is considered mean-reverting if the Hurst exponent is less than 0.5. If it is 0.5, the time series is a geometric Brownian motion (a random walk). If it is greater than 0.5, the time series is trending or persistent. A Hurst exponent of 1.48 indicates the NI time series data is highly persistent or trending revealing long-term memory or dependency.

- Lyapunov exponent (0.00049): The Lyapunov exponent measures the rate of separation of infinitesimally close trajectories, a key quantity to understanding the chaotic dynamics in a system. A positive Lyapunov exponent typically indicates chaos. In this case, a value of 0.00049 suggests the time series data is chaotic and small changes will lead to significantly different trajectories. In other words, the time series data of NI stock exhibits nonlinearity.

- Skewness (-0.1): Skewness measures the asymmetry of the probability distribution of a real-valued random variable about its mean. A negative skewness value indicates the tail on the probability density function's left side (negative side) is longer or fatter than the right side. A skewness of -0.1 for the NI time series data suggests a negatively skewed distribution, indicating relatively more unusually low values than high ones.

- Stochasticity: An entropy value of 7.57 was computed for the time series data of NI, a figure exceeding 90 percent of the maximum possible entropy. This maximum entropy was determined as the logarithm of the number of unique elements within the time series data, that is, log(len(np.unique(time_series_data))). The resulting entropy reveals the time series is highly unpredictable, likely indicating a high degree of stochasticity.

The GRU-based time series model has been implemented to forecast the stock prices for the NI stock, which exhibits the complex patterns as described above. The complete code for implementing the GRU model to predict stock prices is demonstrated momentarily in this section. However, the snippet provided below is just a part of the entire code set. The code provided serves as a guide to constructing and training an GRU-based deep learning model, which is used for predicting stock prices.

```
model = Sequential()
model.add(GRU(units=1024, activation = 'tanh', input_shape=(input_dim, feature_size)))
```

```
model.add(Dense(512))
model.add(Dense(256))
model.add(Dense(128))
model.add(Dense(64))
model.add(Dense(units=output_dim))
model.compile(optimizer='adam', loss='mse')
model.fit(X_train, y_train, epochs=25, batch_size = 25)
```

The provided code outlines the creation and training of a sequential machine learning model using the Keras library. The model comprises a GRU layer with 1024 units as its first layer, followed by several dense layers of decreasing units (512, 256, 128, and 64). The final dense layer's units correspond to the output dimension of the prediction. The tanh activation function is specified for the GRU layer, while a linear activation is implied for the dense layers. The model is compiled using the Adam optimizer and MSE loss function, suggesting it is intended for a regression problem. Finally, the model is trained over 25 epochs with a batch size of 25 on the given training data.

The architecture of the GRU model is crafted with one input layer and five subsequent layers, which can be considered as hidden or output layers depending on the context. The input layer is equipped with 1024 units and utilizes the tanh activation function. The first layer following the input consists of 512 units, and this quantity progressively diminishes until it reaches a singular unit in the final layer. The abundant number of memory cells and layers contribute to heightened accuracy and model generalization. The weight optimization during training is facilitated by the Adam method. Additionally, the employment of the MSE as a loss function enables the model to minimize the total squared deviation between the predicted outcomes and actual values, hence boosting prediction accuracy.

```
import numpy as np
import pandas as pd
import os
import math
import matplotlib.pyplot as plt
```

```python
from datetime import datetime
import pandas_datareader.data as web
from sklearn.preprocessing import MinMaxScaler
from sklearn.model_selection import train_test_split
import tensorflow as tf
from tensorflow.keras.callbacks import ModelCheckpoint, EarlyStopping
from keras.losses import mean_squared_error
from tensorflow.keras.models import Sequential
from tensorflow.keras.layers import GRU, Dense, Dropout


ticker = 'NI'
df = pd.read_csv(ticker + '.csv')


datetime_series = pd.to_datetime(df['Date'])
datetime_index = pd.DatetimeIndex(datetime_series.values)
df = df.set_index(datetime_index)
df = df.sort_values(by='Date')
df = df.drop(columns='Date')


X_value = pd.DataFrame(df.iloc[:, 0:4])
y_value = pd.DataFrame(df.iloc[:, 3])


X_scaler = MinMaxScaler(feature_range=(0, 1))
y_scaler = MinMaxScaler(feature_range=(0, 1))
X_scaler.fit(X_value)
y_scaler.fit(y_value)


X_scale_dataset = X_scaler.fit_transform(X_value)
y_scale_dataset = y_scaler.fit_transform(y_value)
y_scale_dataset_inv = y_scaler.inverse_transform(y_scale_dataset)
```

```python
n_steps_in = 10
n_features = X_value.shape[1]
n_steps_out = 1


X = []
y = []


length = len(X_scale_dataset)
for i in range(0, length, 1):
X_val = X_scale_dataset[i: i + n_steps_in][:, :]
y_val = y_scale_dataset[i + n_steps_in: i + (n_steps_in + n_steps_out)][:, 0]
if len(X_val) == n_steps_in and len(y_val) == n_steps_out:
X.append(X_val)
y.append(y_val)


X = np.array(X)
y = np.array(y)


def train_test_split(data):
train_size = round(len(data) * 0.8)
data_train = data[0:train_size]
data_test = data[train_size:]
return data_train, data_test


X_train, X_test = train_test_split(X)
y_train, y_test = train_test_split(y)


input_dim = X_train.shape[1]
feature_size = X_train.shape[2]
output_dim = y_train.shape[1]
```

```
model = Sequential()
model.add(GRU(units=1024, activation = 'tanh', input_shape=(input_dim, feature_size)))
model.add(Dense(512))
model.add(Dense(256))
model.add(Dense(128))
model.add(Dense(64))
model.add(Dense(units=output_dim))


model.compile(optimizer='adam', loss='mse')


model.fit(X_train, y_train, epochs=25, batch_size = 25)


yhat = model.predict(X_test, verbose=0)


actual_prices = y_scaler.inverse_transform(y_test)
predicted_prices = y_scaler.inverse_transform(yhat)


mse = tf.keras.losses.mean_squared_error(actual_prices[:,0], predicted_prices[:,0]).numpy()
rmse = math.sqrt(mse)
print('RMSE', rmse)
mape = tf.keras.losses.mean_absolute_percentage_error(actual_prices[:,0], predicted_prices[:,0]).numpy()
print('MAPE', mape)


plt.plot(actual_prices, color='green', label=f"Actual {ticker} price")
plt.plot(predicted_prices, color= 'red', label=f"predicted {ticker} price")
plt.title(f"{ticker} Stock Prices-- Actual Vs. Predicted")
plt.xlabel("time")
plt.ylabel(f"{ticker} Stock Price")
plt.legend()
plt.show()
```

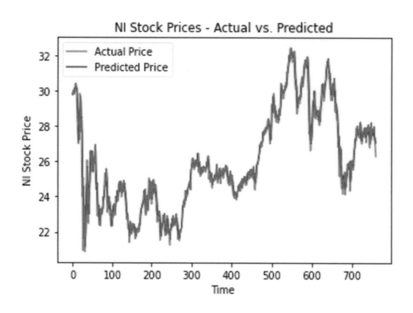

Figure 23: Actual Time Series and GRU-Predicted Time Series for the NI Stock.

The chart above compares the actual time series from the test set and predicted time series. The model produced an RMSE of 0.54. Since the RMSE is a relative measure of the underlying values, the MAPE is best suited to interpret the model's accuracy. The model produced a MAPE of 1.44, indicating there is a 1.44 percent of error in prediction. The lower MAPE indicates the GRU is capable of forecasting the stock prices when the time series data exhibits complex patterns mentioned earlier.

## 12.7 Generative Adversarial Network (GAN)

Generative adversarial networks (GANs) are rooted in game theory, involving two interacting neural networks: the generator and the discriminator. GANs stand as a fundamental cornerstone of generative AI due to their innovative design and functionality. In this model, the generator network is responsible for creating new examples, drawing from an estimated probability distribution. Its goal is to produce data resembling the training set as closely as possible, effectively learning and imitating the probability distribution of the training data. Conversely, the discriminator network acts as an evaluator of the generator's output. It reviews samples and estimates their authenticity, determining whether they are real or fake. If a sample is deemed real, it indicates the sample aligns closely with the training distribution. Conversely, a fake label suggests the sample is a product of the generator's model, deviating from the training set distribution.

In the context of time series, the generator's task is to produce synthetic time series data that are as close as possible to the real ones. The generator could be designed using architectures like RNNs, LSTMs, or GRUs, which are particularly suited for handling sequential data due to their ability to capture long-term dependencies. For example, a generator could be an LSTM network that takes a random noise vector as input and generates a sequence as output. The discriminator has the task of distinguishing between real and synthetic time series data. Similar to the generator, the discriminator can also be implemented using RNN, LSTM, or GRU architectures, taking a sequence as input and outputting a single value representing the probability that the input sequence is real.

Training a GAN for time series data would involve feeding sequences of real and synthetic data (generated by the generator) into the discriminator. The generator and discriminator are trained together in a minimax game: the generator tries to fool the discriminator by generating synthetic data that looks as much as possible like the real time series data, while the discriminator tries to correctly classify the input sequences as real or synthetic. Through this iterative process, the generator becomes increasingly proficient at producing realistic time series data. This can be used, for example, to fill in missing data points or forecast future points in a time series, assuming the generator has correctly learned the underlying temporal dynamics of the data.

In this adversarial setup, both the generator and discriminator networks constantly learn and evolve. The generator endeavors to produce data that becomes progressively more convincing, while the discriminator refines its capability to discern between genuine and synthetic samples. Both the generator and discriminator undergo simultaneous training, with the generator working to create data that can deceive the discriminator, and the discriminator striving to precisely segregate real from counterfeit data. The ultimate objective of a GAN is to generate data that is virtually identical to the real data, and this technology has found extensive applications across diverse areas such as generating images, text, and audio. The generator employs techniques such as upsampling and convolution to fabricate complex data, making it increasingly challenging for the discriminator to label it as counterfeit. This mutual evolution enhances their performance over time, enabling the GAN to produce top-quality synthetic data, nearly indistinguishable from the real ones. Both the generator and discriminator aim to minimize their respective costs. The discriminator's cost promotes accurate classification of data as real or fake, while the generator's cost drives it to create samples that the discriminator erroneously identifies as real. In essence, the discriminator is trained akin to a standard binary classifier.

Let us explore the GAN to forecast the stock prices for the FAST ticker. The figure below visualizes the time series data for the FAST stock from January 2, 2008, to February 10, 2023.

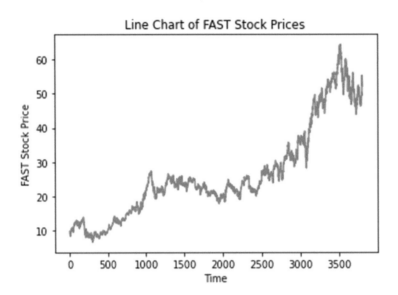

Figure 24: Actual Time Series of the Combined Training Set
and Test Set for the FAST Stock.

The statistical measures provide insights into the properties of the time series data for the FAST ticker.

- ADF p-value (0.85) refers to the p-value obtained from the ADF test. The ADF test is a statistical procedure used to determine whether a time series is stationary or not. A high p-value (> 0.05) suggests the null hypothesis of the ADF test (the time series is nonstationary) cannot be rejected. In this case, a p-value of 0.85 indicates the FAST time series data is likely nonstationary, suggesting it has some time-dependent structure.

- DFA Hurst exponent (1.46): The Hurst exponent is a statistical measure that classifies time series data. The time series is considered mean-reverting if the Hurst exponent is less than 0.5. If it is 0.5, the time series is a geometric Brownian motion (a random walk). If it is greater than 0.5, the time series is trending or persistent. A Hurst exponent of 1.46 indicates the FAST time series data is highly persistent or trending indicating long memory or dependency.

- Lyapunov exponent (0.0035): The Lyapunov exponent measures the rate of separation of infinitesimally close trajectories, a key quantity to understanding the chaotic dynamics in a system. A positive Lyapunov exponent typically indicates chaos. In this case, a value close to zero (0.0035) suggests the time series data is not chaotic and small changes will not lead to significantly different trajectories.

- Skewness (0.91): Skewness measures the asymmetry of the probability distribution of a real-valued random variable about its mean. A positive skewness value indicates the tail on the probability density function's right side (positive side) is longer or fatter than the left side. A skewness of 0.91 for the FAST time series data suggests a moderately positively skewed distribution, indicating relatively more unusually high values than low ones.

Stochasticity: An entropy value of 7.85 was computed for the time series data of FAST, a figure exceeding 90 percent of the maximum possible entropy. This maximum entropy was determined as the logarithm of the number of unique elements within the time series data, that is, log(len(np.unique(time_series_data))). The resulting entropy reveals the time series is highly unpredictable, likely indicating a high degree of stochasticity.

The GAN-based time series model has been implemented to forecast the stock prices for the FAST stock, which exhibits the complex patterns as described above. The complete code for implementing the GAN model to predict stock prices is demonstrated momentarily in this section. However, the snippet provided below is just a part of the entire code set. The code provided serves as a guide to constructing and training a GAN-based deep learning model, which is used for predicting stock prices. The code for the generator is provided below.

```
def create_generator_model():
gen_model = Sequential()
gen_model.add(GRU(units = 1024, activation = 'tanh', input_shape = (input_dim,
    feature_size)))
gen_model.add(Dense(512))
gen_model.add(Dense(256))
gen_model.add(Dense(128))
gen_model.add(Dense(64))
```

```
gen_model.add(Dense(units=output_dim))
return gen_model
```

he code snippet defines a function, create_generator_model(), which constructs a generator model for a GAN using Keras, a user-friendly neural network library in Python. This function builds a sequential model, which is a linear stack of layers, allowing for a straightforward architecture where each layer has a single input and output. The model commences with a GRU layer comprising 1024 units. GRUs, a type of recurrent neural network layer, are well-suited for processing sequence data. Here, the GRU layer uses a tanh activation function and expects input data of shape (input_dim, feature_size), which signifies a sequence length of input_dim comprising feature_size features. Following the GRU layer, the model adds several densely connected layers (dense layers), starting with 512 nodes and then reducing in size through layers of 256, 128, and 64 nodes, respectively. The absence of specified activation functions in these layers implies the use of the default linear function. The model concludes with another dense layer, housing output_dim nodes, which generates the final output. In the absence of a specified activation function, it too defaults to linear. The constructed generator model, gen_model, is ultimately returned by the function. It serves to generate new data within the GAN, with the GRU layer handling sequence data and the dense layers transforming this sequence into the desired output, the dimensions of which are defined by output_dim. The code for discriminator is provided below.

```
def create_discriminator_model():
disc_model = Sequential()
disc_model.add(Conv1D(32, input_shape=(n_steps_in+1, 1), kernel_size=5, strides=2,
padding='same', activation='relu'))
disc_model.add(Dense(230, use_bias=False, activation='relu'))
disc_model.add(Dense(220, use_bias=False, activation='relu'))
disc_model.add(Dense(1, activation='sigmoid'))
return disc_model
```

The provided code defines a function, create_discriminator_model(), which constructs a discriminator model for a GAN using Keras. This model is a sequential model, meaning the layers are stacked linearly. The model begins with a 1D convolutional layer (Conv1D) with 32 filters, a kernel size of 5, a stride of 2, and a same padding. The activation function for this layer is ReLU. This layer expects input data with shape (n_steps_in+1, 1), indicating a sequence length of n_steps_in+1 with 1 feature. Following the convolutional layer, the model includes two densely connected layers (dense) with 230 and 220 nodes, respectively. These layers do not use bias and apply the ReLU activation function. The final layer is a dense layer with one node, which uses the sigmoid activation function. This layer outputs the probability that the input sequence is real, as opposed to generated by the generator. The function returns this constructed discriminator model, disc_model, which will be used in the GAN to distinguish real data from the data generated by the generator. The code for adversarial trainer is provided below.

```
@tf.function
def train_step(self, real_x, real_y, z):
with tf.GradientTape() as gen_tape, tf.GradientTape() as disc_tape:
gen_data = self.generator(real_x, training=True)
gen_data_reshape = tf.reshape(gen_data, [gen_data.shape[0], gen_data.shape[1], 1])
gen_input = tf.concat([tf.cast(gen_data_reshape, tf.float64), z], axis=1)
real_y_reshape = tf.reshape(real_y, [real_y.shape[0], real_y.shape[1], 1])
real_input = tf.concat([real_y_reshape, z], axis=1)
real_output = self.discriminator(real_input, training=True)
gen_output = self.discriminator(gen_input, training=True)
gen_loss = self.generator_loss(gen_output)
disc_loss = self.discriminator_loss(real_output, gen_output)


gradients_of_generator = gen_tape.gradient(gen_loss, self.generator.trainable_variables)
gradients_of_discriminator = disc_tape.gradient(disc_loss, self.discriminator.trainable_variables)


self.generator_optimizer.apply_gradients(zip(gradients_of_generator, self.generator.trainable_variables))
self.discriminator_optimizer.apply_gradients(
```

```
zip(gradients_of_discriminator, self.discriminator.trainable_variables))
return real_y, gen_data, {'d_loss': disc_loss, 'g_loss': gen_loss}


def train(self, real_x, real_y, z):
G_losses = []
D_losses = []


for epoch in range(epochs):
real_price, gen_price, loss = self.train_step(real_x, real_y, z)


if(epoch + 1) > 180:
tf.keras.models.save_model(generator, 'gen_gan_model_%d.h5' % (epoch+1))
self.checkpoint.save(file_prefix=self.checkpoint_prefix + f'-{epoch}')
print('epoch', epoch + 1, 'd_loss', loss['d_loss'].numpy(), 'g_loss', loss['g_loss'].numpy())
D_losses.append(loss['d_loss'].numpy())
G_losses.append(loss['g_loss'].numpy())
#lowest disc loss after 180th epoch
loss_series = pd.Series(D_losses)
min_loss_index = loss_series.idxmin()
return 181+min_loss_index
```

The train_step function is a single training iteration for the GAN. It takes real data (real_x, real_y) and noise (z) as input. The function generates data using the generator network and then reshapes and concatenates the generated data and the real data before feeding both to the discriminator. The discriminator classifies the real and generated data as either real or fake. Losses for both the generator (how well it tricked the discriminator) and the discriminator (how well it correctly classified real and fake data) are computed. Gradients are calculated for each network, and the respective optimizers are used to update the model parameters. The train function iterates over the train_step function for a defined number of epochs. For each epoch, it logs the losses for both the generator and discriminator. Once training reaches beyond the 180th epoch, it saves the generator model and training checkpoint and prints the current epoch number along with the discriminator and generator losses. After training, it identifies and returns the epoch after the 18$^{th}$ where the discriminator had the lowest loss. This might be done to find the optimal point of training where the discriminator was most successful.

The discriminator was trained in an adversarial manner, where the generator tries to generate synthetic data that can fool the discriminator into thinking it is accurate. In contrast, the discriminator tries to distinguish between real and synthetic data correctly. The training process involved iteratively, updating the weights of the generator and discriminator based on their performance in generating and discriminating the data. The full code is provided below.

```
import time
import os
import matplotlib.pyplot as plt
import tensorflow as tf
import pandas as pd
import numpy as np
from tensorflow.keras.layers import GRU, LSTM, Dense, Flatten, Conv1D, Dropout, Bidirectional
from tensorflow.keras import Sequential
from tensorflow.keras.optimizers import Adam
from tensorflow.keras.losses import BinaryCrossentropy
from sklearn.metrics import mean_squared_error
from sklearn.preprocessing import MinMaxScaler
from math import sqrt
from datetime import datetime, timedelta
import math


ticker = 'FAST'
df = pd.read_csv(ticker + '.csv')
datetime_series = pd.to_datetime(df['Date'])
datetime_index = pd.DatetimeIndex(datetime_series.values)
df = df.set_index(datetime_index)
```

```
df = df.sort_values(by='Date')
df = df.drop(columns='Date')


X_value = pd.DataFrame(df.iloc[:, 0:4])
y_value = pd.DataFrame(df.iloc[:, 3])
X_scaler = MinMaxScaler(feature_range=(0, 1))
y_scaler = MinMaxScaler(feature_range=(0, 1))
X_scaler.fit(X_value)
y_scaler.fit(y_value)
X_scale_dataset = X_scaler.fit_transform(X_value)
y_scale_dataset = y_scaler.fit_transform(y_value)
y_scale_dataset_inv = y_scaler.inverse_transform(y_scale_dataset)


n_steps_in = 10
n_features = X_value.shape[1]
n_steps_out = 1


def get_X_y(X_data, y_data):
X = list()
y = list()
z = list()


length = len(X_data)
for i in range(0, length, 1):
X_value = X_data[i: i + n_steps_in][:, :]
y_value = y_data[i + n_steps_in: i + (n_steps_in + n_steps_out)][:, 0]
z_value = y_data[i: i + n_steps_in][:, :]
if len(X_value) == n_steps_in and len(y_value) == n_steps_out:
X.append(X_value)
y.append(y_value)
z.append(z_value)
```

```python
    return np.array(X), np.array(y), np.array(z)


def split_train_test(data):
    train_size = round(len(data) * 0.8)
    data_train = data[0:train_size]
    data_test = data[train_size:]
    return data_train, data_test


X, y, z = get_X_y(X_scale_dataset, y_scale_dataset)
X_train, X_test, = split_train_test(X)
y_train, y_test, = split_train_test(y)
z_train, z_test, = split_train_test(z)


input_dim = X_train.shape[1]
feature_size = X_train.shape[2]
output_dim = y_train.shape[1]
epochs = 200


def create_generator_model():
    gen_model = Sequential()
    gen_model.add(GRU(units = 1024, activation = 'tanh', input_shape = (input_dim, feature_size)))
    gen_model.add(Dense(512))
    gen_model.add(Dense(256))
    gen_model.add(Dense(128))
    gen_model.add(Dense(64))
    gen_model.add(Dense(units=output_dim))
    return gen_model


def create_discriminator_model():
    disc_model = Sequential()
```

```python
disc_model.add(Conv1D(32, input_shape=(n_steps_in+1, 1), kernel_size=5, strides=2, padding='same',
activation='relu'))
disc_model.add(Dense(230, use_bias=False, activation='relu'))
disc_model.add(Dense(220, use_bias=False, activation='relu'))
disc_model.add(Dense(1, activation='sigmoid'))
return disc_model


class GAN:
def __init__(self, generator, discriminator):
self.generator = generator
self.discriminator = discriminator
self.cross_entropy = BinaryCrossentropy(from_logits=True)
self.generator_optimizer = Adam(lr=0.00016)
self.discriminator_optimizer = Adam(lr=0.00016)
self.batch_size = 130
#create empty director with this name
self.checkpoint_dir = './checkpoints'
self.checkpoint_prefix = os.path.join(self.checkpoint_dir, "checkpoint")
self.checkpoint = tf.train.Checkpoint(generator_optimizer=self.generator_optimizer,
discriminator_optimizer=self.discriminator_optimizer,
generator=self.generator,
discriminator=self.discriminator)


def discriminator_loss(self, real_output, gen_output):
real_loss = self.cross_entropy(tf.ones_like(real_output), real_output)
gen_loss = self.cross_entropy(tf.zeros_like(gen_output), gen_output)
total_loss = real_loss + gen_loss
return total_loss
```

```python
def generator_loss(self, gen_output):
return self.cross_entropy(tf.ones_like(gen_output), gen_output)


@tf.function
def train_step(self, real_x, real_y, z):
with tf.GradientTape() as gen_tape, tf.GradientTape() as disc_tape:
gen_data = self.generator(real_x, training=True)
gen_data_reshape = tf.reshape(gen_data, [gen_data.shape[0], gen_data.shape[1], 1])
gen_input = tf.concat([tf.cast(gen_data_reshape, tf.float64), z], axis=1)
real_y_reshape = tf.reshape(real_y, [real_y.shape[0], real_y.shape[1], 1])
real_input = tf.concat([real_y_reshape, z], axis=1)
real_output = self.discriminator(real_input, training=True)
gen_output = self.discriminator(gen_input, training=True)
gen_loss = self.generator_loss(gen_output)
disc_loss = self.discriminator_loss(real_output, gen_output)


gradients_of_generator = gen_tape.gradient(gen_loss, self.generator.trainable_variables)
gradients_of_discriminator = disc_tape.gradient(disc_loss, self.discriminator.trainable_variables)


self.generator_optimizer.apply_gradients(zip(gradients_of_generator, self.generator.trainable_variables))
self.discriminator_optimizer.apply_gradients(
zip(gradients_of_discriminator, self.discriminator.trainable_variables))
return real_y, gen_data, {'d_loss': disc_loss, 'g_loss': gen_loss}


def train(self, real_x, real_y, z):
G_losses = []
D_losses = []


for epoch in range(epochs):
real_price, gen_price, loss = self.train_step(real_x, real_y, z)
```

```
if(epoch + 1) > 180:

tf.keras.models.save_model(generator, 'gen_gan_model_%d.h5' % (epoch+1))

self.checkpoint.save(file_prefix=self.checkpoint_prefix + f'-{epoch}')

print('epoch', epoch + 1, 'd_loss', loss['d_loss'].numpy(), 'g_loss', loss['g_loss'].numpy())

D_losses.append(loss['d_loss'].numpy())

G_losses.append(loss['g_loss'].numpy())


loss_series = pd.Series(D_losses)

min_loss_index = loss_series.idxmin()

return 181+min_loss_index

generator = create_generator_model()

discriminator = create_discriminator_model()

gan = GAN(generator, discriminator)

best_epoch = gan.train(X_train, y_train, z_train)

print("best_epoch", best_epoch)

gan_model = tf.keras.models.load_model('gen_gan_model_%d.h5' % (best_epoch))

predicted_prices_test = gan_model(X_test)

actual_prices = y_scaler.inverse_transform(y_test)

predicted_prices = y_scaler.inverse_transform(predicted_prices_test)

mse = tf.keras.losses.mean_squared_error(actual_prices[:,0], predicted_prices[:,0]).numpy()

rmse = math.sqrt(mse)

print('RMSE', rmse)

mape = tf.keras.losses.mean_absolute_percentage_error(actual_prices[:,0], predicted_prices
[:,0]).numpy()

print('MAPE', mape)


plt.plot(actual_prices, color='green', label=f"Actual {ticker} price")

plt.plot(predicted_prices, color= 'red', label=f"predicted {ticker} price")

plt.title(f"{ticker} Stock Prices-- Actual Vs. Predicted")

plt.xlabel("time")

plt.ylabel(f"{ticker} Stock Price")
```

```
plt.legend()
plt.show()
```

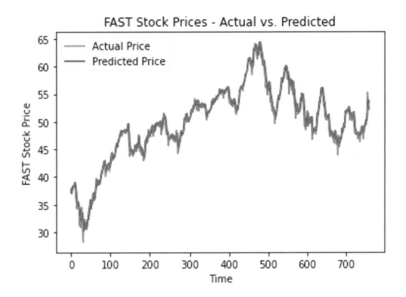

Figure 25: Actual Time Series and GAN-Predicted Time Series for the FAST Stock.

The chart above shows the comparison of actual time series from the test set and predicted time series. The model produced RMSE of 1.05. Since the RMSE is a relative measure to the underlying values, the MAPE is best suited to interpret the accuracy of the model. The model produced MAPE of 1.63, indicating there is 1.63 percent of error in prediction. The lower MAPE indicates the GAN is capable of forecasting the stock prices when the time series data exhibits complex patterns mentioned earlier.

## 12.8   Transformers

Transformers, a class of models that utilizes self-attention mechanisms, have significantly revolutionized NLP, and now they are making inroads into the realm of time series analysis. The transformers model is inherently suited to handling sequential data, given its capability to process input elements in parallel and comprehend long-range dependencies in the data, making it a promising alternative for time series forecasting. The key components that make transformers particularly powerful for time series include the attention mechanisms, positional encoding, decoding, and multihead attention. These elements enable the model to better learn and understand complex temporal patterns, trends, and seasonality, thus offering a sophisticated method for analyzing and predicting time series data.

## An Encoder

In the context of time series analysis, the role of the encoder within the transformer architecture becomes critically important. The encoder is structured in multiple identical layers, each containing two sublayers: a multihead self-attention mechanism and a simple position-wise, fully connected feedforward network. It is crucial to note that these layers work together to transform the input sequence, capturing complex temporal dependencies in the data.

The self-attention mechanism, also known as scaled dot-product attention, allows the model to weigh the relevance of each data point in the sequence based on its context, that is, its relationship with all other data points. It is exceptionally powerful for time series analysis because it does not require sequential data processing, enabling parallel computation, and it efficiently learns long-range dependencies, even for very long sequences. This allows the model to learn how different points in time relate to each other and the output prediction, which is particularly important for complex patterns and seasonality within time series data.

The feedforward layer within the encoder operates independently on each position, applying a linear transformation followed by a nonlinear activation function to transform the output of the self-attention layer. This allows the model to learn intricate, high-level features and patterns from the time series data.

## A Decoder

The decoder plays a critical role within the transformer model, functioning as the component tasked with creating the projected sequence. It accomplishes this by generating future time points sequentially, relying on a stack of decoder layers to do so.

The first core step within each decoder layer is the self-attention mechanism, which echoes its use within the encoder. This layer generates a weighted sum of the decoder layer's hidden states, assigning weights according to the similarity between these states. Unlike the self-attention in the encoder, the decoder's version not only considers preceding positions within the input sequence but also takes into account the already-predicted future time steps. This enables the decoder to generate forecasts that are contextually aware, thereby creating more nuanced and accurate predictions.

Following the self-attention layer is the encoder-decoder attention layer, a crucial element within the transformer architecture. This layer produces a weighted sum of the hidden states that emerge from the encoder. The weights are determined based on the correlation between the hidden states and previously-predicted time steps. This capability allows the decoder to focus on the most relevant parts of the input sequence when predicting future time steps. It essentially provides a bridge between the historical data encapsulated in the encoded input and the predicted future values, ensuring the forecasted output is in alignment with the patterns and trends of the input sequence.

The final component within the decoder layer is the feedforward layer. This layer applies a linear transformation to the outputs of both the self-attention and encoder-decoder attention layers before implementing a nonlinear activation function. This process allows the decoder to extract and learn more complex features from both the input sequence and previously-forecasted time steps.

In its entirety, the decoder produces a sequence of tokens, each representing a predicted future time step. The combined functionality of the self-attention, encoder-decoder attention, and feedforward layers provides the decoder with a powerful ability to learn and adapt to long-term dependencies between past and future time steps. This characteristic not only enhances the transformer's ability to predict complex features from time series data but also ensures a high degree of consistency and accuracy in the predicted output.

# 13

# Reinforcement Learning (RL) for Time Series

While machine learning and deep learning are helpful in time series forecasting, the RL serves differently in the same field of time series analysis. In RL, an agent learns to make decisions by taking actions in an environment to achieve a goal. As such, the agent learns from the consequences of its actions rather than being explicitly taught, optimizing its actions over time to maximize some notion of cumulative reward. When it comes to time series, RL is less about forecasting future values and more about making optimal decisions over time based on those forecasts. For instance, in the context of trading stocks, RL could be used not just to predict future prices (that might be done with an ANN), but to decide when to buy and sell stocks based on these predictions to maximize profit. The main advantage of using RL for this problem is that it can learn complex, nonlinear strategies directly from raw data. This is in contrast to traditional methods that often require strong assumptions about the nature of financial markets.

Time series data can be leveraged to construct trading strategies hinging on certain market events such as fluctuations in the volatility index (VIX). The process follows systematic steps. The agent's status is characterized by an array of features extracted from the time series data. These can encompass attributes like price, volume, and technical indicators. In the context of strategies hinging on VIX shifts, the state description would incorporate the recent alterations in the VIX. The agent's possible courses of action include buying, selling, or retaining the asset. For instance, the agent could be programmed to initiate a buy or sell action when the VIX surpasses a predetermined threshold. The agent's reward is gauged by the profits or losses resulting from its trading actions. A well-timed action, such as purchasing before an increase in price or selling before a decrease, yields positive rewards, while ill-timed actions lead to negative rewards. The agent's policy, or the set of guidelines it follows to determine its actions based on its current state, may initially be random. However, as the agent continually interacts with the environment and learns from the outcomes of its actions, its policy undergoes refinement and improvement over time.

Since, unlike ANN models where the goal was forecasting the prices of stocks on an individual basis, the purpose of the RL is to take action based on the level of VIX, for example, and data point in time series. As such, two time series are used, one VIX time series and the other stock price time series. Initial amount of capital is allocated for each stock. In RL, creating environment that is often used to set up the stage in which the agent will operate. The environment is essentially the world or context in which the agent learns and performs actions. It is responsible for returning responses or reactions to the agent's actions. The role of the CreateEnvironment function is as detailed below.

- Initializing the state space: Defining all possible states the agent can be in. In a game of chess, for example, this would include every possible configuration of the chess board.

- Initializing the action space: Defining all possible actions the agent can take at each step. In a game of chess, this would include all legal moves the player can make.

- Defining transition dynamics: Describing how the environment changes in response to the agent's actions. This often includes some element of randomness or uncertainty.

- Defining the reward function: The feedback signal used to guide the agent's learning. The reward function describes the goal of the task in terms of the states and actions by providing the agent with a reward or penalty (positive or negative reward) for each action.

- Setting any environment parameters: For example, in a stock trading environment, parameters such as initial amount of money, transaction costs, or maximum number of shares the agent can buy/sell, might be defined.

The two functions, Sell Stock and Buy Stock, are utilized to take actions based on the recommendation. Sell Stock method is used to sell stocks within this environment. The method takes two parameters: index, which likely represents the index of a particular indicator in the state vector, for example, VIX; and action, which represents the number of shares to sell.

- Initialize the number of shares to be sold as zero.

- The VIX threshold should be a predefined, which is a threshold on the VIX, a measure of market risk and investors' sentiments.

- If the current VIX is greater than or equal to the VIX threshold, check if the value of the stock at the current state is greater than 0. If the number of shares of the stock currently being held is greater than 0, the number of shares to sell is set to the number of shares currently held.

- If the agent does not hold any of the current stocks or if the current stock's value is 0, the shares to be sold remains zero.

Buy Stock method is used to buy stocks within this environment. The method also takes two parameters: index and action, which represents the number of shares to buy.

- Initializing the number of shares to be bought as 0.
- If the current VIX is less than the VIX threshold, calculate the maximum number of shares the agent can buy of a particular stock with the current cash in hand.
- The number of shares to be bought is the minimum of available amount and action. This means the agent will buy as many shares as it requested through action, but not more than it can afford with its available cash.
- If the VIX is not less than the threshold, no shares are bought, and the number of shares to buy remains 0.

The soft actor-critic (SAC), a RL algorithm, is used to build the model. The SAC aims to improve the reward signal by balancing exploration and exploitation, two critical aspects of RL. The algorithm is based on the actor-critic framework. It uses two separate neural networks, the actor-network for learning the policy and critic-network for estimating the value of state-action pairs. SAC improves the reward signal and overall learning process by incorporating key features known as entropy regularization, soft value functions, off-policy learning, twin Q-networks, and delayed policy updates. The code below is used to build the model.

```
rl_model = SAC(policy="MlpPolicy", env=env_train, policy_kwargs=None, seed=None,
**model_params)
trained_rl = rl_model.learn(total_timesteps=450,tb_log_name='sac',callback=Tensorboard
Callback(),)
e_trade_env = CreateEnvironment(df = trade, vix_threshold = 50, risk_indicator_col='vix',
**env_params)
test_env, test_obs = e_trade_env.get_sb_env()
```

This code is used for training a RL model using Stable Baselines3, a popular machine learning library for RL in Python, with the SAC algorithm, an off-policy actor-critic deep RL algorithm.

- It creates a SAC model. The parameters passed are:
- policy: This is the policy architecture to be used by the agent. Here, "MlpPolicy" is used, which is a type of policy based on MLP, a class of feedforward ANN.
    - o Env is the environment in which the agent will interact.
    - o policy_kwargs are additional arguments for the policy constructor.
    - o Seed is the seed for the pseudo-random number generators. This can be used for reproducing results. When it is set to none, results won't be easily reproducible.
    - o **model_params unpacks additional parameters for the model from the model_ params dictionary.
- trained_rl = rl_model.learn(total_timesteps=450,tb_log_name='sac',callback=Tensorboard Callback())
- This is used to train the SAC model using the provided environment and parameters. The model will learn for a total of 450 timesteps.
- e_trade_env = CreateEnvironment(df = trade, vix_threshold = 50, risk_indicator_col='vix', **env_params) creates an environment for the agent to interact with, The **env_params unpacks additional parameters for the environment from the env_params dictionary.
- test_env, test_obs = e_trade_env.get_sb_env() retrieves the environment compatible with Stable Baselines3 using a method from the CreateEnvironment instance. It also retrieves the initial observation from this environment. The test_env and test_obs variables are typically used later for evaluating the trained model.

RL has been applied for the stock to generate simulated returns. The figure below shows the time series data of the NRG stock from January 2, 2008, to February 10, 2023.

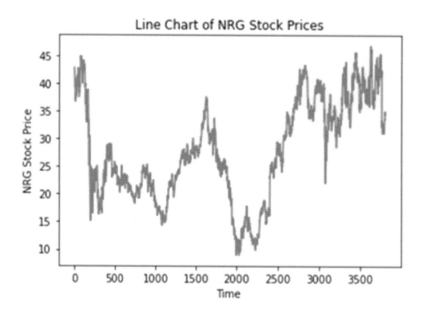

Line Chart of NRG Stock Prices

The statistical measures are generated to assess the complexity of the above time series data. Listed below are detailed descriptions of the statistical measures for the ticker NRG:

- ADF p-value (0.12) refers to the p-value obtained from the ADF test. The ADF test is a statistical procedure used to determine whether a time series is stationary or not. A high p-value 0.12 (>0.05) suggests the null hypothesis of the ADF test (the time series is nonstationary) cannot be rejected. In this case, a p-value of 0.12 indicates the NRG time series data is nonstationary, suggesting it has some time-dependent structure.

- DFA Hurst exponent (1.5): The Hurst exponent is a statistical measure that classifies time series data. The time series is considered mean-reverting if the Hurst exponent is less than 0.5. If it is 0.5, the time series is a geometric Brownian motion (a random walk). If it is greater than 0.5, the time series is trending or persistent. A Hurst exponent of 1.5 indicates the NRG time series data is highly persistent or trending, indicating long-term memory or dependency.

- Lyapunov exponent (0.0047): The Lyapunov exponent measures the rate of separation of infinitesimally close trajectories, a key quantity to understanding the chaotic dynamics in a system. A positive Lyapunov exponent typically indicates chaos. In this case, a value close to zero (0.0047) suggests the time series data is chaotic though with lesser severity and small changes will lead to significantly different trajectories. In other words, the time series data of NRG stock exhibits nonlinearity.

- Skewness (0.05): Skewness measures the asymmetry of the probability distribution of a real-valued random variable about its mean. A positive skewness value indicates the tail on the probability density function's right side (positive side) is longer or fatter than the left side. A skewness of 0.66 for the NRG time series data suggests a positively skewed distribution, indicating relatively more unusually high values than low ones.

- Stochasticity: An entropy value of 7.6 was computed for the time series data of NRG, a figure exceeding 90 percent of the maximum possible entropy. This maximum entropy was determined as the logarithm of the number of unique elements within the time series data, that is, log(len(np.unique(time_series_data))). The resulting entropy reveals the time series is highly unpredictable, likely indicating a high degree of stochasticity.

The figure below compares returns generated by the RL model and the market returns for the NRG stock. The figure shows the model prevented the losses at the beginning of the graph. By doing so, the model achieved cumulative returns of 0.2803 for every dollar, or 28.03 percent. At the same time, the cumulative market returns for the same stock are 14.17 percent. That means the model generated excess returns of 13.86 percent for the NRG stock.

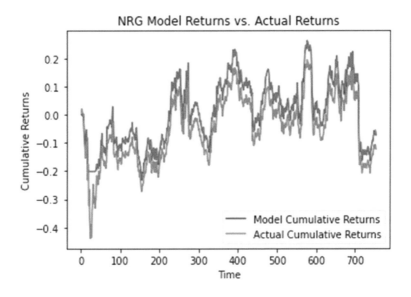

Figure 27: Comparison of Model Returns and Market Returns for the NRG Stock.

The RL models can be used to build automated trading strategies. The automated trading strategy is a set of rules and criteria for buying and selling financial instruments, such as stocks, options, or futures, programmed into a computer system to execute trades automatically based on those rules. The program can automatically buy, sell, or hold the stocks based on the expected direction. Automated trading strategies offer several benefits for practitioners in terms of increased risk management, efficiency, consistency, and reduced costs. Automated trading strategies can help practitioners manage portfolio risk by selling the stock if the prices are expected to decrease to mitigate the losses. Automated trading strategies can help practitioners execute trades faster and more efficiently without manual intervention. Automated trading strategies can help practitioners maintain consistency in their trading decisions and avoid making emotional decisions based on market fluctuations.

# 14

# Computational Aspects of AI Models

AI models, especially those utilizing deep learning techniques, are incredibly complex and require a lot of computational power. This is because they often deal with high-dimensional data. This means the data has many different features or variables. For example, in image recognition, each pixel in an image could be a different dimension, leading to hundreds of thousands of dimensions for a single image. Handling such high-dimensional data is computationally intensive. In addition to high dimensionality, these AI models also need to process large volumes of data to learn effectively. Deep learning models typically learn from large datasets, often comprising millions of data points. Processing this amount of data requires substantial computational resources.

This necessitates using high-performance hardware such as graphics processing units (GPUs) and tensor processing units (TPUs) for training and inference. Because of the high computational demands of deep learning models, high-performance hardware is often required to train and use them for making predictions or inferences. In both training and inference stages, these high-performance hardware components help to speed up the computations. Training involves adjusting the model's parameters based on the input data and the error it makes on its predictions, a process that can be very time-consuming given the complexity and size of modern deep learning models. Inference involves using the trained model to make predictions on new data, which also benefits from the faster computation provided by GPUs and TPUs.

## 14.1   Graphics Processing Units (GPUs)

Traditionally, GPUs were designed for rendering graphics for video games and other visual applications, which requires a lot of simple, parallel computations. This characteristic makes them also well suited for the kind of computations needed in deep learning models. Unlike central processing units (CPUs), which have a few cores optimized for sequential processing, GPUs have hundreds or even thousands of smaller cores designed for parallel processing. This means they can perform many operations simultaneously, which is essential for deep learning tasks, where it is often needed to carry out the same operation on many different pieces of data, for example, multiplying matrices in a neural network.

GPUs have a specific architecture designed to handle the parallel processing requirements of graphics rendering and general-purpose computing tasks. Constructed to manage an extensive level of parallel computations, GPU architecture integrates various elements that streamline this process. These components include streaming multiprocessors (SMs), an organized memory hierarchy, a structured thread organization, the single instruction, multiple data (SIMD) execution model, mechanisms for memory coalescing and caching, as well as control and scheduling units.

## Streaming Multiprocessors (SMs)

GPUs are composed of multiple streaming multiprocessors (SMs), also referred to as compute units in AMD GPUs or shader cores in NVIDIA GPUs. Each of these SMs houses many smaller cores (in NVIDIA) or stream processors (in AMD), which are responsible for executing instructions and performing calculations simultaneously, enabling the high degree of parallel processing characteristic of GPUs.

## Memory Hierarchy

GPUs have different levels of memory hierarchy to optimize data access and transfer rates.

- Global memory: It is the largest and slowest memory available on the GPU. It stores data accessible by all threads but has relatively high latency.
- Shared memory: Shared memory is a smaller, low-latency memory shared among threads within a thread block. It allows for faster data access and communication between threads.
- Constant memory: Constant memory is a small, read-only memory that provides a high bandwidth for frequently-accessed data.
- Texture memory: Texture memory is a specialized read-only memory designed for optimized texture mapping operations used in graphics processing.
- Register memory: Each thread in a GPU has its own set of registers, which are fast, on-chip memory used for storing intermediate values and variables.

**Thread Organization**

GPUs utilize a hierarchical thread organization to execute tasks in parallel.

- Grid: The grid is the highest level of organization, representing a collection of thread blocks.

- Thread blocks: Thread blocks are groups of threads that can cooperate and synchronize with each other. They are executed on an SM.

- Threads: Threads are individual execution units that perform computations. Thousands or even millions of threads can be executed concurrently on an SM.

**SIMD Execution Model**

GPUs utilize a computational model known as single instruction, multiple data (SIMD). In the context of a GPU, this means a single operation or instruction is applied across many different data points at once. To give a simple example, we might have an operation like "multiply by 2," and we could apply this operation to an entire array of numbers simultaneously. That is the SIMD model in a nutshell. This is done within each SM in the GPU. SMs are made up of several CUDA cores (in NVIDIA GPUs) or stream processors (in AMD GPUs), which are grouped together and work concurrently. A group of threads that run on these cores or processors is called a warp in NVIDIA terminology or a wavefront in AMD terminology. In each SM, multiple threads within a warp or wavefront execute the same instruction but on different data. For example, if we have a warp of 32 threads, each thread would execute the same instruction, such as "multiply by 2," but on a different piece of data. This means that in one operation, we can process 32 pieces of data. This is why GPUs are so good at tasks that can be broken down into many small, independent tasks, like graphics rendering or deep learning computations.

This SIMD model of execution enables the massive parallelism of GPUs. Because so many threads can execute the same instruction on different data simultaneously, tasks can be completed much more quickly than they could be with a serial processor. This makes GPUs ideally suited for tasks that involve large amounts of data and require high computational power, such as rendering graphics, simulating physical systems, or training and running AI models.

## Memory Coalescing and Caching

GPUs enhance memory access efficiency through a technique known as memory coalescing. In this process, the GPU organizes threads to access adjacent memory locations in the same transaction whenever possible. This arrangement is beneficial as it reduces the number of memory transactions needed, thereby improving memory bandwidth utilization, the amount of data that can be read from or written to the memory per unit of time. This is a crucial performance aspect, especially for parallel processors like GPUs, as they often have to deal with vast volumes of data. Furthermore, GPUs take advantage of a hierarchical cache memory system to accelerate data access times and reduce memory latency, the delay before a transfer of data begins following an instruction for its transfer. In the memory hierarchy of GPUs, there are usually multiple levels of cache memory, typically L1 (Level 1) and L2 (Level 2) caches. L1 cache is smaller but faster and is located closer to the compute units, while L2 cache is larger but slower and is shared among all compute units. When a computational unit needs to access data, it first looks in the L1 cache. If the required data is not found there (a condition known as a cache miss), the unit then checks the L2 cache. If the data is still not found, only then does it access the global memory, which is much slower in comparison. By maintaining frequently-used data in cache memory, GPUs can reduce the time spent waiting for data transfers from the slower global memory, thereby significantly improving the overall performance.

## Control and Scheduling Units

Control and scheduling units within a GPU are critical to ensuring efficient and orderly computation. These units have the crucial job of managing the execution of threads and distributing tasks among the different SMs. These functions typically operate as three units of work. The control unit plays a pivotal role in managing the execution of threads. It interprets and dispatches instructions for the processor, ensuring that threads follow their execution paths accurately. This encompasses determining the order of operations, managing any dependencies between threads (e.g., if one thread's operation depends on the result of another), and overseeing the resources that the threads require to complete their tasks. Additionally, the scheduler, with a big-picture perspective of all the threads and their workloads, distributes these threads across the SMs. It is crucial for this distribution to be balanced to prevent any SM from remaining idle while others are overloaded. Therefore, the scheduler consistently monitors the workload of each SM and reassigns tasks as needed to maintain an even workload distribution. In some situations, threads might need to synchronize with each other, such as when they need to share data or when one thread's output serves as another thread's input. The control and scheduling units manage this synchronization, ensuring that threads don't outpace each other and precipitate errors.

## 14.2  GPU-Powered CUDA

Compute Unified Device Architecture, or simply CUDA, is a parallel computing platform and programming model developed by NVIDIA. It is engineered to harness the power of GPUs for general-purpose computing tasks that extend beyond traditional graphics processing. CUDA provides developers with a comprehensive software framework, including tools, libraries, and APIs for a wide range of computational tasks. The model extends the C/C++ programming language with added keywords, data types, and directives that facilitate the expression of parallelism and control execution on the GPU. Developers write kernel functions, which are then executed in parallel on multiple GPU threads. These threads are organized into larger structures known as thread blocks and grids for efficient execution. Through CUDA, programmers can offload computationally intensive tasks to the GPU, leveraging its capability for massive parallelism and high-performance computing. This approach leads to a substantial acceleration in computations when compared to traditional CPU-based processing. In addition to these features, CUDA also offers memory management functions and efficient mechanisms for data transfer between the CPU and GPU.

CUDA provides a programming model and platform that unlocks the parallel processing capabilities of GPUs, enabling efficient and high-performance deep learning computations. It optimizes memory access, allows for parallel execution, offers pre-optimized libraries, supports asynchronous execution, and integrates with deep learning frameworks, all of which contribute to making deep learning more efficient on GPUs. By combining the power of CUDA-enabled GPUs, time series forecasting using ANNs can be performed efficiently. The parallel processing capabilities, optimized memory access, asynchronous execution, and CUDA libraries contribute to faster model training, improved prediction speeds, and overall enhanced performance in time series forecasting tasks.

**Parallel Processing**

Deep learning models necessitate the execution of myriad mathematical operations on extensive matrices, such as performing matrix multiplications and convolutions. GPUs, designed with parallel processing in mind, possess thousands of cores capable of simultaneously conducting computations. By using CUDA, developers can craft code that leverages this parallelism, spreading the computational workload across numerous GPU cores. This capability for parallel processing considerably hastens deep learning computations relative to conventional CPUs.

In the realm of time series forecasting, a process that often requires the management of vast volumes of sequential data, ANN implemented with CUDA can exploit the parallel processing capabilities of GPUs. Distributing the computations across multiple GPU cores, parallel processing dramatically speeds up both the training and prediction stages in time series forecasting tasks. Consequently, this leads to expedited model training and inference times, offering a significant speed advantage over computations performed solely on a CPU.

## GPU Memory Hierarchy

GPUs incorporate a hierarchical memory architecture, complete with various levels of memory, such as global, shared, and local memory. CUDA offers control over memory management, enabling developers to refine data access patterns to mitigate memory latency. By leveraging shared memory, a swift on-chip memory accessible to multiple threads within a GPU block, CUDA can lessen memory access latency, thereby boosting overall performance.

This hierarchical memory architecture, consisting of both global and shared memory, can be utilized effectively in time series forecasting. During the training of ANN on time series data, the input data, along with intermediate activations, are stored in GPU memory. CUDA offers control over memory management, which allows the optimization of data access patterns to minimize memory latency. The performance is further amplified through the efficient use of shared memory, which reduces memory access time within GPU blocks.

## Kernel Execution

In the CUDA framework, parallel computations are defined by developers as kernels, essentially functions executed on the GPU. These kernels are structured to be carried out by multiple threads concurrently. CUDA orchestrates the assignment and execution of these threads across the GPU cores, optimizing the allocation of available resources. Developers can initiate several blocks of threads, each housing multiple threads, to maximize the GPU's computational potential.

When applied to time series forecasting tasks using ANNs, kernels, functions executed on the GPU, encompass operations that can be executed in parallel on each element or data batch. Such operations might include forward propagation, backward propagation (during training), and prediction for time series forecasting. CUDA facilitates the distribution and execution of threads across the GPU cores, thereby enabling efficient parallel execution of these operations.

## CUDA Libraries

NVIDIA offers a suite of optimized libraries tailored for deep learning, including CUDA deep neural network library (cuDNN) and CUDA Basic Linear Algebra Subroutines (cuBLAS). These libraries are finely tuned for GPU architectures and provide efficient versions of frequently-used deep learning operations like convolutions, matrix multiplications, and activation functions. Leveraging these libraries allows developers to speed up deep learning computations, eliminating the need to craft low-level optimizations personally.

Furthermore, CUDA boasts dedicated libraries for deep learning, such as cuDNN, that supply optimized implementations of standard operations in ANNs used for time series forecasting. These libraries encompass optimized functions for various building blocks of ANNs, including activation functions, convolutional operations, and pooling. Using these libraries enables developers to gain from the highly-tuned GPU implementations, thereby obviating the necessity for them to create low-level optimizations on their own.

## Asynchronous Execution

CUDA facilitates asynchronous execution, which allows the CPU and GPU to carry out computations in tandem. This concurrent processing and data transfer between the CPU and GPU reduces total latency and optimizes the utilization of resources. Developers have the capability to launch GPU kernels and execute CPU code in parallel, reducing idle time and enhancing overall performance.

Additionally, CUDA's support for asynchronous execution proves beneficial in time series forecasting where both CPU and GPU computations are involved in the training and prediction steps of the model. This feature allows for the overlap of CPU and GPU computations, reducing idle periods and overall latency. The result is an improved performance yielding faster training and inference times.

## Memory Transfer Optimization

Data transfer between the CPU and GPU can potentially create a bottleneck in processing. CUDA offers mechanisms, like pinned memory and asynchronous data transfer, to optimize these memory transfers. Pinned memory removes the requirement for data to be duplicated between the CPU and GPU, thereby reducing overhead. Meanwhile, asynchronous data transfer enables simultaneous data transfer and computation, effectively concealing the latency involved in data transfers.

In the context of time series forecasting with ANNs, the efficient exchange of data between the CPU and GPU is vital. CUDA's provision of mechanisms like pinned memory and asynchronous data transfer aids in optimizing these memory transfers. Pinned memory eradicates the need for data to be duplicated between the CPU and GPU, thus minimizing overhead. Asynchronous data transfer, on the other hand, allows for the concurrent transfer and computation of data. This effectively masks the latency associated with data transfers, contributing to an overall improvement in performance.

## Deep Learning Framework Integration

CUDA is seamlessly integrated with prominent deep learning frameworks like TensorFlow and PyTorch. This integration enables developers to effortlessly compose and execute deep learning code that benefits from GPU acceleration. These frameworks offer high-level APIs and abstractions, simplifying the complexities of CUDA programming and thus making it easier to harness the computational prowess of the GPU for deep learning tasks.

In the context of time series forecasting, popular deep learning frameworks such as TensorFlow and PyTorch feature integrated CUDA support, easing the process for developers to utilize GPUs. These frameworks offer high-level APIs and abstractions that take care of the underlying details of CUDA programming. Therefore, by employing these frameworks, developers can construct time series forecasting models using ANNs and execute them on GPUs smoothly, leveraging the aforementioned CUDA optimizations.

## 14.3   Tensor Processing Units (TPUs)

Tensor processing units (TPUs) are Google's custom-developed, application-specific integrated circuits (ASICs) used to accelerate machine learning workloads. They are designed specifically for TensorFlow, Google's open-source machine learning framework, but can also be used with other frameworks. TPUs are designed to accelerate tensor operations, which are at the heart of many AI and machine learning computations. They can perform a high rate of low-precision arithmetic such as 8-bit, which is often sufficient for many machine learning tasks. This allows them to provide higher throughput than GPUs, given the same power and cost. TPUs are highly optimized for tensor operations, fundamental to deep learning algorithms. TPUs are designed to make deep learning more efficient by leveraging their unique architecture and specialized hardware features. The elements that enhance the efficiency of TPUs for deep learning applications include the matrix multiply unit (MXU), TPU core coupled with TPU mesh, an organized memory hierarchy, precision support tailored for machine learning tasks, specialized hardware optimization for deep learning, high performance coupled with power efficiency, and seamless integration with popular deep learning frameworks.

- Matrix multiply unit (MXU): TPUs are equipped with a dedicated matrix multiply unit (MXU) that excels at performing high-speed matrix multiplications, which are core operations in deep learning models. The MXU consists of a vast array of arithmetic units that can execute multiply-accumulate (MAC) operations in parallel. This parallelism enables efficient and fast matrix computations, significantly accelerating deep learning workloads.

- TPU core and TPU mesh: TPUs are composed of multiple TPU cores, each capable of executing independent operations. These TPU cores are interconnected through a 2D mesh network. The mesh architecture allows for efficient communication and data sharing between the cores, enabling high-speed data transfers. This parallelism and communication infrastructure enables TPUs to process large-scale deep learning models and datasets efficiently.

- Memory hierarchy: TPUs have a hierarchical memory architecture that includes local memory within each TPU core and high-bandwidth on-chip memory known as weight memory (WM). The memory hierarchy minimizes memory access latency and maximizes data reuse. The local memory (activation memory) within each TPU core stores intermediate results during computations, reducing the need for external memory access. This optimized memory hierarchy improves the efficiency of memory operations in deep learning workloads.

- Precision support: TPUs support both 16-bit floating-point operations (FP16) and 8-bit integer operations (INT8). Deep learning models can often be computed with reduced precision without significantly sacrificing accuracy. By utilizing reduced-precision calculations, TPUs can achieve higher throughput and computational efficiency, resulting in faster training and inference times for deep learning models.

- Hardware optimization for deep learning: TPUs are specifically designed and optimized for deep learning workloads. The architecture and hardware features are tailored to accelerate the operations commonly used in deep learning models, such as convolutions, matrix multiplications, and activation functions. TPUs provide dedicated circuitry and instructions to efficiently execute these operations, resulting in significant speedups compared to general-purpose CPUs or GPUs.

- Performance and power efficiency: TPUs are engineered to deliver high performance while maintaining power efficiency. The architecture is optimized for parallelism and throughput, enabling TPUs to process large amounts of data in parallel. The specialized hardware and memory hierarchy of TPUs minimizes data movement, reducing energy consumption and improving overall power efficiency. As a result, TPUs offer a high-performance solution for deep learning tasks while keeping energy consumption in check.

- Integration with deep learning frameworks: TPUs are well-integrated with popular deep learning frameworks like TensorFlow. This integration allows developers to seamlessly train and deploy deep learning models on TPUs using familiar APIs and toolsets. The integration eliminates the need for significant code modifications and simplifies the process of harnessing the power of TPUs in deep learning workflows.

## 14.4   Cloud for AI

The implementation of AI applications presents several challenges, including the need for robust computational resources, scalable infrastructure, and efficient data management, among others. One solution that has proven to be invaluable in overcoming these hurdles is the cloud. Cloud computing has become a cornerstone in the world of AI, providing vital support through scalable infrastructure, robust computing resources, and a plethora of innovative services. The cloud assists AI applications across critical areas: scalable computing power, storage and data management, distributed processing, GPU and TPU acceleration, managed AI services, AutoML and ML pipelines, elasticity and cost efficiency, and collaboration and deployment.

## Scalable Computing Power

AI applications often require substantial computational resources to train and run complex models. Cloud providers offer scalable computing power, allowing users to easily access and provision resources on-demand. This scalability ensures that AI workloads can be executed efficiently, regardless of the size of the dataset or complexity of the models.

## Storage and Data Management

AI applications heavily rely on large datasets for training and inference. Cloud providers offer storage services that can handle massive amounts of data, making it convenient for AI practitioners to store and manage their datasets. Cloud storage solutions also provide features like data replication, backup, and versioning, ensuring data integrity and availability for AI workflows.

## Distributed Processing

Many AI tasks, such as training deep neural networks, benefit from distributed processing to accelerate computations. Cloud platforms provide distributed computing frameworks, such as Apache Spark and TensorFlow Distributed, which can distribute AI workloads across multiple machines or clusters. This distributed processing capability allows for parallel execution, reducing training time and improving overall performance.

## GPU and TPU Acceleration

GPUs and TPUs are specialized hardware accelerators that excel at performing matrix operations required by AI algorithms. Cloud providers offer GPU and TPU instances, enabling users to leverage these accelerators for AI workloads. The cloud's GPU and TPU support significantly speeds up training and inferencetasks, making AI applications more efficient.

**Managed AI Services**

Cloud providers offer managed AI services that simplify the development and deployment of AI applications. These services include pre-built AI models, APIs for NPL, computer vision, speech recognition, and more. By utilizing managed AI services, developers can leverage powerful AI capabilities without having to build models from scratch, reducing development time and complexity.

**AutoML and ML Pipelines**

Cloud platforms provide automated machine learning (AutoML) tools that automate the process of model selection, hyperparameter tuning, and feature engineering. These tools make it easier for users with limited machine learning expertise to build and deploy AI models. Additionally, cloud platforms offer ML pipeline services, enabling users to create end-to-end workflows that streamline the process of data preprocessing, model training, and deployment.

**Elasticity and Cost Efficiency**

Cloud computing offers elasticity, allowing users to scale resources up or down based on demand. This flexibility ensures that AI workloads can efficiently utilize resources, reducing idle time and optimizing cost efficiency. Users can dynamically provision resources during peak periods and scale down during idle periods, paying only for the resources consumed.

**Collaboration and Deployment**

Cloud platforms facilitate collaboration and deployment of AI applications. Multiple users can collaborate on the same project by accessing shared cloud resources and data. Once an AI model is developed, it can be easily deployed to the cloud, making it accessible to users or applications through APIs, web interfaces, or integrations with other systems.

## 14.5   AutoML

AutoML is an innovation aimed at simplifying the machine learning process by reducing the need for extensive manual intervention. The goal of AutoML is to democratize machine learning. This system uses algorithms to automatically handle tasks such as data preprocessing, feature engineering, model selection, hyperparameter tuning, and model evaluation, effectively optimizing the end-to-end workflow. AutoML is particularly beneficial in time series analysis, where it automates the integration of various data preprocessing steps, feature selection, model training, and evaluation. By searching for the best-performing combinations of preprocessing techniques and model architectures, AutoML not only minimizes the time and effort required to build complex workflows but also ensures optimal performance.

## Data Preparation

AutoML systems handle data preprocessing tasks such as data cleaning, missing value imputation, handling categorical variables, and scaling/normalization. They automate the process of preparing the dataset for model training, reducing the need for manual data manipulation.

## Feature Engineering

AutoML algorithms automate the process of generating relevant features from raw data. They can extract common features, create new features, and apply transformations to the data to improve model performance. By automating feature engineering, AutoML saves time and reduces the need for domain expertise. Feature engineering is a critical aspect of time series analysis, involving the transformation and creation of meaningful features from raw time series data. AutoML for time series analysis automates this process by automatically generating and selecting relevant features. It can extract common features such as lagged values, rolling statistics (mean, standard deviation), Fourier or wavelet transformations, and various statistical indicators. By automating feature engineering, AutoML eliminates the need for manual feature selection and generation, reducing human effort and potential biases.

## Model Selection

AutoML algorithms automatically search through a range of machine learning models to identify the best-performing model for a given problem. This involves evaluating various models, such as decision trees, random forests, support vector machines, neural networks, and so forth, and selecting the most suitable one based on performance metrics. AutoML for time series analysis automates the process of selecting the most appropriate model for a given time series dataset. It explores a range of model architectures and algorithms, including traditional statistical models (e.g., ARIMA, SARIMA), classical machine learning models (e.g., random forest, gradient boosting), and deep learning models (e.g., RNNs, LSTM networks). The AutoML system evaluates the performance of different models and selects the one that produces the best results for the given time series data.

## Hyperparameter Optimization

Machine learning models have hyperparameters that influence their performance and behavior but are not learned from the data. AutoML automates the search for optimal hyperparameter configurations by exploring different combinations using techniques like grid search, random search, Bayesian optimization, or genetic algorithms. This optimization process aims to find the hyperparameter settings that yield the best model performance. AutoML automates the optimization of model hyperparameters. Hyperparameters are configuration settings that affect the model's performance but are not learned from the data. Examples include the learning rate, number of layers, number of hidden units, and regularization parameters. Instead of manually tuning these hyperparameters, which can be time-consuming and require expertise, AutoML algorithms automatically search through a predefined space of hyperparameters to find the optimal combination. This helps improve model accuracy and generalization for time series forecasting tasks.

## Model Training and Evaluation

AutoML systems automate the process of training and evaluating machine learning models. They handle tasks such as cross-validation, model fitting, performance evaluation using appropriate metrics, and handling imbalanced datasets. This automation simplifies the model training and evaluation process.

## Ensemble Methods

AutoML often leverages ensemble methods to improve model performance. Ensemble methods combine predictions from multiple models to create a more accurate and robust final prediction. AutoML systems can automatically create and optimize ensemble models by selecting the best-performing individual models and combining their predictions. AutoML often employs ensemble methods to further enhance the accuracy of time series models. Ensemble methods combine the predictions of multiple individual models to obtain a more robust and accurate prediction. AutoML algorithms can automatically build ensembles by selecting and combining the best-performing models from the candidate models explored during the search process. Ensemble methods can improve the stability and predictive power of time series models, particularly in scenarios with noisy or uncertain data.

## Deployment and Inference

Some AutoML platforms also provide deployment capabilities, allowing users to deploy trained models into production environments with ease. This enables the integration of machine learning models into real-world applications for prediction or decision-making.

Printed in the United States
by Baker & Taylor Publisher Services